MY LIFE AND TIMES
OCTAVE SIX:
1923-1930

C.M. in 1928

MY LIFE AND TIMES

OCTAVE SIX

1923-1930

Compton Mackenzie

1967
CHATTO & WINDUS
LONDON

Published by
Chatto & Windus Ltd
42 William IV Street
London, W.C.2

*

Clarke, Irwin & Co. Ltd
Toronto

© Compton Mackenzie 1967

Printed in Great Britain by
T. & A. Constable Ltd
Hopetoun Street, Edinburgh

To my beloved Lily
in memory of our
beloved Chrissie

ACKNOWLEDGMENTS

My grateful thanks for permission to quote letters are due to the following: Lord Reith, Dame Sibyl Hathaway, Lady Davies (Margaret Kennedy), Mr P. G. Wodehouse, Mr Noel Coward; and to Mr Hugh Noyes for Alfred Noyes, Adeline Lady Hankey for Lord Hankey, Miss F. Quiller-Couch for Sir Arthur Quiller-Couch, The Society of Authors for Walter de la Mare, the Trustee of the Max Beerbohm Estate for Max Beerbohm, the Scott Fitzgerald Estate for Scott Fitzgerald, Field Roscoe & Co. for Charles Morgan, the Literary Executor for W. Somerset Maugham, Mrs D. W. Scholes and Barclays Bank Ltd for Percy Scholes, the Trustees of the Letters of T. E. Lawrence for T. E. Lawrence, the Trustees of the John Galsworthy Estate for John Galsworthy, Viscount Samuel for the late Viscount Samuel and to Mr Rupert Hart Davis for Hugh Walpole.

I would like to offer my apologies to those literary heirs whom I have been unable to trace. I hope they will accept this general acknowledgment for material I have quoted.

I am very grateful to the Society of Authors for permission to reprint "The Rectorial Contest" by George Bernard Shaw as an appendix to this Octave.

C.M.

CONTENTS

*

PLATES

*

FORTY YEARS OLD: STILL 1923

THE little island of Jethou is separated from Herm by a deep
channel half a mile wide called the Percée. From the moment I
stepped ashore on its beach on that July morning in the year 1923, so
completely did I cut myself off from Herm that the Percée might
have been the width of the Atlantic. I have told in Octave Five of
the financial stress and strain brought about by my rash decision to
saddle myself with the sixty years' lease of Herm at £900 a year and
of that lease's being taken over by Sir Percival Perry.[1]

How glad I was that I had resisted Sir Percival's plan to grow
poisonous plants on Jethou for the chemical industry and what a
relief it was to reflect that the Crown lease of Jethou was only £100 a
year. I realized when I stepped ashore on that beach that I should
have to work very hard for the next few years if I was going to relieve
myself of a load of anxiety about money. Yet somehow the spirits of
this little island seemed to assure me that I should succeed. The
spirits of Herm had been hostile owing to the island's being ill
wished, as they say in Cornwall, for the next tenant by Princess
Blücher when the Blüchers' lease was annulled in 1914. I invited
those hostile spirits to tempt somebody who had benefited from the
Great War into taking over Herm. Within a few hours Sir Percival
Perry, who had bought the Slough Dump, arrived in a yacht and
finally took over the lease of Herm.

I hesitate to say much about the welcoming spirits of Jethou
because to those without experience of small islands it will sound
like sentimental twaddle. Nevertheless, I have to record my conviction that for the next octave of my life I was protected by the
spirits of Jethou and that when I left it in December 1930 it was
because those spirits foresaw the German occupation of the Channel
Islands in 1940.

The whole extent of Jethou was just under fifty acres and the
name was said to be derived from the old Norse Siethou or High
Island. Yet it was only 262 feet high and the name was as inappropri-
ate as Virgil's epithet for Procida in the Bay of Naples—*alta Procida*.

The island had a long history. It was probably one of the small
islands mentioned by Dionysius Periegetes in the fourth century A.D.
as a resort for women indulging in Bacchic rites. Be that as it may

[1] The late Lord Perry of Stock Harvard.

have been, in A.D. 919 it was presented by Rollo the Norman to
Ranald, his admiral or steersman, who in his turn made it over to
the monks of Mont St Michel in Brittany, from whom it passed to
the Benedictines of Cherbourg. At the Reformation it was seized by
the Governor of Guernsey together with Herm, where there was a
massacre of Catholics, and like Herm it was used as a chase, but not
for fallow deer as the larger island was. Drayton in his *Polyolbion*
wrote of Jethou with its pheasants, swans and conies. The swans had
long vanished by 1923 but the pheasants and rabbits were still there.
I had brought pheasants from Jethou to Herm and I remember
saying to Perry in joke that I was not going to put them into the
valuation and Perry's murmuring 'Thank you very much' in the
tone of one who was grateful even for so small an alleviation of the
financial burden his taking over the lease of Herm involved.

There were far too many rabbits on Jethou; fortunately, unlike the
Herm rabbits, they were not affected by myxamatosis.

In the eighteenth century the Crown let Herm and Jethou for
cultivation and from this time, 1740, dates the great mulberry tree
in the little walled garden. That mulberry tree would have been a
remarkable specimen inland; within fifty yards of the sea it must be
unique. At the beginning of the nineteenth century the Crown
tenant was John Allaire, a famous privateer of the Napoleonic wars.
He built a house the walls of which still remained. Legend said it
had fallen into ruin after people had knocked it about to search for
Allaire's buried treasure, rumoured to consist of banknotes with
which he had papered the walls of his rooms. One authentic souvenir
of John Allaire remained and that was a gun from his privateer
vessel. His descendant the Dame of Sark gave me another in the
shape of a silver teaspoon engraved *Jethou*.

The island was well cultivated until it came into the tenancy of
Sir Henry Austin Lee, who allowed all the arable land and pasturage
to return to wildness. I was glad of this. My expensive lesson at Herm
had cured me of having anything to do with farming.

I knew that if I wanted to indulge my pleasure in building, I
would find indispensable the services of Macdonald, my carpenter
on Herm, and that if I were to indulge my even keener pleasure in
garden-making, Keegan, also with me on Herm, would be equally
indispensable. So I had got hold of a large army hut, which Macdonald had erected above the landing beach. The seven rooms were
divided into two with a kitchen at either end, and here the Macdonalds and the Keegans lived until I left Jethou. The drive sloped

gradually up between gorse hedges to the house Austin Lee had occupied. This was described as follows in the advertisement that lured me away from my projected South Seas enterprise to take Herm and Jethou:

Large hall, dining, living room, 2 large bedrooms, 2 small ditto. Boxroom. Kitchen, Larder, etc. Sanitation is by earth closet.

The advertisement went on:

Behind the house is an old ruined Monastery with a walled flower and vegetable garden running into a little valley full of dwarf trees, and in front of the Monastery is a sunk garden sheltered from all winds, which could be converted into a delightful Flower Garden.

The ruined house of the privateer had been turned into a monastery. The sunk garden sheltered from every wind was in fact fully exposed to the west and south-west. On the other hand the little valley full of dwarf trees was in fact a wood of two acres on the steep slope above the 'monastery', full of ancient Spanish chestnuts, pear-trees, oaks, at least one magnificent ash, and one large walnut. I have never seen anywhere trees of such size almost at the edge of the sea.

Beside the house was a vinery against a high granite wall almost forty feet long and twenty feet wide. Many of the panes were broken and the vine itself had not been tended for years. Outside the sitting-room was a spacious wooden balcony looking across to the rocky peak of Crevichon, an islet of four acres which could be reached across a stretch of sand at the low spring tides with a rise and fall of twenty-nine feet. Even the neap tides were fifteen feet.

Soon after I moved to Jethou I received the following request from somebody in the Natural History Museum in London:

I would be very greatly obliged for permission to dig in the sands at low tides for specimens of a rather rare worm-like creature called Balanaglossus Sarniensis. *The Brit. Mus. collection is rather poor in well-preserved specimens, and I want good material for exhibition. The animal is hard to find and when found to get out whole. One may dig for an hour or two without success as I know from experience.*

I do not remember if that worm-like creature was extricated whole, but just before I left Herm I sent four sackfuls of shells from the shell-beach for the Crustacean tanks in the new aquarium at the Zoo which my friend E. G. Boulanger was supervising. I believe those shells may still be seen.

On the east side of Jethou was another rocky islet called La Grande

Fauconnaire in which plenty of gulls nested but no longer any falcons.

Some fifty yards up from the house was a four-roomed cottage in which Nellie Boyte's father and mother were installed. In the house itself were Nellie Boyte my secretary, and our parlour-maid Honor Everton. Besides the human beings who came to Jethou in that July were Bob, the Old English sheepdog, and Stella, the sealyham, with one of her puppies.

The labour of transporting furniture and over 10,000 books, not to mention over a thousand gramophone records, makes me feel tired to remember. Mercifully the weather remained at set fair throughout the time the operation lasted.

For the first seven weeks I was working at *The Parson's Progress* for twelve hours a day and sometimes longer. It was financially vital for me to let Cassell's have the typescript by September so that it could be published that autumn. There is a lot of talk nowadays about the way everything is speeded up; that does not apply to publishing, when even to publish a book six months after the typescript is received is considered a major feat of technological enterprise.

The writing of *The Parson's Progress*, like that of *The Altar Steps*, involved a good deal of reading to check my ecclesiastical facts. I used to start writing after tea and work till dinner-time. Then from about nine o'clock I worked on till about seven o'clock in the morning. Then I used to walk round the island and get to bed about eight, sleeping on till three in the afternoon.

On the east side of Jethou was a little wood of gnarled and stunted trees, their trunks and branches covered with thick lichen, presumably to protect themselves against the fierce gales which swept across from Sark. One rock was visible in that stretch of water, dark and sinister and well deserving its name—La Pute Noire: the Black Whore.

The enchantment of that little wood never grew less powerful through all the years I lived on Jethou. I have seen nowhere so thick a carpet of bluebells when their chimes were ringing summer in, and in spring along the edge of that little wood were many hoop-petticoat daffodils. These had been planted originally by Austin Lee, and thanks to the oxalic acid which makes daffodils immune from rabbits those golden hoop-petticoats were as numerous as the crinolines of once upon a time. Farther round, a clump of *Narcissus triandrus* had survived and increased. I recall showing them to Macdonald and telling him they were called Angels' Tears and his alluding to them afterwards when trying to recall their name as 'Weeping Saints'.

That little wood marked the boundary for primroses. Beyond it not one showed itself. The slopes south-east and south were covered instead with sea-pinks and white campion, with here and there the sombre green of butcher's broom in which one or two of the island wrens used to nest. The southern slopes were dotted with huge slabs of granite, relics of the time when Jethou supplied the granite for building the harbour of St Peter Port in Guernsey. The flat top of the island was covered in late summer with a deep crimson sheet of bell-heather, the sight of which after working all night on *The Parson's Progress* was as revivifying as wine.

An extract from a letter to my mother in that July reflects my mood:

I'm glad you've settled everything fairly satisfactorily and very glad to hear that you're well—I might almost say and enjoying yourself. Of course misfortune is very exhilarating—like extreme physical pain—if one can use it well.

I was grateful that the efforts I had made to avoid bankruptcy for my mother had not involved my going on the stage and that the Nottingham Repertory Theatre would soon be a misfortune of the past.

That summer J. T. Grein, so long the much respected dramatic critic of the *Sunday Times*, came over from Guernsey to pay me a visit in Jethou. He wrote in the *Christian Science Monitor* of Boston, the nineteenth in a series of 'London Cameos':

"An old friend of his people—particularly of his famous father . . . of his lovable mother (one of a great trio of beautiful sisters who now devotes her life to the Theatre Girls' Club in Soho where she guards and cozies those who work hard for little pay), and of his sister Fay, perhaps the most promising English actress of the younger generation, I went to visit the seigneur of a tiny realm. . . .

"His hours of inspiration strike late at night . . . he cloisters himself in his comfortable writing armchair whose little gateway when closed forms a desk . . . his mental storehouse is so well stocked that he could go on to his nineties, half a century hence. His memory is stupendous. As he talks he quotes. Poetry, prose, French and English—it is all the same to him—he will discuss art and theology with equal ardour, the same penetration. . . .

"Lately he all but threw down the pen to don the toga. At the behest of his mother and sisters, who fought a desperate and plucky repertory battle at Nottingham, he practically decided to tour

England in Shakespearian parts—Hamlet, Richard III, Falstaff, and the character for which nature designed him—Mark Antony. . . . The toga remains in the cupboard, the pen ploughs on night after night."

As I copy these words written forty-three years ago I remember with gratitude that it was not necessary for me to go on the stage and I reflect with equal gratitude that I may hope to fulfil Grein's prophecy. Whether I am allowed to do that or not, he will not have been very far out.

The Gramophone was flourishing, and the response to my proposal to start a National Gramophonic Society to record classical music for its members had been most encouraging. The circulation went up all through that autumn, but so did the printing bill, and the lack of ready cash was a problem. Christopher Stone had been able to find only £300 when he decided in that July to come in, but I am not going to bore my readers or myself by details of the way the financial difficulties were overcome.

Money matters would have been easier for me if Sir Percival Perry had not kept delaying payment of the sum due to me for the valuation of Herm. As late as November 12th I was writing to Victor Carey[1]:

If Sir P. P. hangs about any more over this payment I shall sue him so that Guernsey may have an opportunity of hearing what kind of fellow he is. I will not pay a farthing to the valuers until Sir P. P. has paid the valuation to me by releasing the bill of sale on my furniture and books and my life policy and the balance in cash.

Next day Victor Carey wrote back from the Receiver-General's Office:

I quite agree Sir P. P. has no right to retain any part of the award. . . . I will be ready to take proceedings on your behalf if the whole matter is not settled by the beginning of next week.

On December 3rd, when at last Perry had returned the life policy and paid up the award, Carey wrote:

I heard from your Oxford bank that they had got the assignment safely. I am getting to dislike the K.B.E.'s oily smile. I feel he will yet die a Peer.

The effort to finish *The Parson's Progress* by the middle of September was a terrific strain. On September 11th I was writing to Faith:

---

[1] The late Sir Victor Carey.

My leg has shut up to-day for the first time since Saturday week. It's been perfectly infernal working hours at a stretch in constant pain. The house is full of sonorous grasshoppers who all chirp when the gramophone begins to play. I'm deadly tired and it takes me 10 hours now to produce 6 pages. I've done 400 and still have about 30 to do if I'm to get to London with the MS. by the 17th. I shall have to write my quarterly review of records in town. The paper will have to be late. I'll explain why in my editorial, but I can't do anything except the book at the moment.

' Yet there were compensations for the labour and pain. In the same letter I read:

They're doing a South Sea film on Herm with three palms and a clockwork shark! Nellie has just come back from trying to extract some money out of Perry and gave me a priceless account of a rehearsal. Bob got included by mistake in one picture and it had to be done all over again.

I managed to finish *The Parson's Progress* and reach London with the MS. by September 17th, thus making it possible for Cassell's to publish in November. I found my mother quite unmoved by the Nottingham disaster and completely preoccupied by the Theatre Girls' Club. She suggested my trying the daughter of Mrs Watson, who at that date was helping her at the Club, as a possible illustrator for *Santa Claus in Summer*. The various illustrators Michael Sadleir had tried had all been wash-outs for one reason or another.

Never was made so happy a suggestion. Neenie Watson's illustrations were perfect. I felt that Lewis Carroll could not have been more pleased with Tenniel's illustrations of *Alice in Wonderland* than I was with 'A. H. Watson' as she signed herself.

I shall not go into details about the financial complications of that first year of *The Gramophone's* life. Christopher and Faith worked hard in Newman Street and somehow we survived. My quarterly review of records running to about six thousand words would have been an impossible task if I had not learnt to listen to records being played while I was writing a book. The music was invaluable in preventing my mind from wandering to the problem of money. Without it I should never have been able to maintain my rate of production. I would know at once if Nellie Boyte had put on the wrong side of a record and was listening critically all the while. Yet I was able nevertheless to concentrate on my writing. I shall take this opportunity of saying that the facility with which so many critics credited me, or rather discredited me, did not exist. My aim was to make what I had to say as easy to read as I could. This gave a false impression of facility.

When we are young we are inclined to revere a writer who never lets us forget that he is writing. This was what gave George Meredith his great reputation. Perhaps I might say the same of my own *Sinister Street*. When Tom Jones took Partridge to see Garrick and asked what he thought of this highly praised actor, Partridge replied that he thought nothing of him. "You wouldn't know he was acting." The more difficult a soprano makes it seem to reach that top note the more enthusiastically her audience applauds her. The more faces a strong man pulls when lifting a weight the more impressive seems his strength.

That ability of mine to listen to music while I was writing would be made use of for many years to come.

An echo of the last month of that year survives in the rough draft of a letter to Christopher Stone:

1. Will you impress on the office the importance of always sending any leaflets issued with the records each month. I have not received one from London, so will you see that I get the monthly bulletins for Oct. Nov. Dec. at once i.e. Columbia, Vocalion, H.M.V. and any others.

2. Ask Ridout to send me all Columbia's chamber music records as soon as possible. Tell him that an Encyclopaedia of Chamber Music is in preparation by a set of distinguished musicians and that I have been asked to make myself responsible for the gramophone side.

I interrupt that letter to say a word about that remarkable old gentleman, W. W. Cobbett. He was a leather-merchant who had made a lot of money out of the war, and being an ardent violinist had his own Quartet, in which he was first violin. He had been a member of the Savile for a long time but had only recently taken to using the Club. When he entered for the billiards handicap nobody had seen him play and he was given the top handicap of a hundred. I remember his saying to me with a shake of his ancient head, "I think they've handicapped me rather too favourably."

Indeed they had! He won all his matches with ease.

"Who the hell is this old buffer Cobbett?" Bill Orpen asked. "He started off against me with a break of fifty odd and wiped me out with two more of over forty."

On December 3rd Cobbett was writing to me:

34 Avenue Road,
N.W.8.

Dear Mackenzie

I am devoting next year to compiling a book on Chamber Music of a

Cyclopaedic kind. I wish it to contain all *that pertains to that branch of the art.*

The success of it will depend on my collaborators. . . . I should be immensely gratified if you would (on of course your usual terms) undertake to write about the records of Chamber Music—not from the musico-technical point of view, but just your own brilliant self talking about them. Please do not say No! This is going to be a genuine attempt to give the world something complete. . . .

Yours cordially

W. W. Cobbett

On December 8th he wrote:

My dear Mackenzie,

I am much heartened to receive your delightfully cordial letter. . . . All to whom I have spoken seem to approve unreservedly of the scheme, and with the assistance of the right people I shall perhaps be able to carry it to a successful issue—in time of course. It will not be finished, I expect, much before 1925.

I condole with Mrs Mackenzie upon her bad cold, a trouble with which the august body of medicos seem quite unable to cope.

Yours gratefully,

W. W. Cobbett

On June 18th in 1924 Cobbett was writing:

When will it be convenient for you to let me have the article on records of chamber music? By the way, you said you would accept the same terms as other writers. These are 2 gns for 1000 words (same as Grove).

I was 'listening in' last night to some string quartets. I like Gramophone records better so far. . . .

Cobbett's *Encyclopaedia of Chamber Music* was published and remains a standard work, though that article of mine about the gramophone is sadly out of date to-day. About the same time as Cobbett was planning his Encyclopaedia Dr Eaglefield Hull was completing his editorship of *A Dictionary of Modern Music and Musicians,* to be published by Dent and Sons. On November 27th he wrote:

I wonder if you would be so kind as to write quite a short article of about 150 to 250 words on the Gramophone as a musical propagator for the Dictionary. . . . If so, if you will excuse a stranger holding a pistol at your head in this way, it must be done within the next three or four days.

May I express my admiration of the new paper and hope it will go on and obtain a solid foundation. . . .

B

I sent the following to Dr Hull as soon as his letter reached me:

"The Gramophone will contribute as much to musical education as the printing-press has contributed to the spread of knowledge. The effect of putting such a work as Beethoven's Emperor Concerto complete in the hands of an amateur and thereby making great music an incident of his daily life is incalculable. Moreover, the average man is becoming familiar with the sound of an orchestra through his gramophone. It must be remembered that such an one begins by disliking the sound of an orchestra. Music, as he understands it, is represented by the cornet, the piano, or the violin played with exaggerated *tremolo*. Let him grow accustomed to the sound of an orchestra, and he is as willing to listen to a symphony of Beethoven as to a cheap waltz. One hesitates to suggest that the recording companies should issue records of the cornet in such melodies as the Andante from the C minor symphony of Beethoven; but there is no doubt that by such a trap a still larger public as yet unmoved might be caught in the spell of great music. Meanwhile, let musicians pay as much attention to the Gramophone as a wise mother pays to her children's governess or nurse."

I wrote to Eaglefield Hull with this:

I send you the enclosed at the earliest possible moment, but I am not well placed for quick postal communication. I have written a few words in a great hurry, and if they strike you as a string of silly platitudes, don't hesitate to omit them from the Dictionary.

The power of my paper is growing in a really remarkable way, and I hope that by the end of next year it will be really firmly established.

Dr Hull wrote:

Thank you very much for your nice little article. If you could add another paragraph of about the same length mentioning the sort of sounds which really do come out lifelike, and those that are not yet perfect such as the piano etc it would give an additional value to the work. Can you do this? If so I will hold back the printing presses.

I have no copy of what I must have said about the piano, the double bass and the cor anglais, the three instruments which were still defying the recorders.

And now it is time to get back to that letter I was writing to Christopher Stone:

4. I hope the Edison people are going to send a machine. No doubt they

*appreciate the difficulty of making the British public buy an Edison machine
if they can adapt their own machines to playing Edison 'Recreations'.*

*5. It's time the Sonora did something for us. Have Keith Prowse been
tackled and what do they say?*

*6. You should point out that I am particularly anxious that Chappell's
should not be handicapped by a late start with their Autoplayer as they were
with their Cliftophone. You should suggest they send me their ten-guinea
model, which if as good as you and Faith thought it is just the class of gramophone I can recommend to a certain class of readers.*

7. Wash out World Records.

*8. The Opera list contains nothing but punk, the same with the Polydor
and the Odeon. But who has the old H.M.V. masters or mothers and call
themselves 'Musica' in Germany? Those are the people who have the records
we want. Have the Parlophone people got the Fonotipia matrices? I don't want
to order from Germany a hundred German records if I can get the same records
for nothing in England. Tell Offenbach I will discuss the scheme for Parlophone publicity when I come to London. Only they must put their cards on the
table and say clearly how they stand with H.M.V. That is the snag.*

*I think I've answered all your questions, but I am overworked by corres-
pondence. I'm getting long gramophone letters here at the rate of three a day
and with the* Watch Me *prevented from coming over in the bad weather
we've been having I sometimes get three days' post at once. Besides Gramophone
letters long letters about The Parson's Progress are beginning to arrive. I've
managed to do 71 pages of The Heavenly Ladder. How I don't know!*

*If you can manage to get somebody to lend £1000 to the paper I will accept
it as a personal loan and guarantee repayment by the end of 1925. . . .*

*My main object is to make the Gramophone by the end of 1925 a property
that will bring in a reasonable income for you and Faith. I believe this will
be managed. I am hoping that Ridley[1] will persuade the Bank to leave my
overdraft at £1500 for next year. That will enable me to start next year on
improving the house and garden.*

It was fortunate I had no income tax to pay on Jethou, and indeed
for the whole of the time I lived on that much loved little island I had
only one buff form a year to fill up. That was easy too, for it merely
consisted of my writing 'none' in answer to how many cattle I kept. I
have never sought for an excuse to justify any extravagance in which
I have indulged my creative urge, but I did feel that my freedom

---

[1] Manager of the Oxford branch of Westminster Bank and an invaluable
support in these years.

from income tax made it something of a duty to improve a Crown property and that living as I was as it were in the very jaws of the Treasury I should never give their Lordships any reason to regret their having allowed me the lease of Jethou for life and a year after.

When writing my last Octave I was under the impression that I had met Percy Scholes before I started *The Gramophone*. A couple of letters I have found makes it clear that I did not meet him until March 1924 and that the dinner he had with me off carrots must have been then.

On December 7th, 1923, he was writing from 21 Bedford Court Mansions, Bedford Avenue, Bedford Square, W.C.1:

I so much admire open-mindedness and plain speaking that I was feeling that if I knew you I should like to send you a word of congratulation and thanks for the attitude adopted in your paper. Reading farther, I came across very kind words about one of my little books, and this, I felt, did give me the sufficient excuse I wanted. . . . I am rather wondering why you so emphatically exclude broadcasting from your paper. . . . My own view is that the pianola and gramophone and broadcasting are changing musical conditions in this country. Where, a short time ago, we had one man capable of an interest in a symphony or a sonata, we shall soon have five hundred. What this means, nobody can say. But on the face of it, it seems admirable that fine music should no longer remain the private preserve of a tiny body of initiates.

On December 21st Scholes was writing:

Thank you for your interesting letter. Of course, I, like you, deplore 'this confounded high priest business', and I believe that, like you, I suffer a little because I do not care to wear the robes. I think that what you call 'the little London clique' cannot understand that the music critic of a serious London paper may be none the less competent in that job, although he does write books on music for the man in the street, and even for that man's children.

As for wireless—I know something of the British Broadcasting Company from the outside; in fact they have put me on a programme committee, and I attend a weekly meeting. They are quite prepared to give just as much fine music as the people will take, and it is a great pity that at present the letters received from the consumers represent too largely the 'low-brow' section. Other people ought to write, and write freely. Now you mention it, I dimly remember being on the premises once when a letter from yourself was mentioned, and no doubt that letter had some effect. . . .

This must have been after my meeting with Mr John Reith.

I look forward to meeting you in March. You will note that this flat is but a stone's throw from our O. and C. Musical Club.

I used to stay at the Oxford and Cambridge Musical Club rather than the Savile nowadays when I went to London. This was because I so much enjoyed the company of Mrs Ovens. Mrs Ovens was the wife of a Thames pilot and lived with her daughter in the basement of that former house of the Duke of Bedford. That basement was a little world in itself with an enormous kitchen and level at the back with gardens.

Mrs Ovens gave me an unique experience, for she was in manner, speech and appearance the perfect duplicate of Mrs Gainsborough, whom I had invented in *Sinister Street* and of whom I made the fullest use in *Sylvia Scarlett*. It was almost uncanny, but at the same time reassuring of my ability to create character.

I recall one comic episode. Mrs Ovens's daughter was head house-maid and continuously at war with the Secretary, who was a fussy man. One evening Emily's fiancé was being entertained when the footsteps of the Secretary were heard coming downstairs.

"My goodness, what a to-do," Mrs Ovens told me. "Him and Emily always argyfying as they did, she didn't want Mr Smith to find her Bob down there having tea. 'Oh, whatever shall I do, Ma?' says Emily. 'Hide him in the Duke's safe,' I told her. So she pushed Bob into the safe and slammed the door and Mr Nosy went back upstairs, very annoyed because he hadn't found anything to argyfy about with Emily. But my gracious goodness, what a time we had to get poor Bob out of that safe, because we could *not* find the key. Well, we did find the key at last but not till poor Bob had used up all the air in that safe, and came out looking more like an Egypching mummy than a solicitor's clerk, and which he is. And when my husband came back from Greenwich he created because his tea was cold, with me and Emily trying to undo the door of that blessed safe."

Although I was inclined to groan about my correspondence under the stress of toiling up *The Heavenly Ladder*, that correspondence was a continual encouragement. I record one letter out of the many that compensated for the nagging criticism of copy-cat reviews:

It came from Evanstown, Illinois.

Dear Sir,

Youth's Encounter [as the first volume of Sinister Street was called in the U.S.A.] *gave one who had missed going to college the courage to give up his job and go seeking je-ne-sais quoi from old Mexico to British Columbia. Returning to his home town in the Southern States, Sinister Street, just banished from the chaste shelves of his small town's public library, gave him courage in spite of an approaching twenty-fifth birthday to again give up what his friends called a good job to go to college, earning thereby their general contempt. In uniform he read The Passionate Elopement and spoiled many a sheet of Y.M.C.A. stationery trying to write his appreciation of beauty to its author. Of it—to this day he is inarticulate. Plashers (Guy and Pauline), Carnival, Sylvia Scarlett were read in order named. Enough—to make the point just this—the name of shop and publisher where he may order your volume of verse. And if the point has not been made—no answer then is necessary.*

> *Condensing in a word—years of appreciation—*
> *Gratefully*

BESIDES starting the National Gramophonic Society I had had the notion of a Piano-Player supplement for *The Gramophone*, and what we used to call a pianola arrived on Jethou with a collection of rolls. I had misjudged the pianola's ability to compete with the gramophone; the Piano-Player supplement disappeared after a few months.

Throughout January and February I was desperately trying to finish *The Heavenly Ladder* in time for Cassell's to publish that spring. By the middle of February I was able to feel sure enough of its length to let Cassell's start setting up, and on March 11th I reached London with the final chapter, the book being published in the middle of April. I had had the usual amount of pain during that stormy winter. I find in two letters apologies at different dates for not replying sooner to a letter because our boat had been unable to cross from Guernsey for three days; during four months of gales posts interrupted by a day were frequent. Not that I minded these interruptions; it was a relief to have even twenty-four hours' holiday from letters.

I am not going to inflict on contemporary readers accounts of the almost innumerable sound-boxes and machines which arrived on Jethou for me to try: the hi-fi experts of to-day would wonder how we could have tolerated let alone praised the reproduction of music at this date. However, I cannot resist recalling a visit from Percy Wilson, who was our 'expert' judge of gramophone mechanics and who, I rejoice to say, is still an expert of *The Gramophone* forty years on, advising a readership of nearly 80,000 all over the world instead of the nearly 8,000 of 1924. The reason for Wilson's visit was that a Welsh parson called Griffiths had sent me a rubber-neck with which the sound-box was attached to the arm of a gramophone and which he claimed much improved the reproduction. As I remember, he had made the discovery by accident when something had gone wrong on his own machine. I was sceptical when that rubber-neck arrived but the moment I tried it out I realized that it really did improve the reproduction. Wilson was equally sceptical when I gave him the news to the London office but was persuaded by me to come to Jethou and be converted. I have forgotten what was the record I put on, but I know that in the middle of it Wilson leapt up

from his chair and shouted 'Got it!' It was like the 'Eureka' of
Archimedes. Apparently it was a drum-tap he had sought to hear
from various sound-boxes without success. Wilson's endorsement was
all I needed. In due course we were selling what I called 'The
Lifebelt' and every reader who bought one wrote to thank us for the
boon of that 'Lifebelt'.

My one diversion during that strenuous winter was growing a
beard, which I kept for nine months. Of that beard I wrote:

"In the end I had to give it up as one gives up keeping a dog in a
city through the difficulties of providing it with proper exercise.
Before I had a beard I thought it would save me the trouble of
shaving every morning. It is a delusion that beards look after themselves any more than gardens. They require careful weeding to
remove white hairs which affect them as daisies affect lawns. They
require almost incessant trimming, and every barber has his own
idea of how a beard shall be grown. You can enter his shop looking
like a Vandyck; you may leave it looking like a nail brush. You can
go in with the trim appearance of a British naval officer; you may
go out again more like a goat than a man. But as goat or man, Vandyck or nail brush, women all deplored my appearance. They said
it aged me; I did not yield. They said it was a pity to spoil my profile;
I held firmly to my beard. They used arguments against my beard,
which, being now clean-shaven, I should blush to repeat. And then
one evening a woman asked me while we were dancing together if I
did not think it looked a little undignified for a man with a beard
to fox-trot. It was in one of those ballrooms lined with mirrors. I
looked. I hesitated. I had to admit that she was right. It did look
undignified; it even looked ridiculous. The next day I cut it off. I
had to decide between boards and beards, and the boards won. I
could not give up dancing in the flower of middle-age. I sold my
birthright, not for a mess of pottage like Esau who, however,
remained a hairy man, not for a woman's embraces like Samson,
but for the pleasure of waddling round a crowded garish room to the
accompaniment of music. Let it be remembered, though, that it was
the woman who tempted me."

The growing of that beard made me feel suitably venerable to
accept Martin Secker's invitation to be godfather to his son Adrian;
in that April I presented him with a mug and by the font made as
many rash promises on his behalf as a parliamentary candidate.

Just as I made a mistake in Octave Five by pre-dating my first
meeting with Percy Scholes, I made the same mistake over my first

meeting with Lord Reith. It was not in fact until the beginning of this April.

> 2 Savoy Hill
> Victoria Embankment
> W.C.2
> *April 8th 1924*

Dear Mr Mackenzie

I understand that you are now in town and at liberty to come and see our studios. I shall be pleased to make your acquaintance, and show you round to-morrow afternoon about 4 p.m. . . . This place is easy to find if you make for the Embankment entrance to the Savoy Hotel.

> *Yours very truly*
> *J. C. W. Reith*

Soon after this I received the following letter:

THE BRITISH BROADCASTING COMPANY
LIMITED

Directors	2 Savoy Hill
Lord Gainsford (Chairman)	Victoria Embankment
and eight more names below	London, W.C.2
Managing Director	
J. C. W. Reith	*12th April. 1924*

Dear Mr Mackenzie

I am looking forward to welcoming you here one Thursday morning in June to give a talk during the hour's transmission of Gramophone Records. Perhaps you would let me know if you have any preference as to the programme, so that I can arrange to have the necessary records available.

Your suggestion re a night of classical music with popular titles is an excellent one, and I should like to adopt it in the near future for a special programme. I should be very happy to have your suggestions on this on the lines which we discussed. There is, as we know, a tremendous lot in a name, and if a thing can be called 'The Rustle of Spring' instead of 'Characteristic Piece. Opus 124', it will make all the difference.

> *With kind regards,*
> *Cordially yours,*

FOR
THE BRITISH BROADCASTING CO. LTD.
> *R. F. Palmer*
> DIRECTOR LONDON STATION

Faith and I with Nellie Boyte left for Capri at Easter; as soon as possible after our arrival I sent Mr Reith the article I had promised him.

I received from him this acknowledgment:

Dear Mr Mackenzie

Thank you for your letter of the 23rd enclosing your article, which I have passed on to the Editor of the Radio Times. He hopes to be able to insert it in the issue of May 9th.

I also enjoyed our talk very much, and I am looking forward to seeing you again.

Yours sincerely

J. C. W. Reith

In an acknowledgment from the joint editor of the *Radio Times*, Herbert Parker, I am amused to see at the top of the page of writing-paper THE RADIO TIMES in large capitals sprawling across a fore-shortened map of Great Britain in which are the names of the various stations beside what look like gallows—Aberdeen, Glasgow, Newcastle, Manchester, Birmingham, Cardiff, Bournemouth and London. In rather smaller capitals it is described as The Official Organ of the B.B.C.

I think it is worth reprinting that article as a reminder of the past:

"Yesterday afternoon [I write these words in mid-April] I was sitting on a terrace that overhung the Mediterranean. A gentle wind slipped in and out of the Aleppo pines, and from the water far below the voices of the swimmers came up with the sound of summer in their mirth. We had endured four days of Easter travelling. Every boat and train and hotel had been packed. It was pleasant to sit here warm and idle after all that confusion of noisy tourists and changing weather. In the course of conversation I told my host that early in June I should be broadcasting some remarks about gramophone records and to my amazement he asked me to let him know the exact time and date so that here in Capri he might listen. My mind travelled back across the Bay of Naples, drove along the clangorous Naples streets to the railway-station, crashed up in the train through Campania to Rome, dealt with the complication of changing trains, settled down to the long journey from Rome to Paris in the wagon-lit, puffed up through Italy into the Mont Cenis tunnel, puffed out of the tunnel and up through France, drove across Paris in a taxi-cab, grappled with the dirt and crowds of the Gare du Nord, rattled along the dreary track between Paris and Calais, survived the immemorial odour of the Channel boat, beheld the white cliffs of England strung across the horizon like distant washing hung out to dry, puffed on through Kent until it reached Victoria, swept along in a taxi-cab to the Savoy, and ended its long journey in the studios of the British Broadcasting Company.

"There, in a quiet room, even the windows of which were hidden by grey draperies to deaden the echoes, I should stand and speak about a yard away from the kind of instrument one sees in an optician's shop; here in Capri on this terrace overhanging the Mediterranean pine-shadowed, warm, murmurous with the mirth of swimmers far below, my friends would hear what I had to say.

"Of course, there is nothing more miraculous in being heard in Capri when one speaks from London than in being heard in Aberdeen: and if mere mileage is to count, it is much less miraculous than sitting up until three in the morning to hear a man talking at ten o'clock in the evening in America. But somehow this was the first time that the miracle was really brought home to my imagination. We have come to take so much for granted during this last quarter of a century into which has been packed more human ingenuity than into all the many millions of years before it. We have become like the children of rich parents and are no longer capable of appreciating the marvellous toys that are showered upon us.

"I feel that if I read in to-morrow's paper of a distinguished Czeckoslovakian engineer who had invented a rug like the rug in the Arabian Nights on which one would sit and be immediately transported wherever one wanted to go, I should not be at all astonished. I should just mention that someone had invented a rug for going anywhere at once and say how strange it was that such an invention had taken so long to perfect and that I must get one as soon as the price was at all reasonable.

"When I read the diaries or the letters of our grandparents and note what an amount of stupefaction they lavished upon such an edifice as Paddington railway station, and when I remember how the sight of a bone-shaking safety bicycle drew every little boy and girl to stare at it wide-eyed, and how the first pneumatic tyres induced other little boys and girls a year or two later to run along the kerb shouting 'Pneumatic Tyres! Pneumatic Tyres!' as though the rider had descended from another planet, I feel ashamed of the nonchalance of our modern imagination.

"Yet for the future of the human race broadcasting is as heavily fraught with potentialities as the discovery of printing.

"I suppose that at the end of the fifteenth century people asked themselves what was going to happen to literature under the influence of the printing press, the strange new monster that threatened individual expression. And certainly at the present moment many people are asking what will be the effect on literature of broadcasting. In a way, it is a return to the more primitive method of publicity when the bard stood up and recited his own epic. But it is a return with a difference, for whereas formerly the audience was limited to a few hundred listeners, the audience of the contemporary bard may be several hundreds of thousands and within the next few years it may easily be several millions.

"Personally I view such a prospect with complete optimism. Poetry has been slowly expiring under the influence of the printed page; but, though I fear it may be too late, it is just conceivable that the spur of recitation by the poet himself may yet recover it. Poetry was never meant to be read; it was meant to be heard. The recitation by the poets of their own verses will test them more severely than the best hand-made paper; and while broadcasting will provide them with a larger audience than they have ever dreamed of, it may act as a check on over-production.

"Any extension of the facilities for obtaining literature is in the long run an advantage to literature. At first the tendency is to help what is second-rate; but a public whose mind has been more nicely nourished will become surfeited with bad food. Yes, I look forward with hope to getting rid of a lot of worthless printed matter with the growth of broadcasting; indeed, the publishing trade now badly needs a Malthus or a Marie Stopes.

"Young women and young men produce books in these times as a hen lays eggs in Spring. It is true that few people read their works, but I am hoping that with the growth of broadcasting nobody will read them. And when we examine the case of music we have grounds for optimism, even within one year we can already see the tremendous improvement in the quality of music that is being issued by the gramophone companies; whatever may be the effect on literature there is no question at all that the effect on music is going to be entirely beneficial. For my part, I believe that we are moving toward a point of human development when it will be possible only in music to express the complicacy of human emotion.

"The great obstacle in the way of music has always been the difficulty of obtaining it. It is pathetic to think that an inadequate instrument like the piano should have represented practically the whole of the mechanical facilities which music received during a hundred years of mechanical progress in every direction.

"When finally the gramophone arrived, it was allowed to remain perfectly unprogressive by those who exploited it. As usual, the public was blamed; we were told that the public did not want good music and that it would not buy good records. It is hardly necessary to point out that this was nonsense; as soon as the gramophone companies began to provide good music in sufficient quantity, they found not merely that Wireless, their mighty new competitor, was not going to ruin them, but that it was actually going to assist them.

"I had occasion last year to deplore what I thought was the rubbish that the British Broadcasting Company was offering the public in the way of music. It seemed to me lamentable that such opportunities for education should be neglected; all that is changed now, and I affirm with respect and gratitude that no great financial corporation has ever shown itself so eager and so willing to help the cause of art.

"I believe many listeners write from all over Great Britain protesting against what they consider is the highbrow music that is being offered them. Presumably, some of the malcontents will read these words of mine and if any of them are so far honouring me, I beg them to pause when next they want to grumble at being given a performance of good music and to ask themselves if they really are anxious to remain in a state of barbarism. I beg them to doubt their own perfection and to bring themselves to wonder if they are not still capable of learning. Let me assure them that their fellow men who derive a sharper pleasure from a symphony of Beethoven than from some silly little tune of the day (which is after all only attractive because it is a repetition of a hundred and more catchy little tunes before it) are enjoying an infinitely greater pleasure than they themselves have ever experienced in their lives.

"Such men would probably write and protest with equal vigour if they were compelled to read nothing but nursemaids' novelettes. Yet, musically, they are in the condition of the nursemaid. Wireless has given these men an opportunity to raise themselves if they will only have the humility to realise that they want raising. People like them gain the general public a bad reputation; and yet the general public has the only really infallible taste, for it must never be forgotten that a work of art becomes what is called a classic not by the verdict of a few dank-haired critics, but by the capacity for enjoyment it can give to the general public in every generation.

"I doubt if 'Yes, We have No Bananas' would have been the success it was if the public ear had not been prepared for its rhythm

by Handel's Hallelujah Chorus. And what about the success of
'Lilac Time', in spite of the fact that before it was used for a musical
comedy every tune in it was Schubert's Op. something or other?

"Complacency is the great foe of Art, just as it is the enemy of
Religion and the destroyer of Love."

The truth of what I wrote in 1924 would be demonstrated during
the Second World War when the public were driven into buying
gramophone records of good music because the recording companies
took the opportunity of getting rid of all their unsold stock of good
music. Hence the boom in good music after the war, greatly helped,
of course, by the long-playing record, a boom which is still resounding. On the other hand, the publishers took the opportunity of
getting rid of all their second- and third-rate literature, and a decay
in literary taste set in which has not yet been stopped. What I wrote
then about the need of a Malthus and a Marie Stopes for the publishing trade is more than ever necessary. The present trend of publishing
is to follow the disastrous example of the newspapers by merger after
merger; this will end in the future by books being turned out like
plastics.

Those last few weeks in Casa Solitaria made Faith feel sad, but
Capri had given all it could give to me and was already seeming
something in the past, although it would have given me so much and
would remain vividly in my mind for the rest of my life.

Those weeks of spring and earliest summer in Capri are not as
vivid as earlier days. I was too much preoccupied with the desperate
need to get through the next years and reach calmer financial waters.
Before I left London Miss Kennedy Jones, the Editress of Pearson's
Home Magazine, had asked me to write a serial for them. I suggested
as a possibility telling the story of Stella. She read *Sinister Street* and
wrote to say how much she liked the idea of telling the story of
Michael's sister. So I sent her a synopsis from Capri, when she wrote
back to say that her directors disapproved of what she called the 'free
love episode' before Stella married. They felt it would wound the
susceptibilities of their readers. I then proposed a story called pro-
visionally *A Study in Green* which was to be founded on the story of
Madeleine Smith. She approved of that idea and asked for a first
instalment. I was anxious for the money a serial would bring in and
foolishly wrote that first instalment. This again was turned down by
her directors as likely to shock the readers of the *Home Magazine*
and I refused to waste any more time over them.

Toward the end of that wasted May Pinker wrote to say the *Daily Mirror* was keen for me to give them a serial and that the editor would like to talk about it when I came back to England next month. He would not want to begin the story before November.

I fancy that it was this spring when I had a verbal battle with James Agate, but it may have been later on this year.

The *Yorkshire Observer* reviewed a novel of his called *Blessed are the Rich* in the course of which the reviewer said that Mr Agate seemed to have been reading Mr Compton Mackenzie not wisely but too well. This drew a letter from Agate protesting that he had never read a word I had written, whereupon the reviewer asked why then did Mr Agate write in *Blessed are the Rich* of Mr Compton Mackenzie's 'showy harlots' if he had never read anything he ever wrote. Agate now wrote that it was not necessary to read an author to know what he wrote about. It was not necessary to read Plato to know that he wrote about the immortality of the soul. It was now up to Mr Compton Mackenzie to demonstrate that his harlots were not showy.

I had written so far when I decided to have another search through my scrapbooks to see if any letters survived from this battle and managed to find three which establish that it was in October of this year.

The first is from me:

"Sir, Mr Agate, as far as I am concerned, may protest the parthenogenesis of his egg until it is addled by time, or until—a more distant prospect—he writes a good book. I am not going to brood upon it in order to find out whether I have or have not fertilized a writer for the rest of whose work I have a profound contempt.

"I grudge Mr Agate his virginity no more than I grudge the captive parrot hers. Yet, perhaps I may be forgiven for feeling a little chastened by the thought that even one sentence of such pretentious writing could be attributed to my influence. It is hard to be accused of seducing such an over-dressed hussy as Mr Agate's muse, compared with whom no harlot I have ever known is half as 'showy'.

"Whatever faults Mr Agate might find in my novels, should he, as a critic, be visited by a momentary doubt of the morality of condemning an author on hearsay, he would never find me guilty in them of sneering at contemporary novelists; and if in future he will imitate nothing except my good manners in this respect I shall not have to correct him so brutally a second time.

Compton Mackenzie
Isle of Jethou, Channel Islands."

To this James Agate replied:

"Sir, In my novel 'Blessed are the Rich' I asked whether a low-class walker of the streets is of less interest than one of Mr Compton Mackenzie's 'showy harlots'.

"The implication was that the life-history and misfortunes of be-draggled wretches are as full of human interest as those of expensively begowned and bejewelled demi-mondaines. In being accused of imitating Mr Mackenzie's technique, I admitted at once that I had not read that writer's novels, and had merely dipped for an illustration into the stock-pot of general and transmitted knowledge.

"If Mr Mackenzie had denied the quality I attributed to certain of his characters I should have tendered an apology. But Mr Mackenzie does not deny that quality, and is content to say that his harlots are not half as showy as 'such an overdressed hussy as Mr Agate's muse'.

"In the ensuing medley of vulgar and virulent abuse I gather that I am accused of sneering at the writer. I submit, sir, that there can be no sneer in applying to certain of an author's characters an adjective the correctness of which he himself endorses. I submit, further, that my book contains no criticism of Mr Mackenzie's art which, again on hearsay, I must rate very highly.

"But, sir, surely those who would give a lesson in manners should themselves be above reproach. Mr Mackenzie—who couples my name with the words 'captive parrot'—calls me 'a writer for the rest of whose work I have a profound contempt'.

"I take it that condemnation as sweeping as this must be based on a thorough knowledge of the work condemned—otherwise the passer of sentence falls into the pit he would dig for another. I have published eight books besides 'Blessed are the Rich'. One is a war book, one a novel, two are general essays, four are volumes of dramatic criticism.

"I challenge Mr Mackenzie to say that he has read 'the rest of my work' or even one book out of each category. I challenge Mr Mackenzie, here and now, to say before he has time to send to the main-land for a copy of my novel 'Responsibility' whose and of what nature that responsibility was. I accuse him of the very crime which he, without foundation, alleges against me.

"On the other hand, if Mr Mackenzie assures me that he has read even one of each kind of my books so comprehensively damned by him, I shall unhesitatingly accept his assurance. But I shall at once proceed to ask him what quality of writing has persuaded him to waste so much of his valuable time upon the perusal of work for which he has a 'profound contempt'. On one or other horn of this dilemma I submit that I have my mentor impaled.

"I presume, sir, you have no objection to my reproducing this controversy in my next book of essays. I shall call it 'A Further Study in the Gentle Art'. I take it that there is nothing in Mr Mackenzie's letter which he would be ashamed to see in more permanent dress.

James Agate
55 Doughty Street, London, W.C.

Agate had recently succeeded Sydney Carroll as dramatic critic of the *Sunday Times* and never hesitated to come down with a heavy hand on some young actress who had written to protest against a sneer at her expense. I felt he needed a lesson and I wrote:

"Sir, I did not intervene in this 'controversy' until Mr Agate himself deliberately trailed his coat before me. I thought that his attitude was insolent, and I treated him as I shall always treat insolence.

"Among the several hundreds of characters I have drawn there are perhaps half a dozen harlots. None of them is 'begowned or bejewelled'. One of them is that 'bedraggled wretch' in whose portrayal Mr Agate is interested', and her history occupies pp. 964-976 of Sinister Street.

"To return to Mr Agate's own work. I have read a volume of theatrical criticism called 'Buzz-buzz', a novel called 'Responsibility' and a good deal of his work in 'The Sunday Times'. I read that paper because Mr Edmund Gosse and Mr Ernest Newman adorn its pages; and though I may deplore the intrusion of Mr Agate's fluted Corinthian columns, I must plead guilty to what I suppose is a morbid indulgence in a debased style, or perhaps a mere curiosity about what is being produced on the London stage.

"Still I ought to have qualified my remark about the rest of his work by adding 'as far as I have read it'. My copy of 'Responsibility' is at Capri, and I frankly admit that I have not the slightest recollection who, the author excepted, was responsible for what; though I do perfectly remember that the book struck me as turgid, pretentious, and horribly self-conscious.

"Will Mr Agate declare that he has never read a word of Meredith? Contrariwise, can he have read one word of Whistler? It seems rash to emulate so great a wit by publishing this 'controversy' in a book. It will savour of the schoolboy who proudly exhibits to his com-

c

panions the marks of the cane. However, Mr Agate's juvenile
exhibitionism is his own affair.

"Mr Agate is apparently under the impression that I likened him
to a parrot. If he will re-read the sentence in a calmer frame of mind
he will find that I did not. Had I wished to liken him to any bird I
should have chosen for reasons that ornithologists will appreciate the
hoopoe.[1]

"But it is time to direct this unseemly dispute toward an urbane
conclusion. Let me remind Mr Agate, who in a novel has sneered at
two of his fellow-novelists, one of whom is a woman, of the following
words, written by Miss Jane Austen in 1798: 'I will not adopt that
ungenerous and impolite custom, so common with novel-writers, of
degrading, by their contemptuous censure, the very performances to
the number of which they are themselves adding.'

Compton Mackenzie
Isle of Jethou. Channel Islands."

(This correspondence must now cease. As Mr Compton Mac-
kenzie says, it is time to direct it 'toward an urbane conclusion'. Editor.)

One cannot imagine any newspaper to-day allowing a couple of
authors to take up space with such 'controversy' as Agate called it,
but, I may add in justice to his memory, he did not mispronounce it
contróversy.

Norman Douglas and Charles Scott-Moncrieff were both in Capri
that spring and up in Anacapri Francis Brett Young was working
hard to finish a novel he was writing by June.

Louis Golding, a tiny little man in a grubby jersey, had arrived in
Capri, and had taken a cottage close to Francis's villa where he was
writing one of those many books he would write. He was continually
running up to Fraita to borrow paper from Francis, who did not
think it reasonable.

"Dog doesn't eat dog," I agreed. "No author should prey upon
another author's paper."

But my most vivid memory of those last days in Casa Solitaria is
of a golden oriole among the cherry-trees of Anacapri full-laden with
ripe fruit above the yellowing corn of June.

I had just written that sentence when *The Times* arrived, and
opening it I read that Magdalen had gone down into the Second
Division of the Summer Eights. For over a hundred years Magdalen
had never been out of the First Division, and indeed for well over

---

[1] Which fouls its own nest.

sixty years was never out of the first three colleges. The lilies of Magdalen have drooped; the scarlet blazer of the cox must now be the colour of rust. Yet why do I sigh? The many firsts in the multitudinous schools of to-day will seem more important to contemporary Magdalen than bumps.

Back in London by the second week in June I went to Savoy Hill to give my first broadcast in the weekly transmission of gramophone records every Thursday from one to two o'clock. It would have been Rex Palmer who greeted me when I arrived with a bundle of records all of which I have forgotten except one.

"Where's your script?" I was asked.

I explained that I always spoke off the cuff. Rex Palmer shook his head.

"I hope it will be all right," he said. "But broadcasting is different from after-dinner speaking."

He led the way to a big studio at the end of which was a gramophone with an armchair beside it over which hung a microphone.

"Try to imagine that an old friend is sitting in that armchair, and talk to the microphone as naturally as if you were talking to him. You don't feel too nervous?" my producer asked.

I assured him I did not feel at all nervous.

"Ah, well, it won't matter much if you do dry up. There's nobody listening at this hour except the women washing up."

I was to hand each record as I came to it to somebody who would put it on the gramophone; I did not have that to bother about. A minute or two before we started I was asked if the presence of a Sunday school treat being shown round Savoy Hill with a parson would make me nervous. I replied that on the contrary a visible audience would be a help. So off I went, commenting on each record before it was put on, the first of a stableful of disc jockeys in the future.

One of my records was a ten-inch Vocalion of Lionel Tertis playing a viola solo.

"I always have a rather sentimental feeling when I am playing a record of Lionel Tertis because that great viola player and I were both born in that . . ." I was on the verge of saying 'that grubby old town beside the North Sea' when I had a vision of one of the leading citizens of West Hartlepool listening and writing to complain of the epithet . . . "both born in West Hartlepool which stood up so gallantly to the cowardly bombardment by the German fleet in the war."

I think I can claim that broadcasting came naturally to me and that I was fully conscious from the first of that hidden audience.

It would have been about that date that the Archbishop of Canterbury was persuaded to broadcast. In one of the heavily draped small studios he was to give a talk, but when he faced the microphone he was overcome by the equivalent of stage-fright and after opening with "My dear friends" could only ejaculate "Goo! Goo! Gah!" until they had to cut him off and put on gramophone records for the rest of his quarter of an hour.

The first volume of *The Gramophone* was complete with the May number. The circulation was rising all the time, but until we could raise our advertisement rates I realized that this rising circulation would involve us in loss. I decided we must put a break on circulation and at the same time double the revenue from sales. Everybody connected with the paper thought I was taking a rash step, but I insisted; doubling the price only resulted in the June number's circulation remaining the same as May. After that it continued to rise steadily every month. Moreover, with new advertisement contracts for the second year we were able to charge more for them. The Press all over the world was very generous in congratulating us on the success we had achieved in our first year. I had thought it would be a good idea to obtain publicity by having a test of the various gramophones on the market. This was to take place at the Steinway Hall on June 14th. There were to be two classes, one for machines of £25 and under, the other for machines above that. H.M.V. and Columbia naturally felt they could not afford to compete, but without them fifteen machines were entered. These gramophones were concealed from view throughout the tests, and they played the records I had chosen for the ordeal in a different order for each. Neither the judges nor the audience knew what machines were competing, nor which of them was playing at any time. The verdict was to be given by the joint votes of the judges and the audience, and it was encouraging to find how slightly they disagreed.

The judges were Marie Novello, Alfred Kalisch, Peter Latham, Alec Robertson, Francis Brett Young, and Percy Scholes. Scholes, true to his democratic principles, would agree to judge only the cheaper machines. He was not prepared to encourage machines costing as much as £63. The cheapest machine was the Decca Portable which had been the solace of so many trench-weary men when they were out of the line. Sad to say, it was placed last in the opinion both of the judges and the audience. Nobody guessed then that the Decca Portable would two or three years later give its name to the great company which to-day has only E.M.I. as an equal.

Of the judges Peter Latham was for many years one of *The Gramo-phone's* most valued critics and Alec Robertson, who at this date was one of the musical advisers to H.M.V., is to-day the musical editor of *The Gramophone*.

I spoke just now of the ordeal for the machines; it was nothing like the ordeal of the judges and audience. The hall was packed and the test lasted for over four hours with a brief interval to get some refreshment.

Back in Jethou I found that Macdonald had carried through with the help of Edwin, his sixteen-year-old nephew from Alderney, the installation of a water-closet in the house and another in the cottage. There was nothing Macdonald could not do and do well. His next job was to fence in the sunk garden and about a quarter of an acre beyond it so that I could plant various sub-tropical shrubs without their being blown out of the ground by wind. I had a lot of seedling acacias raised by Basil Leng from seed obtained from a nurseryman in Adelaide. He arrived from Tresco in the Scilly Isles with various echiums which became a feature of the islandscape—among them a crimson bugloss rising to fifteen feet. I had been impressed by the way the orange groves in the Sorrentine peninsula were protected from the wind by laths and we followed that example on Jethou. The advantage of this was that the wind was filtered through and did not hit a high wall and come down on the other side with vicious force.

I had managed to sell the *Aphrodite* to Lady Boot by now. I had hoped for £2,000 but had to accept £1,500. At the last moment after the price had been agreed I received a letter to say that there was a faulty screw somewhere and that unless I accepted £1,400 the purchase would have to be cancelled. Dame Florence Boot, as she was called in the registered transfer of the motor-yacht, might have been a match even for Sir Percival Perry. The sale of the *Aphrodite*, the decision of the *Daily Mirror* to accept my suggestion for a serial, and the progress of *The Gramophone* upwards made me feel justified in planning for Macdonald to build a library in place of the dilapidated vinery, but I decided to wait until next year before he started.

I have spoken of the birds and flowers of Jethou; the intimacy into which a small island endows them for him who lives on it. The same is true of the butterflies and moths. One seems to recognize them as individuals. From that summer of long ago I recall the graylings sunning themselves with their folded wings tilted over almost flat on the ground (does any other butterfly do this?) and seeing a female brimstone with folded wings who looked so much like a leaf that a fly had alighted on her under the impression that she really was a leaf. Dark-green fritillaries and green hairstreaks came to the island; I recall watching one of the latter laying her eggs on the gorse bushes beside the drive. The most exciting visitors were the convolvulus hawk-moths that used to flap against the window of a lighted room and sometimes manage to get in. I also saw what was probably the island's last black rat. Nowadays the old English black rat has been displaced by the big brown rats of Norway which are prepared to eat anything and which with rabbits, sparrows, woodpigeons and starlings will probably be the only examples of wild life in Great Britain in another hundred years at the rate with which farmers are exterminating insect and bird life with insecticides and fertilizers. However, if the insects vanish, human beings will be a hundred years nearer to the perfect Insect State into which mankind seems set on evolving.

That April in Capri I had received the following letter from College Street, Dublin:

A Chara

Possibly you have already heard of the Literary Competitions of Aonach Tailteann by which we hope to give a much needed impetus to literature in this country both in this year and in the years to come. Aonach Tailteann is of course the first revival of the ancient Tailteann Games which were held many thousands of years ago at Tara in the old Gaelic days. It will be revived this year in August, and has aroused immense interest among Irish people in all parts of the world.

Dr Oliver St J. Gogarty suggested to me that you might care to act as judge in one of the Literary Sections. The Sections are: Drama, Novels, Prose, Poetry and Short Stories. We are anxious to have men of your experience and international reputation as judges in the Literary Competitions, and Dr Gogarty felt sure that you would be prepared to act in conjunction with another littérateur as judge in the novel section. It will not be heavy work, I can assure you, as I fear the quality of the entries is not very high, but I would certainly like to have your opinion on them, and I know the entrants would be very satisfied too.

Perhaps you could let me know at your earliest convenience if you can see your way to do this.

Is Mise do Chara

M. J. Murray, Chairman Literary Committee

P.S. Other judges include W. B. Yeats, Æ, Padraic Colum, James Stephens etc.

In the middle of June half the novels arrived and in the first week of July the rest of the twenty-four entries, all in typescript. With that invitation came a letter from my old friend Oliver Gogarty.

I had first met Gogarty when he was up at Worcester College, Oxford, for a year or two after taking his degree at Trinity College, Dublin. He was now the leading throat specialist in Ireland and a Senator of the Irish Free State. He was also the greatest wit of the wittiest city in the world and a raconteur of the first class. He was the Buck Milligan of James Joyce's *Ulysses*. He urged me to accept that invitation to the Games and said that I could be the guest of Tim Healy, the Governor-General at the Viceregal Lodge, with G. K. Chesterton. Others who had been invited were Augustus John, Sir Edwin Lutyens and Sir Henry Hadow, who had been a tutor at Worcester and was now Vice-Chancellor of Sheffield University.

I cannot remember looking forward to anything more keenly than that visit to Dublin, and yet it was much more colourful than even I had anticipated.

Augustus John and I decided to cross from Birkenhead rather than Holyhead, which meant arriving at North Wall in the middle of Dublin instead of at Kingstown. Sir Henry Hadow was also on board, but he went early to his bunk, leaving John and me to sit up talking into the small hours.

Oliver Gogarty was at North Wall to meet us and we were told that the first function would be a dinner of welcome to the distinguished visitors at the Metropole Hotel. I was faintly surprised when Augustus John appeared wearing brown Harris tweed trousers below tails and a boiled shirt.

"I forgot to pack my black trousers in London," he told Gogarty.

"Couldn't Dunsany lend you a pair of his?"

John was staying with Lord Dunsany about fourteen miles out of Dublin.

"I wouldn't ask a teetotaller to lend me his trousers," John growled.

"Well, well, don't bother about those trousers," Gogarty told him. And being Ireland nobody else bothered about them.

"I've got a great joke on over Augustus," Gogarty murmured to me. "I've told Augustus that Dunsany is a fierce teetotaller and for god's sake not to ask him for a drink and I've told Dunsany that Augustus is a fierce teetotaller and for god's sake not to offer him one. I wonder how long Augustus will stand it."

It was not for long. Two or three days later Gogarty was giving a breakfast at 15 Ely Place, the house with a large garden where George Moore had lived.

"Who do you think is in my bed?" Gogarty said. "Augustus! I went to the bathroom to shave this morning and when I came back Augustus was asleep in my bed. What finished him off was when Dunsany started to explain how to play the great Irish harp, and that without a drink. After they went to bed Augustus climbed over the wall of Dunsany Park and walked the fourteen miles to Dublin. He arrived here while I was shaving."

At the top table of that banquet for three hundred guests I saw a huge figure in pale blue robes and a turban covered with pearls. This was the Jam Saheb of Nawanagar, the immortal 'Ranji' himself, who had just bought an estate in Connemara. C. B. Fry was with him.

When speech time came, one of the speakers was the Jam Saheb, who said how happy he was to have acquired Ballynahinch Castle in Connemara and how much the people there reminded him of his own Rajputs, courteous, wise and loyal. It was a good speech and as that huge resplendent figure sat down the Commander-in-Chief of the Free State Army rose. At that moment the municipal gas and electric people decided to have their two-minutes' strike to protest about something or other, probably wages. Unperturbed in the absolute darkness the Commander-in-Chief went on with his speech in Gaelic, after a minute of which Augustus John lent over to me.

"What's going on?" he asked.

"It's a Free State General making a speech in Gaelic," I whispered.

"Thank God, I'm only drunk," said John in a tone of relief. "I thought I'd gone mad."

Then the lights came on again.

As we gathered at the Viceregal Lodge to get into the cars that would take us to Croke Park for the opening of the Games, Tim Healy warned us we should probably be shot at on our way.

"I shall be all right, sir," I said confidently. "I'm in the car with G.K. and no shot will reach me."

As I write that, I recall the expression on the face of a little Portuguese monsignore to whom G.K., on being presented, prepared to genuflect, under the impression he was a bishop. An approaching avalanche would not have alarmed him more.

"He's not a bishop," I hastily murmured to G.K. and the avalanche was stayed.

I realized when I saw painted in huge green letters on one of the walls we passed 'Death To The Murder Gang' that Tim Healy's remark might not be so far out after all. There were Republicans still in prison, and Kevin O'Higgins, the Minister of Home Affairs, the strong man of the Free State, had roused bitter hatred by refusing to reprieve Erskine Childers from being shot in reprisal for the assassination of Michael Collins. I had tea with Kevin O'Higgins that August. It was one of those grey days of the West and as I walked along the laurel-lined drive to his house I felt the doom that was hanging over him almost physically. His brother, Tom Higgins, a naval surgeon, had become a dear friend of mine at Tenedos when he was there with the governor, Captain E. K. Loring, after the old battle-ship *Ocean* was sunk in the Dardanelles. Tom Higgins had stayed with us in Capri. I recall his scoffing at Kevin as a would-be Mussolini; no two brothers could have been less alike. I can see Kevin in that shadowy sitting-room ceaselessly smoking cigarettes, the shadows in his sombre eyes. Later he became Minister of Justice and was assassinated on his way to Mass in July, 1927.

I was introduced to John McCormack that afternoon at Croke Park. As he shook my hand he said:

"I suppose you think I sing nothing but rubbish."

I told him that, so far from that, I was anxious to write an article in *The Gramophone* commenting on every one of the records he had made in the same way as I had written about Caruso.

"No doubt one song 'Oh, don't you remember sweet Alice, Ben Bolt?' could be called sentimental rubbish, but your record of it took me back to my first enchanted reading of *Trilby* when I was in my teens."

At that moment a friendship began between us that would last for the next twenty years.

McCormack gave a concert at the Theatre Royal for the funds of the Games. I had to leave for some function while he was singing his sixth encore at the end. As I came out into the lobby W. B. Yeats, dressed as a Senator in frock-coat and silk hat, came out.

"A wonderful concert, eh?" I observed.

"Wonderful! Wonderful!" Yeats agreed in those hieratic tones of his. "But oh, the clarity of the words, the damnable clarity of the words."

One of the privileges I remember vividly in looking back to that August of forty years ago is of sitting up every night with Tim Healy after the rest of the Viceregal party had gone to bed. I think G.K. would have liked to sit up too but Mrs G.K. always took him off to bed by half-past ten at the latest.

I regretted this because I had welcomed the opportunity of getting to know G.K. He had left St Paul's about a couple of years before I reached it but his younger brother Cecil had been a great friend, and friends of G.K. like E. C. Bentley were still there in the summer term of 1894.

I foolishly did not make notes of these talks with Tim Healy which lasted sometimes till three in the morning, but I recall a few fragments.

On one occasion he said:

"You Scots were lucky because you had a Bannockburn. We never had a Bannockburn in Ireland."

On another occasion Tim Healy took a sip at the bottle of 'Johnnie Jameson' between us, that Irish whiskey with an 'e' which I enjoy so much when I am not in Scotland.

"Tell me, I know you've thought quite a lot about these things, in the matter of indulgences would you be inclined to follow the Jesuits or the Redemptorists?"

"Well, sir, if I were seventy, like you, I think I'd probably pay more attention to the Redemptorists than I do now."

Tim shook his big white beard.

"Ah, I thought you'd say that."

On another evening he was going back to the days of Parnell, whose influence he did so much to destroy after he had been his devoted supporter.

"I remember going to Mr Gladstone at the time of that miserable Parnell business and I said to him, 'Sir' " . . . Tim paused and looked at me gravely . . . "You know, we all of us always called him 'Sir'."

Nothing has brought to my mind a clearer impression, whatever Queen Victoria or Disraeli might have thought, of the grandeur of that G.O.M. I feel to-day that if Mr Gladstone had been handling our entry into the Common Market not even General de Gaulle would have been able to withstand him. Let me quickly add that I have for General de Gaulle a profound admiration, believing him to be almost the only great stateman left in Europe in this year 1965.

It may have been that same evening Tim Healy said to me:

"You know, God forgive me, but I don't believe that in our hearts we really wanted Home Rule. We used to enjoy ourselves at Westminster, we didn't have our fingers on the pulse of Ireland, and then those young men swept us away in a night."

He was alluding to the Sinn Fein election in 1918; he had been the first of the Nationalist members to grasp what was happening, and that was why he was now Governor-General of the Irish Free State.

One day the Governor-General took me out into the grounds to look at a limestone obelisk on the face of which was carved the figure of a tree. Underneath was the following inscription:

Erected in 1856 by
H.E. the Earl of Carlisle, K.G.
Lord Lieutenant of Ireland
to mark the site of a tree planted in January
1856, by Jemima Countess of St Germans,
the wife of his predecessor.
The tree did not live long.

On the opposite side of the base were some verses:

1856
Poor tree, a gentle mistress placed thee here,
To be the glory of the glade around.
Thy life has not survived one fleeting year,
And she too sleeps beneath another mound.
But mark what diff'ring terms your fates allow,
Though like the period of your swift decay:
Thine are the sapless root, and wither'd bough:
Her's the green mem'ry, and immortal day.

Just beyond the obelisk was a stone to mark the burial place of King Edward VII's Irish terrier, Jack:

Here lies
JACK
King Edward's
Favourite Irish terrier
who only lived twelve hours
after reaching his native land.
He died at the Viceregal Lodge.

"And we paid for that," Tim Healy observed as he put his hands behind his back and flapped the tails of his coat in a familiar gesture before turning and walking back with me to the Lodge without another word.

On another day the Governor-General took me to see his house at Chapelizod on the banks of the Liffey. There he had an electric installation fed by the waterfall of a dam.

"George Wyndham used to call my house Heliopolis," he told me with a chuckle.

One more story of Tim Healy which was not told me by himself.

A famous surgeon of Merrion Square called McArdle was co-respondent in a divorce suit. James Campbell, the late Lord Glenavy, appeared for the plaintiff; Tim was representing the surgeon. McArdle was listening to the proceedings in the body of the court, and Campbell was saying as he stared hard at McArdle:

"I do not know if the co-respondent has had the audacity to be present in this court to-day, but if he has let me tell him that the wrongs he inflicted on my client have brought tears to my eyes."

In a flash Tim Healy was on his feet.

"My lud and gentlemen of the jury, you have now witnessed the greatest miracle since Moses struck the rock."

Some argument between the Labour Government and the Irish Free State Government was going on in that August; Arthur Henderson and J. H. Thomas came over to Ireland to iron it out. I was walking up and down the terrace with 'Jimmy' Thomas on a blowy morning and Thomas kept trying to light his pipe.

After several failures I offered him the shelter of my coat by pulling out the lee side of it.

"Oh, I know how to light my pipe in a wind," said 'Jimmy' Thomas, "I used to be an engine-driver."

"You haven't been very successful so far," I told him, and in the end he had to surrender his pride and take advantage of my coat.

I recall saying to J. J. Walsh, the Minister of Posts and Telegraphs, after Thomas and Henderson went off, that I hoped he had been firm about keeping all broadcasting rights in the hands of the Irish Free State, and being relieved to hear that he had had the foresight to do so, though I doubt if he realised at the time quite how vitally important a monopoly of broadcasting would be.

There was a big dinner-party one night at the Viceregal Lodge. By mistake when the invitations were sent out there were not enough ladies to go round and Mr Doyle, the Controller of the Household, a much respected and well-loved Dublin publican, asked four of us without our wives if we would mind not taking in a lady and sitting all together at one end of the table. The four 'bachelors' were Ned Lutyens, Cecil Baring,[1] Baron Palmstierna, the Swedish Minister in London, and myself. The Swedish minister was looking very gloomy when we took our seats.

"What's the matter with you?" Ned Lutyens asked in that irresistible voice of his. "You're looking very sad."

[1] The late Lord Revelstoke.

I recalled that note of light persiflage from a packed lunch with Sybil Colefax[1] when I was sitting next Walter de la Mare.

"Tell me," Ned Lutyens had said from the other side of the table, "Why do all you poets write such nonsense?"

Dear Walter de la Mare was less prompt with his reply than Baron Palmstierna.

"Well, Sir Edwin, I know that this is a young country and I know that perhaps yet they have not been able to understand about protocol. When I come to the Lodge the sentries pay no attention but when that Afghan comes they click-click and present arms. They do not realise that I am the doyen of the diplomatic corps here."

The 'Afghan' to whom the Swedish Minister alluded was Prince Mirza Riza Khan, a Persian poet and representative of his country at the League of Nations. He was wearing an astrakhan fez and sitting next the Marchioness McSwiney, the wife of a Papal marquis who had a very large and exuberant handlebar moustache.

"But this evening," the Swedish Minister continued, "it has been too much. I was to take the Marchioness McSwiney in to dinner, an intellectual and very distinguished lady, when just as I am offering her my arm, she is taken away from me and given to that Afghan to take in."

"Never mind," said Ned Lutyens, "you're still our greatest little Swede. In fact I'm going to call you Baron Mangel-Wurzel with a hyphen."

At this point Cecil Baring hurriedly intervened to invite the Swedish Minister to visit Lambay, that island rather bigger than Herm for which Lutyens had designed one of the finest houses even in his achievement.

When the signal was given by Lady Lavery, who was sitting on Tim Healy's right, for the ladies to retire, they were followed through a large ante-room to the drawing-room where all would assemble after the post-prandial interval for port and brandy and cigars and male conversation.

Presently Miss Healy appeared in the doorway of the farthest drawing-room. The Governor-General looked up and beckoned the Controller of the Household.

"Mr Doyle, Miss Healy seems to be making signals of distress. Will you kindly go along and see what she wants?"

The Controller went along and soon came back.

"It's his Highness, your Excellency. He's sitting there in the

1 The late Lady Colefax.

drawing-room and embarrassing the ladies."

"Did you not tell his Highness I was anxious to have an opportunity of talking to him?"

"I said just that, your Excellency, and he wouldn't budge."

The Governor-General looked across to me.

"Mackenzie, you're a young man of tact. Will you kindly go along and explain to his Highness how anxious I am for a few words with him."

So I went along to the drawing-room where I found the Persian prince and poet sitting on a pouffe in the middle of a circle of obviously irritated ladies.

"For heaven's sake get him out of here, Monty," Hazel Lavery whispered to me.

I approached the Prince.

"Altesse, son Excellence n'a pas eu le plaisir d'une entretien avec vous. Il espère que vous lui donnerez un tel plaisir."

The Persian poet replied firmly in tinny Levantine French.

"Non, non, je ne viens pas. Toujours chez moi après le diner je lis la posèie à mes femmes et je lirai mes poèmes maintenant."

With this he took a slim volume from the pocket of his jacket.

"Écoutez, mesdames, s'il vous plaît," he commanded in a voice no Sultan could have made more authoritative.

I gave up and returned to apprise the Governor-General of my defeat.

Soon after that dinner Colonel Grant Morden and his wife arrived to stay at the Viceregal Lodge. He was the member for Brentford and Chiswick, one of those rich Canadians who in various ways have flowered financially in Great Britain. I pause to ask why it is always Canadians who buy up British newspapers rather than Australians. Grant Morden had just bought the *People* and Tim Healy was hoping that its influence would be exercised in trying to get some common sense about Ireland into popular British opinion. I was not less interested than the Governor-General in Grant Morden because he had just bought the Vocalion Company and in him I saw a useful competitor to spur on H.M.V. and Columbia to produce more and more symphonies, concertos and string quartets. Spur is the word, for Grant Morden was a devoted fox-hunter and M.F.H.

I recall an evening when we went to a hunt ball and Grant Morden let it be known that he was looking for a horse. Unfortunately for those who hoped to sell him one, the Colonel was attracted to a merry widow and was no longer looking for a horse. He was so pressing in his attentions that when he suggested driving her home in the viceregal car she demurred until she was sure that Mr Doyle and I would both be in the car. It was dawn when we reached her house on the outskirts of Dublin and the sun was up before Mr Doyle and I managed to persuade the Colonel to go home. The Controller of the Household had been charged by the Governor-General to look after him. It must have been past six when we got back to the Lodge, and as we entered Grant Morden said:

"I think a bottle of champagne would be welcome after that long drive."

"I'll see about it, Colonel. We'll go along to my room," Mr Doyle suggested.

As we were walking along the corridor past the big lift I heard a voice above say:

"Is that you, Grant?"

As a horse twitches to throw off a fly the Colonel's neck twitched.

In the Controller's little room there was no champagne.

"I'm sorry, Colonel, but I've only got a bottle of whiskey and a bottle of brandy."

"I don't drink much except champagne nowadays, but brandy will do," said the Colonel as he poured himself out half a small tumbler; neither Mr Doyle nor I felt able to tackle neat brandy at six o'clock in the morning. The Colonel was made of tougher stuff; he poured himself out another half glass.

"Did either of you hear something as we passed the lift?" he asked presently.

I said I thought I *had* heard a voice.

"That must have been Mrs Morden. She's kind of restless now at night. I'd better go up. Do you mind if I take this bottle up with me, Mr Doyle? She might get off to sleep if I gave her a sip of brandy."

With this Grant Morden picked up the bottle of brandy and walked out of the room to take the lift like a five-barred gate.

"He's quite a character, the Colonel," the Controller observed.

"He certainly is," I agreed.

"That was a '93 Cognac," said Mr Doyle with the faintest touch of regret in his tone at such a cognac's being drunk at six o'clock in the morning.

One of the pleasures of that thronged fortnight was meeting James Stephens, who was working at the Dublin Gallery. It was Tom

Bodkin who introduced us. How improbable it would have seemed then that years later I should be broadcasting with James Stephens, and even more improbable that I should appear on television in Tom Bodkin's *This is your Life*. Eamonn Andrews was then a Dublin infant not yet two years old. The picture of the author of *The Crock of Gold* between G. K. Chesterton and Lennox Robinson opposite this page shows his likeness to the leprechaun he remained all his life. In 1924 Tom Bodkin was still Secretary to the Commissioners of Irish Charitable Bequests and was trying to extract from the British Government the pictures Hugh Lane had bequeathed to the Dublin Gallery. I had met Lane nearly twenty years earlier in the Carfax Gallery of Robbie Ross, a tall slightly effeminate man who had just put up the money for a young Irish pianist to go to Vienna and study under Leschetizky. I was able to tell Bodkin that even then Hugh Lane had been set on collecting pictures for the Dublin Gallery. When he went down with the *Lusitania* he had failed to sign a codicil to his will and on a technicality the British Government refused to give up the pictures.

These powerful 'no' men behind the scene of British politics and bureaucracy provide an answer sometimes to what seems the incomprehensible hebetude of the British Government over some question of art. I remember dining in 1946 with the late Lord Glyn when the late Lord Jowitt, then Lord Chancellor, was also a guest. In the smoking-room after dinner I said the right way to handle the situation in Greece was for a British cruiser to arrive at the Piraeus with the Elgin marbles and give them back to Hellas. It would be a gesture the Greeks would never forget.

"No!" shouted 'Bill' Jowitt, and shot up in the air from the armchair in which he was sitting.

I had been planning a letter to *The Times* with a few signatures of painters, sculptors and authors of eminence advocating the restoration of the Elgin marbles. I knew now it would be pointless. There would be other 'no' men like Bill Jowitt who would make sure that the Elgin marbles remained in the British Museum, buried out of sight though they were at this date because the British Museum had used the wrong stuff to clean them and it was feared ruined them in consequence. Mercifully, they were at last restored from the clumsiness of the restorers.

The photograph of that group in Ely Place was taken at a garden party given by Oliver Gogarty. He was at this time mad on archery and in a green jacket showed us what a good shot he was. I went for

At 15 Ely Place, George Moore's House
left to right : G. K. Chesterton, James Stephens, Lennox Robinson,
W. B. Yeats, C.M., Augustus John, Edwin Lutyens

Christopher Stone, C.M., Félicité Fairfax-Ross and Faith Mackenzie
in the library at Jethou

Jethou from the air

several hair-raising drives with Gogarty in his car, but when he suggested taking me for a spin in his aeroplane, I refused. My nerves had suffered enough from his furious driving, talking all the while and taking his hands from the wheel from time to time to illustrate one of his inimitable tales. The prospect of his doing this when I was up in a plane with him was too much for my nerves to contemplate.

That wonderful time at the Viceregal Lodge came to an end, but the enjoyment of Ireland was to be prolonged by an invitation to stay with Hilda and William Nolan at Corbawn, their house in Shankill. William Nolan was head of the great Irish publishing firm of Browne and Nolan; Hilda Nolan was a beautiful American from Salem. Their son Allen, a small schoolboy home for the holidays from Downside, is now head of the business. With that American determination to show and be shown the sights Hilda Nolan introduced me to the Irish countryside. My mother lacked that American quality, but her elder sister Ellen, who had been playing Richard III at the age of four to great audiences all over the United States, was worried at the age of ninety because she had not seen Iona and travelled there from Santa Monica in California.

One expedition we made was to Aughavanagh, high in the Wicklow mountains, the home of Captain William Redmond, the son of John Redmond. He was member of the Dail for Waterford, an ex-Irish Guardsman saddened by his father's failure to realise the great hopes of the Irish Nationalists.

Aughavanagh was a large, lonely house on top of the view in every direction. I was astonished to see in a sheltered corner by the house the largest *Crinodendron hookerianum* or *Tricuspidaria* I have ever seen, covered with a myriad of those flowers like cut rubies; that dark Chilean evergreen filled me with awe. I thought of the two tiny *Crinodendrons* I had planted on Jethou in the shelter of the privateer's ruined house and wondered if they would ever rival this noble giant.

I turned over the pages of the press-cutting albums that William Redmond showed me in which were recorded those Irish gatherings in the early 'eighties in Chicago and New York and so many other American cities. This very month I had been introduced to John Devoy, who had served penal servitude as a Fenian in 1867 and spent the rest of his liberty in America until he came over for the Tailteann Games to see an Ireland that was at last free. And then I was shown a number of record albums full of old Celebrity discs with white and green and pale blue and lavender and yellow labels, all

D

of them by this date a monotonous red, like the varicoloured horse-buses of once upon a time, but costing much less now than when they were first issued.

We talk of upsetting the apple-cart. How many people have literally upset an apple-cart? I had driven in to Dublin with Hilda Nolan to do some shopping. In a side-street sloping down to Sack-ville Street, Hilda jumped out to go into a shop, leaving me in the car. Suddenly the car began to move. I had not the faintest notion how to put on the brake and the car glided down. Mercifully just as it reached Sackville Street its further progress was stopped by a donkey-cart full of apples being led along by an old woman. The cart was not actually turned over but the apples with which it was loaded were scattered all over the road. Being Ireland, matters between myself, Hilda, the apple-woman and the Civic Guard were soon amicably settled.

I was anxious to see Smith's nursery at Newry just over the North Irish border. In the fifteen years since I had bought so many rarities from that nursery for the garden in Cornwall it had become almost a wilderness, and Smith himself was too old to bother. However, I ordered an *Eucryphia pinnatifolia* or *glutinosa* for Corbawn; I hope the white petals of its hawthorn-scented flowers still strew the ground beneath in August.

We made an expedition to Co. Kerry to stay for a night at the Glenbeigh Hotel run by jolly Captain Shea. Beyond the hotel wide sands stretched for three miles along dunes to the Dingle peninsula, on which even on the calmest days the Atlantic breakers thundered. I was much taken by a house at the head of Loch Caragh where the Republicans had made their last stand against the Free State army. DOWN WITH VICTORIA'S TANS AND BLACKS was painted in sprawling green letters on a ruined cottage close by.

Enquiries from a solicitor at Tralee told me that a General Franks, now serving in India, had first refusal of Lickeen House. Captain Shea suggested I should take a furnished house called Ripley Lodge belonging to a Mr Fitzjames Shute. I decided that for £105 it would be worth while to rent it for a year from next October so as to be on the spot if Lickeen became available.

I left Corbawn with much regret. My stay there had been the perfect climax to my time in Ireland, in recalling which I have left out so many people about whom I should have liked to write.

Faith went back to Capri in September to superintend the evacuation of Casa Solitaris. I knew that she did not want to leave Capri and when Axel Munthe wrote to suggest I should take San Michele at £200 a year with the right to sublet I was tempted. However, finally Faith felt it would be too much of a responsibility and decided she should prefer to spend her time in Capri in the *villino* she had taken, La Carmela.

When Faith left Newman Street, *The Gramophone* moved to 58 Frith Street, Soho. Douglas Parrish brought some capital into what was now Gramophone Publications (Ltd) and I signed a contract to remain as Editor, write a monthly editorial and a quarterly review of records of not less than six thousand words. I cannot remember what money I received, but I know it was very useful and temporarily lightened the financial strain. The *Daily Mirror* people expressed themselves pleased with what I had written of *Coral* and I guaranteed to finish the serial for them to publish in November.

I think it was to celebrate his acquiring Vocalion that Colonel Grant Morden gave a dinner at Heatherden Hall, Iver Heath. I know it was a white-tie affair and that we ate off gold plate. He had a large swimming-bath with travelling-rings above it, and after dinner in his tail-coat he swung himself from ring to ring to the end of the bath and then back again. He wanted to know what I thought of an idea put before him by a young Spanish grandee who was staying at the Ritz.

"I think this young fellow has hit on quite a bright notion. He has a whole lot of small gramophones disguised as something else. One looks like a lamp, another like a flower-bowl and so on. He has about a dozen of these models with him at the Ritz; you and I will go there to-morrow and have a look at them."

At the Ritz Grant Morden asked for Count Somebody. The head porter told him the Count would soon be in and sent a boy up to let the Colonel into his room.

I was doubtful of the advantage to be gained by disguising a gramophone as something else.

"But it works," said the Colonel and proceeded to turn them all on. They had no sooner started than he thought he would visit the Count's loo, into which he disappeared, leaving me in the middle of about a dozen gramophones all playing and all disguised as lamps or flower-bowls. The records were still playing when the Count came in, and looked at me with suspicious astonishment. As he could speak hardly any English and I could speak no Spanish I could only point to the loo and say in Italian "E dentro, il Colonello", hoping it would be a bit nearer to Spanish than English. I was much relieved when the Colonel emerged, buttoning the last button of his braces. We heard no more of those disguised gramophones.

Colonel Grant Morden continued to sit in Parliament until 1931 and died in the following year. He was then only just over fifty. Such abundant vitality should have endured longer.

When I got back to Jethou I wrote a long appreciation of every one of John McCormack's records in the H.M.V. list; it appeared in the October *Gramophone*. He wrote to me from Esher Place, Surrey:

What is there to say that will adequately express to you my deep appreciation of your most flattering article? Know in any event that you have the very deep appreciation of an artiste who has always striven to do his best in whatever he has tried to do. I believe if a thing is worth doing at all it is worth doing well, and rubbish is after all a relative term, especially in music. After all if a song makes the hearer the better for having heard it, if it takes the mind of his audience away from the Sturm und Drang of life I believe it has fulfilled one of the principal reasons of its being. In that way songs like Mother Machree and such like which are musically rubbish have their place in the general musical scheme of things: I would like to have a chat on Sunday after the concert over a cold bottle on this interesting subject. By the way I am asking the Musical Courier of New York to print the article in full. Have you any objection?

> *Again my heartfelt thanks*
> *Yours most sincerely and in friendship*
> *John McCormack*

P.S. By the way if you notice any difference in the size of my head on Sunday, you are certainly to blame. So there.

John McCormack was terribly nervous about that concert at Queen's Hall. He was getting anonymous letters denouncing him as a traitor and threats that he would be hooted off the platform. During the war he had been nationalized as an American citizen. This was a logical step for an Irishman to take in protest against the outrageous treatment of Ireland by the British Government, but the distorted presentation of the troubles in Ireland by the British Press stimulated the skunks who exude anonymous letters.

I begged John not to worry about fanatical oafs and to feel sure that he would receive the enthusiastic welcome he deserved from what would be a crowded audience of well-wishers. He asked me if I would sit with his wife and daughter at the concert, and naturally I was proud to agree.

John McCormack went to early Mass on that Sunday morning and remained in church until it was time for him to reach Queen's Hall. I sat in the middle of the front row of the circle between his wife and daughter. When John appeared he was as white as a dead man, and Lily McCormack put out her hand, which I seized and held tightly. There was no need for apprehension. From every part of the Hall the reception was thunderous, and then a complete hush as John, still deathly white, began with that lovely high note to sing 'O Sleep, why dost thou leave me', the aria from Handel's *Semele*.

That evening John gave a terrific dinner party at the Carlton. There must have been a couple of dozen of us at least, but I am ashamed to say I can remember only one of the guests. That was Madge Titheradge, who was sitting next to me. From the stage shop we were talking I recall only one remark:

"So Fay is married to a Quartermaine. I'm married to a Quartermaine. They take themselves very seriously."

When the party broke up about one in the morning my host asked me to stay on because he had something he wanted me to hear. That was his recording for H.M.V. of *lieder* by Brahms and Schumann.

"I think I ought to show them I don't *always* sing rubbish."

I should like to add that his public bought them as avidly as *Kathleen Mavourneen*; alas, they did not.

The Old Men of the Sea which had been running as a serial in one of the Cassell magazines was published at the beginning of November.

I wrote to Faith in Capri.

The notices of the Old Men are either superlative in praise or blame. The D. Telegraph says it is like a bad revue. But the D. Graphic says "As Dr Johnson said of Goldsmith, so do we all say to-day of Mr C. M. that he touches nothing that he does not adorn . . . the truth is he has brought it off again. He enters every man's domain without fear and proves himself a king in every walk of literature." That's really handsome! It's a relief to find a reviewer who does not warn me against trying to be too versatile. I'll do a detective story next, and then a ghost story.

I certainly could not complain of what the notices said about *Santa Claus in Summer* when it was published that autumn. Except for one or two women reviewers who wrote children's stories themselves, they were more than kind. Some of them went so far in praise as to say it was the best thing of its kind since *Alice in Wonderland*.

It was published on the same day as *When We Were Young*, and it was A. A. Milne's book with Shepherd's enchanting illustrations which swept the Christmas market. Nevertheless, *Santa Claus in Summer* was out of print a year or two later, and a new edition without A. H. Watson's illustrations was published by Blackwell. This too went out of print and *Santa Claus in Summer* was next re-published by Dent, with the original illustrations and a delicious jacket by A. H. Watson. That edition is still in print.

One letter about *The Old Men of the Sea* from the Purser of R.M.S. *Elmina*, Sierra Leone gave me particular pleasure:

Few novelists appear to take so much trouble to verify details of ship life, and it would seem that either you have been a sailor or that you have been very well advised. There is, however, one unimportant slip which in the general excellence may be forgiven, but of which you may not be ungrateful. See page 134 on which you make your passengers crowd in the forepeak. *'On the forecastle' would appear to be indicated here. The forepeak is an unpleasant, dark hole of a place, directly at the bow of the ship, under the forecastle and usually approached through a trap, or 'scuttle hatch'.*

I tried to express my gratitude for that encouraging letter by sending Mr W. Thomas a copy of my book with the mistake corrected. I am glad to think that 'forepeak' has vanished from *Paradise for Sale*, which is the name given to *The Old Men of the Sea* in a new edition of it published by Macdonald. *Paradise for Sale* was a chapter heading and the French translation was called *Paradis à Vendre*. I thought that after Hemingway's *Old Man of the Sea* it would be wiser to change the original title.

In his letter of acknowledgment Mr Thomas wrote:

May I suggest to you, with the idea of being mildly useful as well as grateful, that West Africa—an astounding country—is still waiting for a careful and conscientious writer to exploit. 'White Cargo', 'Sanders of the River', 'Capt. Kettle' etc are all the worst kind of inaccurate twaddle.

Nobody, nobody, but Mary Kingsley has ever written about W.A. with the faintest real understanding. There is a rich mine of legend and adventure awaiting a man such as yourself.

I wonder what Mr Thomas would write about West Africa to-day.

In this October I signed at the Savile an agreement with Mr Fitzjames Chute to rent Ripley Lodge for a year from November 1st. The house-agents in Dublin wrote:

Dear Sir,

Thank you for the agreement signed by yourself and witnessed by Sir

William Orpen, Painter of Pictures. We have it in contemplation when the tenancy is over and the agreement has become an expired document, to cut off that portion of it containing the two signatures and to put it amongst the things we value.

Yours faithfully

Jas. H. North and Co.

Where in the world but in Ireland would one get such a jolly acknowledgment from a firm of house-agents?

I got rid of my beard before the *Daily Mirror* sent down a cameraman to take photographs of me for the advance publicity of *Coral*.

"I wish you'd take a picture of me sweating to get this confounded serial finished instead of making the public think I spend the whole of my time emptying lobster pots and walking about Jethou with a tame goose."

However, I must admit that they were a very good set of photographs and one of them did show me putting a record on one of our gramophones.

It was about now that T. E. Lawrence was collecting the hundred-odd subscribers for *The Seven Pillars of Wisdom*. Robin Buxton had let him know I wished to be one of them and I received the following letter:

Clouds' Hill

Moreton

Dorset

6 x 24

Dear Sir,

It's rather alarming, your wish to subscribe to my book. I hope you realize that it's not in the least a work of art? I'm not a writer either by trade or instinct, and I'm afraid lest the writers who have asked for copies (yourself, H. Walpole, Wells, Shaw and Hardy) may be under a misapprehension on the point. To pay thirty guineas for a bit of obscure military-political history would annoy me very much, but perhaps your bank balance is enormous.

Robin Buxton has taken your cheque but he will give it back if on second thoughts you wish to recover it. I have about ninety of the hundred or so subscribers needed.

Yours sincerely

T. E. Lawrence

Of course I'd like your subscription: but I don't want you to pay because you have been misled by rumours as to the book being lively or obscene or indiscreet—or interesting! It is uncommonly long, dull and petty.

On the other side of the page, he wrote,

Particulars about the book are:—
Some 600 pages

60 illustrations, by all sorts of artists: about 100 copies of the complete work: as many as are required to pay all the bills for printing and binding. Some free copies of the text, promised to the fellows named in the book. Maximum of these perhaps fifty—probably much less.

No review copies and no library copies (I hope). An American (and incomplete) edition of about ten copies. The printing will take a long time yet—the book should be delivered some time next year.

The cost of the thing is mainly in the chromo-litho blocks. Thirty of them.

T. E. L.

I wrote to assure him that I *did* want the book and had another letter from Clouds' Hill.

Dear Mr Mackenzie
Yes, balance when the book arrives. I hope I warned you that it would be a long time yet. G.B.S. when he heard that I was keeping my book private, groaned because he'd never hit on that as an advertising dodge. And when he saw my letters of dissuasion said that the greed of them was indecent. It seems so. But what can I do?

Yours sincerely

T. E. Lawrence

On the 1st November I reached Ireland with Nellie Boyte, Honor Everton, a chauffeur and a Morris car. I am amused to find among the relics a County of London Licence for Edward Montague Compton Mackenzie of the Savile Club to drive a Motor Car or Motor Cycle for a period of twelve months from October 21st 1924 until October 20th 1925 inclusive. Fee of 5s. Received. I do not know when this light-hearted permit for anybody to become a public danger ceased to be obtainable; I read almost with a shudder an allusion in a letter to the suitability of the sands of Glenbeigh for learning to drive a car. I am glad to say that the 'Pages for Renewal of Licence which must not be removed or defaced' are virginal.

Ripley Lodge, beautiful though the view, was not a success. The beds were as hard as cement. The chairs were liable to collapse if one sat down in them too suddenly. At the end of the month something happened to the cistern and water came pouring down the stairs. What made the discomfort of Ripley Lodge hardly noticeable was my obsession with the hope of securing Lickeen.

On November 24th I was writing to Faith:

If a General on the N.W. frontier of India doesn't exercise his option I can have it, though it won't be ready for occupation till next summer at earliest because it was shot up by the Irregulars and the inside has to be rebuilt. It is situated by the head waters of Caragh, about four miles up the lake from where we are now, the most divinely lovely situation—a perfect house for us because it has 4 or 5 rooms separated from all the other rooms by a corridor. The Caragh river comes foaming and tumbling down under an ancient grey bridge opposite into the lake which is only the width of the river at this point. The house is reached through the loveliest woods and wherever you look there is a mountain panorama of great beauty, about three miles away. It simply beggars description.

The woods are mostly beeches, all golden and silver at this season, with great Scots pines, rowans and spruces among them. There is an 8-acre meadow surrounded by woods. It is said to be the best woodcock shooting in Europe and the earliest salmon fishing in Ireland—mid-January. So the place could always be lettable at different seasons.

The rent will be £150 which includes 30 acres of woodland for one's own pleasure apart from the shooting over 700 acres of woodland and 4000 acres of moorland. I shall have an option of purchase within 10 years for £3100. But all depends on this General on the N.W. Frontier.

Lickeen House reminds me in some ways of Lady Ham. Not like it in appearance, but the same kind of atmosphere. I think you'll be enchanted by it. There is a large flat lawn in front of the house with rhododendrons scattered in isolated clumps, and beyond all that about half-a-dozen of the largest Monkey Puzzlers I have ever seen, and what is more in fruit with dark cones, the which I have never seen before. And such woods with great boulders among them and carpeted with the saxifrage called London Pride.

On December 5th I was writing from Ripley Lodge:

It doesn't look as if I shall get Lickeen. The General is holding on to his option.

I'm going to Dublin next week to hear Galli-Curci and address the first meeting of the Gramophone Society. Then to the Glasgow Gramophone Society, London for five days and Jethou by December 20.

I'm still feeling tired but am gradually recovering from the effort of Coral. The worst of it is I have to brace myself to begin another book soon and I'd like a year's holiday. I'll do my best to reach Capri in January and will stay for a fortnight, but I may have to be working. The Mirror people have been good with their advance publicity for Coral and I have not had to blush once.

The Galli-Curci concert in the Theatre Royal, Dublin, came immediately after her tremendous success in Glasgow. Unfortunately she sang flat once or twice in Dublin, but apart from that her voice and personality failed to attract her audience. I went round to see her at the Shelbourne Hotel after the concert. I see her still, sitting among four large trunks.

"What an audience!" she exclaimed. "*Miserabile! Miserabile! Che popolo apatico!*"

I looked across to her husband, an unexciting man whose first name was Homer.

"May I talk frankly alla signora?"

"Sure, but don't make it too long because we have to catch the boat-train from Kingstown."

"The train?" I echoed in surprise. "Won't you be going by car?"

"Do you know what they asked to get us and our trunks to Kingstown by car?" Homer exclaimed.

I forget what the sum was but it seemed to me a very minute fraction of the thousand guineas the diva had received for that concert.

"And I always feel sick in the train," she said in a sad voice. "But it cannot be helped. And we will be glad to get away from Dublin. I have never sung to an audience so cold. In Manchester and Liverpool and most of all in Glasgow they were so wonderful."

"Glasgow is certainly one of the warmest audiences in Great Britain," I agreed. "But Dublin is just as warm an audience. I think it was partly your fault, signora. You slipped round the corner of the curtain in that beautiful golden dress you were wearing and slipped back again behind it so quickly that the audience did not realise it was you and so didn't give you the reception you would have had."

"They were so cold," she said with a shudder.

"That was partly because you sang too many popular English songs like *Just a Song at Twilight* which the audience here did not want to hear."

"But in Glasgow . . ."

"Glasgow has not had to endure what Dublin had to endure from the English a short while ago."

In Ireland I had hoped to meet Stephen Mackenna, with whom I had been in correspondence over gramophone matters, but he could not get away from his great translation of Plotinus down at Bere Regis in Dorset. He had written from there in November:

A Chara, A great pleasure and honour to hear from you. Yourself and H.G.W. are the only two Engl. novelists I read ever and for the both of you I look out eagerly; in your own art and substance I delight, hugely. . . . Of course there's the music side but I don't know anything about that, only to be ceaselessly hearing, insatiably, yet utterly incapable still of pronouncing a judgment or even, if the truth were told, of recognizing the development of a theme: my love of music is like the loving of God, an absorption without reason giveable!

Long may you and your works and Your The Gr. live to delight us.

S. Mackenna

I never did meet Mackenna but I rejoice to see the volumes of that great translation of Plotinus on my bookshelves as I write these words.

I was again enjoying the hospitality of the Nolans at Corbawn and James Stephens took Hilda Nolan and myself to see G. W. Russell. Stephens had already been disappointed at not being able to talk with Stephen Mackenna and myself about the best sound-boxes, which as he wrote was as important a matter as the best safety-razor. Now unfortunately Sean O'Casey arrived to talk about his last play with Æ and was evidently so resentful, and so rude to Hilda Nolan, that we soon left. I regret I never had a chance to meet Sean O'Casey when he was in a friendlier mood.

Just after that visit to Æ, I disgracefully abused the hospitality of William and Hilda Nolan by having one of my bad goes. The visit to Glasgow had to be cancelled. My temperature went up to 105 on one night and I was told afterwards that I had spent the whole night talking about cormorants. Perhaps I had been imagining that Sir Percival Perry had come into the room. However, I quickly recovered and, back in London, I was writing to Faith in mid-December:

Gramophone will keep me here for a bit. For January alone we've got from H.M.V. the Jupiter symphony and the 4th of Beethoven (complete), the Schumann Concerto (Cortot) and a Bach sonata (Primrose). From Columbia the Brahms C minor symphony. It's really terrific nowadays and our beloved Gramophone is getting all the credit for the music the recording companies are giving us. I must say I do feel a little proud of what we have managed to do in eighteen months. I hear much praise of your Verdi article; and I'm looking forward to Rossini, Donizetti and Bellini.

Alice and Christopher are taking another house near Horsham and Alice now wants Christopher to be a master at the Bluecoat School!! I told her we couldn't spare him as London Editor of the Gramophone and that she really must try to realize this job would become more and more important for him as time went on.

I got back to Jethou before Christmas and was delighted with the progress Macdonald had made with the house. Sometime after Christmas the engine of the *Watch Me* was out of action and we were completely cut off for over a week.

FORTY-TWO YEARS OLD: 1925

On January 18th I was writing:

The Watch Me's all right again and I'm in communication with the world. It was rather pleasant to be cut off, though it gave me a stiff day catching up with the Daily Mirror's crossword puzzles. However, I'm up to date now with every word. You really ought to go in for crosswords. I see no chance of getting out to Capri before the beginning of February. It's quite fine here now and I had a lovely day for my birthday. There's a mound of letters owing to the congestion of the mail.

The *Daily Mirror* was one of the first papers in Britain to go in for crosswords and as they had been sending me the paper every day since *Coral* started I had found them an admirable sedative after hard work. Until then I had been accustomed to play patience before turning over to sleep. Now I found a nightly crossword less of a physical nuisance. Patience involved shuffling and the cards were apt to fall off the bed-table. That crossword habit would last for the rest of my life. Apparently crosswords had been popular for a while in mid-Victorian days but had died out. Then they were revived in America and from America they reached the United Kingdom. Another ten years would pass before *The Times* started its daily crossword, and I take this opportunity of expressing my gratitude to those mysterious setters who still beguile me.

I am sometimes asked by young people what is the best way to start to write. Naturally I always tell them the only way is to find out for themselves, but I sometimes add that when they can supply correctly the missing word of a quotation from some poet with which they are unfamiliar they may begin to feel they can write.

The hard work I had put in on *Coral* was rewarded by the unfailing consideration of the editor of the *Daily Mirror*. British editors had not yet acquired the habit of trying to write serials in the editorial office. To-day that habit, to which has now been added the worse habit of trying to write books in the publisher's office, is endemic in Great Britain under the steady Americanization which 'escalates' all the time.

Here is a pleasant letter to get from an editor:

In passing the final instalment of 'Coral' I have been touched anew by your beautiful description of the death of Iris. It has a note of simplicity which makes it a rare scene in contemporary literature, and I should like to express to you some part of the pleasure it has given me to be able to print such a story as 'Coral'.

My readers however I am afraid will accuse you through me of hard-heartedness in letting the child die at all! But of course she had to die!

And here is another:

I was asked to call at the Faculty Office to-day, and found them a little disgruntled at the description 'grimy place' and 'dusty old clerks'. It isn't grimy, they say, nor are the clerks dusty, though there was one dear ancient gentleman to whom I was introduced who has been there over sixty years, and is a gay dog still. I said I would mention the matter to you, and that you would be sure to remove any derogatory impression when 'Coral' came out as a book. . . . All confessed to being admirers of Mr Compton Mackenzie's work, so the interview terminated without loss of esteem on both sides.

It was a week into February before I was able to reach Capri, and I was rather depressed by the tiny villa Faith had found for herself below the Via Tragara. I had managed to get out to her all the Rossini, Bellini and Donizetti records she wanted for her articles and she was in correspondence with various Italian helpers.

One day the following letter arrived:

Grand Hotel Quisisana
Capri

Dear Mr Mackenzie

I am an American writer, and one of the most enthusiastic admirers of your work—so much so that when I was twenty-two I wrote a novel called This Side of Paradise *which was much more* Sinister Street *with trimmings of* Tono Bungay *than anything else. At least a hundred reviewers said so too but the book made Princeton romantic almost with the secondhand glow of your Oxford. Three years ago I went to Granchester (for Brooke) and to Magdalen (for you) with almost the feeling of a sacred pilgrimage.*

I'm here for a night and I'm terribly anxious to see you if only for a few minutes. If you're in the middle of a book and were driven mad just last night by other bores who wanted to ask you if 'Lily lay along his bended arm as if asleep' was exquisitely cribbed from Rossetti say so and I'll understand. But, on the contrary, if you can come here for a drink with me or let me sit in your garden for five minutes I'll be awfully happy.

Sincerely

F. Scott Fitzgerald

I had not yet read any of Fitzgerald's books but found him an extremely attractive man and we had a long talk. He reproached me for disappointing my admirers by writing books merely meant to make people laugh. I reminded him that the greatest writer in the English language had not considered it beneath his dignity to make people laugh with plays like *The Comedy of Errors.*

"Have you ever thought," I asked, "that it's imperative for rising young writers to decry comic books because none of them can write them? It's time you produced another Mark Twain in America."

I do not remember what Fitzgerald replied to this, but one remark of his I do remember.

"You've no idea," he said, "how shabby Europe looks to an American."

And this was said not in a tone of contempt but of compassion.

That brief last return to Capri is a cloud in my memory, apart from that meeting with Scott Fitzgerald which until I checked up on his movements I supposed had occurred at Easter 1924.

I always feel I made my last farewell to Capri at the beginning of that June and that this February visit in 1925 was but the brief visit of a ghost. I did not see Capri again until I flew round the isle of Capree in the summer of 1947.

A letter has survived, written to Faith by Mrs Boyte from Jethou on March 5th:

It was very sad that Mr Mackenzie should arrive back so ill, but as he says fortunate that he reached here before having to go to bed, which he did about 3 hours after arriving with bronchitis. We were most anxious for 3 or 4 days, especially as the terrible weather lasted and Dr Carey could not be got across. Luckily it took a normal course with the warmth and what remedies we had and by the time Dr Carey was able to get to him he was a little better and I am very glad to say the improvement has continued and as at last the weather has improved too and there is lovely sunshine, but he is not to get up for at least a week. Dr Carey said he didn't wonder we had been worried as the bronchitis had been acute and that he must take great care. He is longing to be in the garden where the scillas and daffodils are all out and the primroses are getting plentiful. So it will be nice for him when he is able to go out. . . . The new balcony covered with glass will certainly make Mr Mackenzie's room much warmer. We all lead a very quiet life here and yet there is always something to do and the time passes quickly. I really think we must soon get better weather as during the time Mr Mackenzie was in Italy and since his return it has been one incessant gale, and torrents of rain. The fowls are laying well now and some pullets hatched out (all white Wyandottes) last October are now laying. The goose is also laying. . . . I shall wear you out, but Jethou is all there is to write about.

Yours faithfully

Priscilla Boyte

On the day Mrs Boyte wrote that letter a telegram arrived from G. K. Chesterton:

Sorry to be nuisance but find printers insanely insist copy next Tuesday sending this on chance

The next day came another telegram:

Please forgive rude mad mysterious telegram if it arrived before letter which explains Chesterton

The explanatory letter arrived at the same time:

Top Meadow

Beaconsfield

March 2nd

Dear Mr Compton Mackenzie

I have been meaning for a very long time to take the liberty of troubling you with this letter; but unfortunately I am the sort of person who can think of a letter a long time before he writes it; and think of a person very often indeed without getting to the point of informing him of the fact. I have never forgotten the great pleasure I had in making your acquaintance in Dublin and have always wanted to renew it if you would allow me to do so. I am sorry we never combined in the way you suggested in a protest about the Irish business; but the truth is that I myself rather came to the conclusion that things were going right, relatively speaking, without us and that rubbing it in might possibly put them wrong; I mean that the English have in their hearts lost all belief in the Orange nonsense and yet, if challenged, could hardly avoid pretending to believe in it more than they do. I may have been wrong in this; and if at any time you feel that something of the kind is needed, I should be only too much honoured to be associated with you in the matter.

But the real truth is that I put off writing to you until I could write, as I can now, to tell you that I am really going to bring out the paper with which I am glad to remember you expressed sympathy. You were even so kind as to say that you would write something for it; and I am bothering you now to ask you if you have anything you might possibly send me for the first number, which we hope to bring out on the nineteenth; or if not for one of the immediately following issues. I remember you said something about defending the romantic

*side of the war against the sham realists and materialists; which would be
quite along our lines. But anything else from two to three thousand words, or
shorter, a short story or sketch or essay on anything would do as good. We can
only pay about the ordinary rates of these weekly intellectual rags like the New
Statesman and the Nation, but I would make a push to get a little more for
people of distinction like yourself; and the money, whatever it is settled to be,
will be quite safe. For I am glad to say we have at last got the capital sub-
scribed which justifies us in starting, and we are going to start.*

*I have deliberately made this letter of a suffocating dullness; for I am so
unbusinesslike a person that when I do talk business I cease to be a person at all.
But I am sure you will understand that I am asking your help for things in
which you and I are both believers;* coheredes et sodales in terra viventium.
*I believe the next twenty years are going to be, in the most solemn sense, great
fun. This snobbish sceptical orthodoxy is being stormed like the Bastille; and
we shall have all the fun of being rebels with the consolation of being loyalists.*

Yours very sincerely

G. K. Chesterton

I was not able to appear in that first number of *G.K.'s Weekly*
but as soon as possible I sent him a comment upon the fashionable
denigration of Rupert Brooke, and I made it as offensive as I could.

Coral was published in March, and was naturally handicapped
from the reviewing angle by having appeared serially in the *Daily
Mirror*. However, reviews did not worry me because I was always
deep in the writing of another book when they arrived.

Some time about now I must have written to Alfred Noyes, commenting on what I thought was the unfair way he was being treated
by the critics. I find in a letter from him:

*I'm really concerned about the way in which values are being manipulated
by the 'literary' weeklies. A short time ago a complete stranger wrote to me,
enclosing a very laudatory notice of himself from the 'Times Literary Supplement' and telling me, quite frankly, that he was going to 'pay me out' (for the
success of my books) in a sketch he was writing. It was a crazy letter with this
particular passage underlined heavily, and the Supplement had praised him in
terms that would have made Dante blush. If this is what we are coming to
and men of that calibre are to be exalted by deft manipulation and frag-
mentary quotation, it means that those who have any regard for real values
must do something to expose it.*

I recall that just about the time *Coral* was published I read with
immense enjoyment and admiration *The Constant Nymph*; I wrote to

E

tell Margaret Kennedy as much. She replied from St Ives in Cornwall on March 26th:

*Thank you so very much for your letter: it has given me great pleasure. I'm
so excited to learn that you were all over the moon when you read Chartreuse de
Parme for the first time because I was and I have not, on the whole, met many
people who feel about that book as I do.*

*I am interested in your remarks about London's slang. I am not very certain
of Cockney idiom and I have not lived in London very much and have had to
pick up the remarks of stray charwomen and people; and that is never so good
as living among them, as one is apt to get expressions a little out of their
context. I think bad language is an awful problem in a book, don't you? I hate
blanks because they spoil the look of a page. I hate inaccuracy. My publishers
won't let me be accurate, the only oaths which are considered printable suggest
a curate falling over a coal scuttle. Yet if one is writing about people who swear
what is one to do? Thanking you again for the kind things you have said.*

That letter of mine to Margaret Kennedy was the first I ever
wrote to an author I had never met, and the next I should write
would be to Rosamond Lehmann. *The Constant Nymph* was drama-
tised and put on at the Haymarket where it had a great success. I was
disappointed by the play. I felt Noel Coward was all wrong as the
young man and although Edna Best brought off a *tour de force* as the
nymph she was not my idea of her. It is time to say that the better
the book the less satisfactory a play it makes. The reader has already
endowed the characters with life from the ability with which the
author has fed his imagination. He does not want to see that life
taken from them by actors.

I had made up my mind by now that Ripley Lodge was a mistake,
but I had to remain the nominal tenant of it until next October. I
sold the Morris car in Ireland. Allen Nolan arrived to spend his
Easter holidays with us, and to this day he remembers that Easter
holiday on Jethou forty years ago as vividly as if it were yesterday.

We had a gathering of gramophone experts that Easter, Percy
Wilson among them. A letter from Nellie Boyte to Faith says:

*We have had a gramophonic 7 days and used 6 packets of needles (each 200)
so have played 600 records, 1,200 sides.*

I was working hard at the lecture I was due to give to the Musical
Association at London University on April 21st. The subject was
'The Gramophone: its past, its present, its future'. I cannot remem-
ber where the lecture was given or anything about the audience, but

it was printed and in a footnote I read, "Since I gave this lecture a new system of electrical recording has been introduced and the results promise to be excellent." I shall not claim that I realized then what a complete revolution electrical recording would be for the gramophone.

I went to Jethou to work hard on *Rogues and Vagabonds*, but was fetched back to London in a hurry by news of my mother's grave illness. She was now seventy-two and in those days double pneumonia at that age was a grim prospect. She was in a nursing-home on the other side of Nevern Square from our house, Number One. I was told when I arrived that there was little chance of her pulling through. Then I went up to her room. Her mind was wandering and she recognised me not as I was now but as I was when I was two years old. Then suddenly her mind was clear.

"I'm afraid I wasted a great deal of money at Nottingham," she said, "but I couldn't possibly have continued as Bode's partner. I think it's time now I left this world."

"No, it's not yet time. You can't desert the Theatre Girls' Club."

She put out her hand which I grasped.

"Perhaps he's right," she murmured to herself.

"I know I'm right." And then I said something she used to tell me I had once said to her when I was two years old.

"Monty cannot be told."

"But you were always very good if it was properly explained to you why you ought to do or not do something or other."

"Well, you won't be able to explain to me why you should leave this world. So I'm afraid you'll have to do what I want, not what you want."

From that moment she got rapidly better and would stay in this world for another fifteen years.

Back in Jethou I continued to work hard on *Rogues and Vagabonds*.

I told in an earlier Octave of the curious confirmation I was given in this year of how much of my writing was thought out in sleep. I had sought in vain for a simile for heavy rainfall in 1911 when I was writing *Carnival* in Church Row, Hampstead. It was now that I dreamed of Napoleon leading French troops along Charing Cross Road and realized that the bayonets glittering in the arc-lights provided me with my simile. I woke up and I wrote in *Rogues and Vagabonds* a scene that would enable me to use that simile I had been searching for at the back of my mind for fifteen years.

My chief diversion for a while during work on *Rogues and Vagabonds* was watching the hunting-wasps at their business in front of the vinery, on the demolishment of which to build a library and two bedrooms Macdonald was about to start. I did not even know that the fascinating performance I watched for the first time in my life was the work of wasps; I thought they were large flies.

The wasp would excavate a hole for herself, to which she would return carrying a paralysed fat green caterpillar of the large-white butterfly, which she would pack down into the hole to be fed on by her grubs until they became wasps. She would then close the mouth of the hole, carefully smoothing the earth over it and sometimes putting a little stone on top. She would then remain by the hole and if another wasp came near it she would fiercely attack her.

A letter to me from Geoffrey Vevers of the Zoo says:

I think the flies you have must be 'Hunting Wasps'. I saw some on Sunday along the cliffs on the South coast of Guernsey and caught one which I enclose in paper marked A. It is one of the Sphegilae and is Ammophila Sabulosa. See Fabre's 'Hunting Wasps' translated by T. de Mattos.

In the B paper are 3 specimens of British Ichneumons. The wing venation is the chief difference. . . . We can let you have budgerigars at from 7/6-10/6 a pair according to quantity and Golden and Amherst Pheasants at £2 a pair. . . . When you have your aviary fixed up, I will send you a breeding box for your man to copy.

I sent off at once for all of Fabre's enthralling books about insects and am grateful to those hunting-wasps which introduced them to me.

After the success of the gramophone tests last year at the Steinway Hall I thought it would be a good idea to hold a gramophone congress, as I called it. It was held on July 8th in Caxton Hall and was thronged all day by enthusiasts. Sir Richard Terry opened it with an admirable speech and I had the pleasure of introducing him to the congress. When the exhibition of machines, sound-boxes and gadgets of all kinds closed at five o'clock the enthusiasts went off to refresh themselves for the tests; they began at 5.30 and went on till 10.30 with an interval of an hour during which Marie Novello and Helen Henschel sang and a string quartet was played.

Back on Jethou I managed to finish *Rogues and Vagabonds* and was taken aback when Newman Flower wanted me to make it post-war. I wrote to him on August 3rd:

Pinker tells me you're worried that Rogues and Vagabonds begins in 1829, but it couldn't ever conceivably be post-war. The story forbids that. What I said to him was that it could probably be made to begin in the middle, but that such a beginning would involve a retrospect of the family history and would not suit serial form.

The other alternative is for serial purposes to cut out the first four chapters and begin with chapter five. The book is long enough to stand that excision. But can it possibly be made post-war? The subject necessitates the passage of time and contemporary theatrical life does not provide the necessary background.

The other book called The Golden Egg (*but I am now thinking of calling it* The Cheshire Cat) *would have begun with the war and come down to the present. You saw a synopsis of it (good synopses are impossible for me to write) and I think it will make a serial. One of the characters in* Rogues and Vagabonds *will appear in it as the profiteer. But you said definitely that you preferred to have* Rogues and Vagabonds *first. I think* Rogues and Vagabonds *has a better chance of popularity than* Coral. *I've put every ounce I could into its production and my intuition is that it will be successful. I had the same intuition about* Poor Relations *which, you will remember, you refused as a serial, and it did 36,000.* Coral *has done what I prophesied it would do.*

You behaved so very decently over the ecclesiastical trilogy that anything I can possibly do I will do. But it would be a physical and mental impossibility for me to transform Rogues and Vagabonds *into a post-war book.*

The reason for my feeling fairly confident about *Rogues and Vagabonds* was that it was a true story. I knew that the critics would probably accuse me of deliberate sentimentality and certainly I should never have brought myself to write what one may call a Cinderella story unless it had happened as I told it. It was luck that her mother had told me the story of that Gaiety girl daughter of hers, Rosie Boote[1] once upon a time.

I was planning to write a huge novel in seven volumes to be called *Our Seven Selves* but in order to have the two years clear which I should require for such an undertaking I had to get my finances clear. It was vital for me to produce two books a year now. The need to do this made me almost hate those books. Yet when I re-read them now at intervals as they are re-published I am agreeably surprised to find that they show no trace of the strain under which I wrote them. Many reviewers kept shedding crocodiles' tears over the decline of Compton Mackenzie, but I was unaffected and now when I am re-reading through my press-cutting albums for *My Life and Times* I am astonished to find how vicious some of those reviewers were; I had completely forgotten them. I knew at the time that I was writing

---

[1] The late Rose, Marchioness of Headfort.

against the mood of the moment, but by retiring to a small island of my own I was untouched by this mood. I could at any rate feel sure that my founding of *The Gramophone* had changed entirely the attitude of the recording companies and that I had been useful to music. It was gratifying to receive a letter like the following from Japan:

On the end of last month, I received your 'Gramophone' june number and when I saw my letter appeared in it with tears of joy, I was very very glad because I have never such a cheer since I was born, for my name is printed first time in Honorable your country, I thank you so much.

Moreover by this chance makes me to know many English gramophone enthusiastic friends, all who read my letter in your magazine, and kindly lettered to me for help my collection and study, such kindly offers also owing to your benefits, I thanks again.

To-day I received seven your National Gramophone Records (Beethoven, Debussy and Schubert) all were safe. Here I am hesitate to write about the beauty and the perfect of the records, because I think with such my clumsy sentence will spoile its value and also I couldn't write how to express its admiration and gratification.

Since one month ago when I received your letter dated 15th, May told me that the records will reach you safely very soon, so every day I wait eagerly for its arrival and at last I couldn't endure to wait, then often I went to the Post Office to enquire about the Foreign Parcel Post. (Perhaps you laugh, but please imagine my faithfulness to you with this.)

Please write me when arrive next Schonberg Sextet and continued Schubert Trio records, but also total price and postage of all back numbers of the 'Gramophone' before Nov. 1924.

Now I am eagerly to select from many Japanese gramophone shops for representative Japanese instrumental records which I intend to send you, so when reach thise one to you, please use it when you or your friends need or want real oriental music. I will write with it some story or expranation of its music and with photographs of instruments, if I could.

Once I beg to write you 'THANKS',

Yours most faithfully

Hajime Fùkaya.

We now had correspondents from China to Peru, from Spitzbergen to Invercargill.

Nevertheless, the capital required for *The Gramophone* was still a problem and in my need to pay my mother's creditors, pay off my overdraft, and find the money to improve the house and garden at

Jethou I was tempted to sell out my shares in *The Gramophone*.

It was when I was feeling pessimistic that a letter from Quiller-Couch cheered me:

> The Haven
> Fowey
> Cornwall
> *28th September, 1925*

My dear Mackenzie:
  Greetings!
  I have a suit to make to you. I want for an Oxford Book of English Prose a passage from your Passionate Elopement. It's the one about the 'Basket of Roses Inn' and you must give me leave as you love me. Forgive a dictated letter, as my eyes have given out, for the rest, all is well at Fowey except that you are too long absent.

> *With our best regards,*
> *Yours ever,*

Forgive a dictated letter.   Q

I had not seen Q for nearly ten years, and so I could feel that his inclusion of my name in the Oxford Book of English Prose was his endorsement of my career as novelist, the very beginning of which he had so generously encouraged.

Early in October I went up to Glasgow to fulfil two speaking engagements. Little did I dream that those two or three days in Glasgow would be fateful in my life.

The first engagement was a talk to the Glasgow Gramophone Society, great supporters of *The Gramophone* from the first number. The second engagement was with the Trinity Literary Society. Last year when I was laid low in Dublin I had had to break that engagement. The Trinity Literary Society was the creation of that remarkable man the Reverend H. G. McClelland, the Minister of Trinity Congregational Church in Claremont Street. McClelland had originally been an actor but abandoned the stage to become a Congregational minister. As such he had travelled all over the world and managed to get captured by Bedouin when he was wandering about Trans-Jordania. In 1912, disguised as a tramp, he had explored the underworld of London and had written authentically about the destitute. Three years later he became Minister of Trinity Church, where he had built up the Literary Society with a membership of over 1,200 and had persuaded almost every prominent figure in English literature to lecture for him. Some years later proceedings were taken against him under some gambling act for starting football pools in Glasgow. He was certainly a pioneer.

In 1925 he had recently married a widow with three or four beautiful daughters and I stayed in his comfortable house in Kelvin- side. The church was packed out for my lecture and except for another Congregational chapel in Manchester it had the best acoustics of any place in which I have spoken. According to McClelland the only speaker who had managed to be almost inaudible was A. S. M. Hutchinson when he had given thoughts from *If Winter Comes* and readings from it.

One of the pleasures of that Glasgow visit was meeting again Norah Duncan, now Norah Dunn, and being introduced to her daughter Doris, aged eighteen, and anxious to go on the stage. I was back in Switzerland at the beginning of my third Octave a quarter of a century ago and then back in the King's Theatre at the second performance of my play *The Gentleman in Grey* when Doris had been a baby in arms.

I had the privilege of meeting J. S. Phillimore, the Professor of Humanity at the University, perhaps the most popular professor the students of Glasgow ever had. I had heard much of Phillimore from Sandys Wason. Together they started *The Spirit Lamp* in 1891; it was bought later by Alfred Douglas. Phillimore was the greatest all- round classical scholar of the time—equally accomplished in Greek and Latin. When he was President of the British Association he shocked academic opinion by saying that a new translation of Plato was needed. Neither G. B. Shaw nor H. G. Wells knew Greek; the most suitable person for the job would be myself. Phillimore's death a year or two after this was an irreparable loss to the University and to humane scholarship. The contemporary habit of calling agnostic humanitarians humanists is one more irritation for the humanists of once upon a time. Grating barbarisms like 'sociology' and 'homo- sexual' are inevitable with the growing ignorance of Greek and Latin, but there is no excuse for giving an old word a new meaning. I have yet to meet a Renaissance figure among the self-styled Humanists of our day.

The Rectorial campaign was in full swing, the candidates being Austen Chamberlain, G. K. Chesterton and Sidney Webb. G. K. was standing as a Liberal and I was asked to speak at a meeting of his supporters in the University Union. G. K. was very narrowly defeated by Chamberlain, Webb being far behind. Among my papers I find a faded copy of *The Student Leader*, No. 2, October 1925, one penny. This has a picture of Sidney Webb with a message underneath from Ramsay Macdonald advising the students of Glasgow University to vote for Sidney Webb as their next Lord Rector. The rest of the number is devoted to an 'Exclusive Article' by George Bernard Shaw dated August 4th from Scourie in Sutherland. On the back the Glasgow Alhambra announces a personal visit of Sybil Thorndike and her London Company in Bernard Shaw's masterpiece *Saint Joan*.

Shaw's entertaining article may be read in the appendix, and it is indeed well worth reading.

McClelland had written to tell me that "two young Editors—Hedderwick of the *Glasgow Citizen* and Heddle of the *Bulletin*" would be lunching with us. One of them mentioned the forthcoming sale of the Leverhulme estates in the Outer Hebrides at Knight, Frank and Rutley's Auction Room in Hanover Square, and gave the list. I wished at that fateful moment that I had any chance of acquiring the Shiant Islands, and all the way down to London I spent a restless night in the train, thinking about them.

Back in London, A. E. Russell, literary editor of the *Daily Express*, asked me if I should like to write a serial for the *Evening Standard*. Cassell's were still trying to serialize *Rogues and Vagabonds* under their contract with me, and I had agreed to continue *Buttercups and Daisies*, which I had laid aside after writing the first chapter in the spring of 1923 for their last book under the present contract. I told Russell about *Fairy Gold*, the title I had chosen for the book I had been calling *The Cheshire Cat*. I was proposing to use Herm and Jethou for the story but set them off Lyonesse and make the mainland Cornish. Russell liked the idea and the prospect of an unexpected £1,000 made me feel justified in bidding for the Shiants. I asked Nellie Boyte's brother, Charlie, who was with a firm of estate agents in Sloane Street, to go to the auction in Hanover Square on October 22nd and bid up to £500 but not more. £500 would be the utmost to which I could go. I did not expect for a moment that a bid of £500 would secure the islands but that if by chance it did I should accept it as a sign from fortune about my future.

One of Knight, Frank and Rutley's valuers, M—, who came to Herm, was a *Gramophone* fan and had been unable to acquire the second number before it was sold out. I managed to get hold of one and he was grateful. I had asked M— whether he thought I should stand a chance of getting the Shiants for £500: he thought it was most improbable.

I went back to Jethou and on the first day of St Luke's Summer the *Watch Me* came over early on a calm and rich October morning with a telegram:

Fire away with Fairy Gold am writing Russell

In the mail bag was a letter from Charlie Boyte:

I am pleased to say I succeeded in purchasing the Shiant Islands for you this afternoon for the sum of £500. . . . The circumstances in which I bought them were somewhat peculiar. . . .

M— phoned this morning, saying he was sure it was useless for me to bid for you as Lord Leverhulme's son had instructed Sir Howard Frank to see that he obtained this Lot. He desired for sentimental reasons to reserve this small portion as a memento of his father's interest and also because he was now Viscount Leverhulme of the Western Isles.

However, I decided to attend the auction.

I put in a bid of £300 to bring it back to me in £50's at £500. The bids went in quick succession and I put in my top figure, and Sir Howard knocked it down to me.

I then left the Auction room and M— joined me in the passage in a great state of mind to ask me if it was correct that I had secured the Lot. I told him that this was so and he said that Sir Howard had knocked it down in error.

There was some argument between Sir Howard Frank and one or two indignant would-be purchasers. I heard one man say that he had offered £550 for this Lot before the Auction and had been assured by Sir Howard Frank that this figure was no use. . . .

It occurs to me that Sir Howard knowing me by sight, mistook me for one of the 'Boosters' and knocked it down to me under the impression he was thereby reserving the Lot.

Presently I was glad to receive a letter from the tenant of the islands, Malcolm MacSween, Baker, Tarbert, Harris. I had heard that he had put in a bid for them and I was afraid he might bear me a grudge for having outbid him.

Sir,

I write this note to introduce myself as I understand you are now my proprietor. . . . I myself had a small offer on them, but was not extra keen on account of recent reasons I need not touch at present.

These islands are extraordinarily difficult to work, being so exposed to the Elements. A person cannot always make a landing after reaching them.

I will be going out in November for dipping the sheep and if you could come out here, you could go out with us, when you could explore what you have bought during the time of our dipping. Of course there are very few birds just now except 'Barnacle Geese'. You will find us what we are any time you like to come.

Meantime I am
Your obedient servant
Mal^m MacSween

I wrote back to say that I was deep in a book and therefore would not be able to come up yet awhile. I asked him a lot of questions and ended:

I suppose you couldn't persuade some amateur photographer to risk his life by taking a few snapshots for me? . . . I am glad I did not deprive you of something that you were very keen on, and I much appreciate your writing to me.

Malcolm MacSween replied on November 23rd:

I put off answering your letter until my return from the Shiants. I am pleased to say we got on very well and had a good 3 days outing. I always look forward to any time I have to go out as if it was a foreign holiday.

Now for your queries. Yes, you can always get rooms at the Tarbert Hotel. In July and August they sometimes are short of bedroom accommodation. But we will not see you without a Bed. I have not a guest house but I could give you a bed equally as good as you could get in an hotel. "So much for that".

Yes I have about 200 ewes on the three islands. But they are capable of grazing another 200: if I could afford to get them. The trawler crews have been stealing a good many from these islands. But since we caught them at the game last August and reported the matter the Police authorities are keeping an eye on them, and last week for the first time since I became tenant 4 years ago we did not lose more than 2: when we used to lose as many as 30 in 3 months. I made up my mind to give the islands up as hopeless until we really found out the cause of our heavy casualties.

From the moment I read these words I declared war in my mind on the Fleetwood trawlers who were the chief culprits, but the story of that war waged by John Lorne Campbell and myself must wait for the next Octave.

I do not keep a shepherd. It is too lonely a spot for a shepherd. I couldn't get anyone to go. There was a shepherd on some time and the stone wall of the house is still as good as the day when he left. Only that one of the gables fell off a bit. We have two small fishermen's huts in which we stay. Fishermen do go there during the winter to catch lobsters which are very plentiful. But as for salmon! It was simply an auctioneer's dotch [that 'dotch' the first sign of the Gaelic speaker in his letter] *to catch the worm. These islands are the breeding ground of hundreds of seals and you know how salmon and seals agree to share a coast. "The former are always devoured by the latter." I never saw any signs of salmon or trout. But plenty of lythe can be got in May and June.*

No, I do not think the landing can be improved on how nature has left it. But a capstain *fixed on the top of the beach could help in hauling up a boat. The water is quite shallow in shore but the terrible motion would not leave anything unturned. The beach is an isthmus between House Island and Garbh Island, composed of stones. The water sometimes covers the isthmus.*

I got the loan of a small camera and for the first time in my life I tried to take Photos. I enclose herewith the entire spool for yourself to develop. I haven't the faintest idea of how this is done. If you can take some of them I should be delighted to receive the one in which our 82 year old skipper sits with our lunch on his knees.

There are barnacle geese staying on Mary Island during the winter and they are very destructive. Six of them eat as much grass as one ewe. They feed on the grass and their droppings poison the soft parts of the ground and later on in the season cause rot in the sheep's feet. Of course if a person with a gun were staying for a while on the Islands they would be scared off. It was since the shepherd left the Islands they made their winter quarters here.

But early in April the Puffin comes, always on a Sunday night and remains for a week to clear out his burrow and prepare his nest. All of a sudden the whole crowd millions in numbers clears away again for 10 to 12 days, when they again come back in a body, this time to a dry clean burrow and they remain on until early in August when the young puffin is able to fly. There are several other specimens. But the Puffin is really the one prominent attractive bird.

I think I have written enough this time and will await your further consignment of queries which I will be always pleased to answer. I am quite sure of this that you will really enjoy a trip to these ancient islands and any time you come I will make it my business that you will get out to them as comfortably as possible.

Meantime I remain

Yours sincerely

Malcolm MacSween

I felt in reading his long letter that Malcolm MacSween was going to be a man after my own heart. That intuition was to be richly confirmed when I met him for the first time a few months later. I had another letter in December:

I am in receipt of the snaps, for which I am much obliged. Now, for your answers.

No, there are no rabbits. But there are worse than rabbits Rats which came ashore from a Norwegian ship that was wrecked on the islands some 20 years ago. I got a few cats put out and the rats have dwindled.

There is the finest of drinking water on House Island and there is a fairly sized burn on Garbh Eilean and enough for us to get plenty water for dipping with in the middle of the summer.

I am not in the photograph. It was myself who was at the back of the camera. As I am sure the rest of the picture could tell. Of course it was my first try: perhaps it will be better next time.

Yes, I understand there is plenty of peat in the Garbh Eilean. It was there the shepherd used to get his supplies. But as to how he managed to come down from Garbh Eilean to House Island with a bag of peats on his back is a conundrum.

However he was managing it, and the peat bags are still to be seen there: he also planted and raised good crops of potatoes, barley and oats, cabbages and etc. about his house, the walls of which we use for a Fank. It's about 8 feet high, of stone and lime construction.

There is also a lot of 'mint' growing naturally on House Island. We sometimes put a little of it in the tea which gives it a grand flavour.

As I read that my mind went back a quarter of a century to Tetuan where in the crowded market place I drank for the first time tea flavoured with mint.

The archway in the cliff is a natural tunnel through which a boat can go. There is no drinking water on Mary Island. Those wild geese make a mess of it. Mary Island is all green grass and quite flat once you come to the top. But gey stiff to climb; there is heather on the other 2 islands. As for the smaller Rocks about them, they are of no use. Except one. It will keep 5 sheep all the year round, and I gave the use of it to the Old Skipper. Simply because I liked him to be with us. Him knowing the Islands so well. Landing places etc, and I understand he has had the use of them from 3 tenants now in 60 years. Just for piloting them about the Islands and he is still as strong and hearty as ever and him 82 years of age. The big man sitting aside him is his nephew. He is an able hand about these shores. He is for the last 30 years every winter fishing lobster about the Islands and stays 14 days each time before he goes back to the lobster agents with his fortnight's catch. He sometimes gets as many as 100 dozens in the fortnight. Lobsters are very plentiful there and as for Seals they are there by the thousands. [These were not the great Atlantic seals.]

Your island Jethou is almost the same shape as Mary Island, but I rather think Mary Island is larger. It does not look a bit rough as for landing. I am sure they are much the same as to that part.

Yes, I agree it is all Americans and Englishmen who possess the whole Highlands. . . .

I think I have answered all your queries and shall be pleased to answer any others you may have.

With kind regards

Yours sincerely

Mal. MacSween

In September of this year the *Daily Express* published a series of articles by various writers called 'My Religion'. I was the only one who committed himself to a positive religion. Hilaire Belloc and G. K. Chesterton had both refused to contribute because they were Catholics. I asked the Editor if he had any objection to a simple statement of my belief as a Catholic, and he pressed me to make it.

This article let me in for a lot of correspondence, much of it in the shape of tracts from hopeful and earnest Protestants, some of it anonymous with the usual obscenities. Among my letters was one from Sir Ray Lankester of whom I had written:

"Dear wise Ray Lankester, communion with whose profound knowledge and beautiful common sense is one of the pleasures of contemporary existence, once told me that he could not understand how I had managed to surrender so completely my individual judgment as to profess Catholicism. It would be insincere to pretend that I cannot imagine a conflict between my reason and the authority of the Church. That may develop at any moment. All that I can affirm now is that my reason has not yet been called upon to struggle with my faith."

From 44 Oakley Street, Chelsea came Ray Lankester's letter:

I must send you a line to thank you for your most kind and flattering reference to me in your article on your religion in the Daily Express. The article interested me very much. I wish I could write out in an adequate form my own notions on the matter of religion. But I am not strong enough nowadays for the task. I am afraid I should shock and even hurt many readers—for really I think the incessant discoursing about 'Science' and 'Religion' as two commensurate philosophies is mis-leading. It appears to me that the creeds and mythologies often called religion are truly and historically the survival of the primitive illusions and efforts at explanation of natural things—when spirits and demons and an endless variety of special gods and devils were imagined by our struggling ancestors on the way from life to man. Those who doubted this or that demon or god and the powers of its self-appointed representatives—the priests and 'medicine men'—were the first 'men of science'. They have gradually built up and handed on a systematic enquiry into the truth of the pretensions of the spirit-worshipping crowd and their masters— the priests and wizards.

The contest goes on to-day as of yore. The men of science have in the last 2000 years gained an ever-increasing strength—but still the fantastic and suffocating beliefs of man's childhood dominate the rich and the poor and we are governed by ignorance and superstition. We are still an immense way from the healthy use of our intelligence: we neglect it, even refuse to exercise it. The Kingdom of Man is open—ready—waiting for him—but he has still too much of the ape left in him and clings blindly to his primeval dreams and terrors—E pur si muove!

P.S. I am very weak in the legs now—go out in a bath chair! and I can not write more than a few lines in a day—or even a week. Good luck and all happiness to you!

A volume called *Voices from the Hills* was published that autumn in aid of a Gaelic Bazaar held in Glasgow. To this I contributed an article called *Looking Northward*, a few excerpts from which will illustrate my frame of mind after I had acquired the Shiant Islands:

"I can scarcely remember the time when I was not a perfervid Gael, but I have never attempted to express the passion of race in words. The consciousness of being landless in Alba, coupled with ignorance of the language, forbade me out of pride to assume what I should have felt would appear no more than the trappings of a mock romanticism. So this is actually the first time I have ventured to speak of something that has long lain nearer to my heart than rank or fortune or reputation. If the exiled Gael has been a frequent sorrow for poets, I can recall no poet who has sung of an exile between whom and his country stretched not the bitter estranging sea but time itself. Yet although over a century and a half had passed since that younger son from whom I sprang, like so many other sons of Alba, left his country, and though my grandfather to placate disapproving relatives had abandoned his own name when he went on the stage, I was always even as a child of three most insistent that I should be called Mackenzie and not Compton. Indeed, through all my childhood I insisted so successfully on this that from the time I went to a public school at eleven not merely myself but also my brother and sisters were never called by the assumed name to which my father more filial than myself clung.

". . . If only when I was eight or nine some Gaelic enthusiast had come my way what a pupil I should have made! The fire in my heart was never cherished or fanned by any individual; my love of race had to subsist as well as it could on a play called Rob Roy. I begged my father to put this stirring affair into his repertory and was much depressed by his failure to grant my request, especially when he told me that as a young man he had often played Rob Roy himself during stock seasons at Kilmarnock and Kirkcaldy. . . .

"On my seventh birthday an aunt gave me Scott's *Tales of a Grandfather*. Here at last were the enchanted pages for which my soul had been yearning. I was no longer flattering my imagination with the 'let's pretend' of novels and plays, but nourishing it now with solid ineluctable facts. Naturally the behaviour of the Mackenzies was of paramount importance, and how my pride surged when in the Clan map at the end of the volume I saw their territories—all Ross and Cromarty in pale yellow with Mackenzies sprawling right across them, and only here and there a few Rosses or Munroes or Urquharts intruding. Nor was Ross-shire broad enough for their acres. I rejoiced to see the name reach from Loch Seaforth to the Butt of Lewis. How many times I pursued the thread of their history through that thick volume. There were moments of mortification. I can see myself now reading by the school-room window at the top of a tall London house, the small print beginning to blur in the grey November dusk. My mind is troubled by Seaforth's battle with Montrose at Auldearn; and when in '15 the Mackenzies, held up by the Earl of Sutherland and his accursed Whig clans, were prevented for a whole month from joining forces with the Earl of Mar there are tears in my eyes. I turn over the sticky pages of India paper to console myself for the failure of my Chief by reading of the battle of Glenshiel and of how he was carried wounded from the field. Darkness descends upon the London room. The gas is lighted, and I search out a more comfortable subject. The '45 must be postponed for another day when I can bear to read the lamentable story. I recover my spirits by cutting down Covenanters with Dundee and unhorsing English knights at Bannockburn.

"When I was sixteen my legitimist sympathies found some expression by joining every legitimist society that existed. I lived in a world of white roses and white cockades, and then little by little I allowed modernity to smirch those loyalties and ridicule their lost and fragrant causes. I count myself a fool now in middle age, because I understand at last that what seemed the shadow was the substance, but that what offered itself as the substance was indeed no more than a mean shadow. . . .

"I shall always regret that I did not gain possession of the Shiant Islands before Osgood Mackenzie died, so that I could have written and reminded him of our meeting at Compiègne in 1903, because it was to that meeting I owed my determination somehow to obtain land in the country of my forefathers. He himself writes in *A Hundred Years in the Highlands* of sailing over to the Shiant Isles and camping out on them as a boy, and it would have pleased him, I think, that one of his name should own them again after a lapse of eighty years. . . ."

The Editor of the *Evening Standard* was as encouraging and considerate about the serialization of *Fairy Gold* as the Editor of the *Daily Mirror* had been over *Coral*. It was to start at the beginning of December, which meant I had to forget about the Shiant Islands and go to work immediately in top gear.

I have written in Octave Five of Sylvia, my Siamese kitten who kept me company while I was writing *The Altar Steps*, and of her sad death. I now had a second Sylvia who never left my side at night while I was writing *Fairy Gold*. I pause for a moment to give thanks for what cats have done to sustain me in my work—Twinkle at Burford, Tootoose in Cornwall, Pauline in Capri, the first Sylvia in Herm, the second Sylvia in Jethou, and even now as I am half-way through this Sixth Octave an adorable white and tabby cat called Blandine who has taken the place of my stone-deaf white cat Blanco, lost in a thunder-storm while I was writing Octave Five.

Publishers about now were being more difficult than editors. Stokes published *Coral* in the U.S.A. under protest and we took advantage of that to suggest cancelling the last book owing under the contract Martin Secker had made with them. George Doran of Doubleday Doran made a contract to publish simultaneously the whole seven volumes of *Our Seven Selves*, which I proposed to finish in 1930. Cassell's did not think simultaneous publication feasible but were willing to publish volume by volume. This created the problem of how to adjust British publication with American. Doran was most reasonable and the problem was solved somehow. Cassell's now decided to publish *Rogues and Vagabonds* in the autumn of 1926 and were able to sell the serial rights to the *Sunday Chronicle*. They

F

were to do *Fairy Gold*, with which they were pleased, in the spring.

To anticipate, Doran did not like *Fairy Gold*, but again was most reasonable. I am glad to reflect that I too was reasonable. I find in a postscript to one of Eric Pinker's letters:

I wish all the clients were like you; the business would be real recreation all the time.

That November came a voice from the past in a letter written from Brisk Island (Townsville P.O.), North Queensland:

You will no doubt remember my name as the publisher of Ranger Gull, Reggie Turner, and the Scarlet Pimpernel. Ill health compelled me to relinquish publishing, and here I am living the real simple life on one of the small islands of the Palm Group. I write to congratulate you on 'The Gramaphone' [which like a quarter of our correspondents, including at first my own wife, he spelt with an 'a' instead of an 'o']. . . . *Arthur Greening*.

The rest of a long letter was taken up with gramophone matters.

I was back in Reggie Turner's rooms in Clement's Inn, having just escaped from the oppressive quotidianity of school, listening to Ranger Gull, the author of *The Hypocrite* which had seemed such a revelation of the world when I was sixteen. I never met Greening but remember Reggie Turner's wondering whether another publisher might be better for him and perhaps send at least one of his novels into a second edition.

That autumn a young accountant from our firm of auditors gave a rather disturbing picture of the financial side of *The Gramophone*. To our gratified surprise he said he should like to leave his own job and work for the paper in whose future he had confidence. In 1926 Cecil Pollard became business manager, and the position *The Gramophone* holds to-day is due to his enthusiasm, integrity and skill. His son Anthony, not yet born in 1925, would in due course devote his life to the paper.

It was our policy to offer the members of the National Gramophonic Society an opportunity to choose what they wanted most of three or four proposed pieces of music. This autumn the subscribers had selected Elgar's Pianoforte Quintet as a recording they should welcome. I thought it would be a great coup if the composer could be persuaded to play the piano himself. Sir Edward Elgar had to refuse. He wrote from,

Brooks's
St James's Street, S.W.1
Nov. 17th 1925

Dear Compton Mackenzie,
All thanks for your letter—but I never play the pianoforte. I scramble through things orchestrally in a way that would madden with envy all existing pianists. I never did play really. I must not begin now. Your offer is flattering however.
Mrs Alfred Hobday or, failing her, Mrs Kinsey both play the quintet well.
Best regards   *Yours sincerely*
                                                    Edward Elgar
In fear I have put 'esq' but I feel it's wrong to address an Overlord so—but I know not the exact title.

I had been successful in getting enough of *Fairy Gold* written for the *Evening Standard* to start the serial in December and I prayed I should keep well enough not to let the Editor down. I had stipulated before the serial was accepted that I should have to write it as a book and had made it clear that such a book would be too long for a serial. The Editor should be at liberty to cut as heavily as he found necessary.

When we were at Ripley Lodge we had been great friends with two English women who had a little house beside Caragh Lake in which they had lived all through the troubles and been raided both by the Irregulars and the Black and Tans. They used to talk of their experiences as if they were amusing interludes in their quiet existence.

I was heartened to get a letter from one of them some days after the first instalment of *Fairy Gold* appeared:

Your story came like dew upon a thirsty land. There had been before it a frightful farrago of impossible deeds and people so that your cool scholarly tones broke like chimes upon an unruly playground. I am so glad you sent it to the Evening Standard which is our paper since the sad end of the poor dear Pall Mall. . . .
I wonder if you know the tragedy of Lickeen? The stiff necked tenant to whom the Trustees would not play false played false to them in the end and left the place on their hands. . . . People are all so sorry about Lickeen and you. Far preferable to your Northern Islands!

I have no doubt that if I could have had Lickeen a year ago I should have taken it and the second half of *My Life and Times* would have been far different.

THOSE first few months of my forty-fourth year were a trying
time. On February 1st I was writing to Faith:

*I finished Fairy Gold last night. 585 pp of manuscript or half as long again
as Rogues and Vagabonds. The Evening Standard are cutting heavily now,
poor dears.*

A fortnight later I was writing:

*Back again from town, and have been writing letters since 4 p.m. It's now
1 a.m. and I've still a good few to get through. Now I have to write 2
children's stories, 3 articles and the first instalment of a serial for Tit-Bits
before March 1. What a life! . . . Fairy Gold turns out to be over 150,000!
They're cutting it to ribbons now in the E.S. It would be madness for me to
come to Capri in my present state of nervous exhaustion. I should just have
attack after attack in scirocco.*

I was laid out with violent pain all through the last half of February
and had to write and tell Pinker that I must cry off a serial for
Tit-Bits.

I find a typed copy of a letter I wrote to the Editor:

*It really was a great wrench having to write to Pinker that I did not feel
up to our serial at present. . . . I am at the moment completely fagged out and
I did not feel that it would be fair to make the necessary effort to provide you
with an opening instalment you would probably like unless I felt sure I could
maintain the story at the same level.*

Faith, faced with the prospect of giving up Capri altogether, was
writing gloomily. D. H. Lawrence was there with Dorothy Brett at
the beginning of March. I was sending my love to him in a letter and
hoping his plan to visit Jethou in August would materialize.

Faith would write of that visit.[1]

"When Lawrence asked me to dine alone with him . . . I went
gladly because I enjoyed his company, and when we discussed
Monty I let him talk more frankly than I would have allowed any
one else to do, 'because', I wrote in my diary, 'I know he loves him'.
And of course I talked myself, warmed by Capri wine, and his
sensitive understanding and the glow of kindness in his deep eyes.

[1] In *More Than I Should.*

To me that night he seemed an angel, and I gave him some of the secrets of my heart which hitherto had never been let loose. Unfortunately some months later a short story appeared in one of the popular magazines which he could not have written if I had not dined with him that night in Capri. A malicious caricature of Monty, and a monstrous perversion of facts, yet the source of it clearly recognizable."

When Faith was upset by this story I thought she was imagining a grievance, for I could not see in it the faintest resemblance to her or me and as there was no resemblance to our background, which, as I told Faith, there certainly would have been if Lawrence had been writing about her and me, I urged her to give up worrying.

I find a letter from a friend of Faith's in that olla podrida of femininity in New Mexico which Lawrence stirred continuously. I quote one extract before I destroy it:

I don't mind what you do with my letters. Lorenzo always blows his nose in his letters, so I am hardened to the fate of letters.

But there—don't bother any more about the story—after all think of poor Lorenzo with that old four poster banging away at him—that is heart-rending if you like. He has been ill but is now recovered. Frieda is still pounding away at me after all this time.

Cassell's were to bring out *Fairy Gold* at the end of April, and it was depressing to hear from Pinker that George Doran did not like it now. However, after I agreed to let him have it without any advance, he promised to do his best for the book.

The next blow was the loss of the *Watch Me.* I find a letter of March 1st to Faith from Nellie Boyte:

It was such a sad day for us on Friday and we all feel we have lost a good friend in the Watch Me.

The last galleys of Fairy Gold didn't turn up on Wednesday as expected. Kemp knew Mr Mackenzie was anxious about them (we had sent him back to Guernsey early on Wednesday to see if they had been left in the P.O. because sometimes the mail is not properly sorted before it's collected) and so on Thursday he put out on a morning of heavy westerly squalls. At lunch time the punt was blown 40 Yards across the beach and her sides were smashed. So it was impossible to get out to the Watch Me until the tide was low. Then they used Basil Leng's cockle to get aboard her and lower the extra anchor. Then the wind veered to N.W. She must have broken loose at high flood and drifted on to the N.E. point of rocks. It was ghastly to see her masts just out of the water at high tide and with such a swell and run of tide it was altogether impossible to reach her. We watched anxiously for fear she would drift out to sea and be finally lost. But at low tide the wind dropped to a complete calm and it was possible to reach her over the rocks and dismantle her of everything worth saving. Zabeila and his boy came over from Herm and they all worked like niggers to get the engine out, and just as the tide was coming in all round them they succeeded. The engine weighs over 7 cwt and we got it over the rocks inch by inch on planks. It was a miracle the engine was not smashed, as it was tightly wedged on the big rock that had gone right through her side. Next morning she was smashed to atoms and nothing of her remains but the skeleton of her ribs wedged in the rocks. Mr Mackenzie came down and helped all the afternoon . . . we are seeing about another boat. As Sir P. is still away, the Herm boat is bringing Kemp with mails and milk. Mr Mackenzie was in bed with pain but is better to-day and busy on his introduction to Mr Scott-Moncrieff's translation of the Chartreuse de Parme.

I was lucky enough to get a new boat almost at once, a bargain at £165. She was an Admiralty sailing pinnace and we were able to fit her with the engine of the *Watch Me*. She had been running trips to Herm last year, but this year Sir Percival Perry was running his own boats to bring tourists every day. I called our new boat *Melusine* and she served us well.

A husband for Sylvia arrived about now. I was writing to Faith:

Michael is a priceless cat, more interested in his food than his future wife. He is a philosopher and only gets excited over paper balls, which he retrieves. I put the covers of records round his and Sylvia's necks. They were both amused until they saw each other dressed up like a knight in armour. Then they both spat and growled at each other, neither being able to make out what the other was. It was too absurd. I go out walking with the pair of them following like two diminutive lions close at my heels. Sylvia won't let him sit on my lap. Otherwise she isn't jealous; she gets annoyed with his matrimonial failures, but he's only a baby—10 months old. He's the colour of an otter.

My next worry was a letter from Christopher Stone resigning his London editorship on *The Gramophone* because he felt he had been responsible for the financial mess-up by having too much confidence in somebody. I refused to accept his resignation and fortunately by now Cecil Pollard was getting things straightened out and our office at 58 Frith Street into better order.

The General Strike at the beginning of May started a day or two after the publication of *Fairy Gold*. Faith was in Paris on her way back from Capri. I was writing on May 2nd:

> *For goodness sake don't leave Paris until this strike is settled. England will be hell. I've provisionally cancelled all my engagements. I suppose this will kill Fairy Gold dead. Only two notices so far. The Morning Post said that having already written the best modern story of young love in Guy and Pauline I've now written another even more lovely and alluring. So that was good.*

A day or two later I was writing:

> *Sylvia's kittens are expected hourly. It's an anxious time. Michael is depressed because she won't let him be sentimental about the future. He sits and gazes up at her until she boxes his ears. He keeps trying to get into the basket prepared for her accouchement but this is forbidden.*

In another undated letter I was writing to Faith:

> *I'm glad you're having a good time in Paris. Yes, the play with Guitry and Yvonne Printemps must be lovely. Encouraging notices of Fairy Gold till the strike stopped them. Only 8 but all very good. Best since Poor Relations.*
>
> *Sylvia had her kittens yesterday. Five! One has a double-kinked tail. All of them snow white.*

That double-kinked kitten was called Stumps; he and his brother Baron in the same litter would both live to 18 and Sylvia herself would reach 22.

In the middle of June Faith and I went up to stay at the comfortable hotel presided over by Mrs Cameron in East Loch Tarbert, Harris. Just before we left, Christopher rang up to say we were making a mistake in going by Inverness. Alice knew the Tarbert Hotel well in old days. Luckily I knew enough geography to know that there was Tarbert, Loch Fyne, as well as Tarbert, Harris.

We went by train to Inverness. It was crowded and slow because the railways had not even yet recovered from the effects of the General Strike. After a night in Inverness we drove to Kyle of Lochalsh by way of Glenmoriston and Glenshiel. For me that drive was one long fulfilment of a childhood's dream—the seven men of Glenmoriston with the Prince, the battle of Glenshiel in 1719, Eilean Donan Castle, still as the English frigates had left it after bombardment, and finally Kyle of Lochalsh, where we stayed the night at Simon Mackenzie's inn.

Next morning we went aboard the *Plover* and on the quay at

Tarbert I met for the first time my tenant Malcolm MacSween, whom I felt immediately that I had known all my life. He was the small dark man of the West, and to Faith's pleasure much more like an Italian than her idea of a Scotsman. He was sorry to tell us that Mrs MacSween was laid up in bed and so unable to offer the hospitality she would have liked to offer.

Mrs MacSween was a Mackenzie from Wester Ross, the granddaughter of four Mackenzies. Their house in Tarbert was called Caberfeidh, and over the door were the horns of the Mackenzie stag. I have believed for a long time that the crests of the big clans derived from totems—the Campbell boar, the Macdonald lion, the Matheson bear, the Maclean seal, the Mackenzie-Fraser stag. It is significant that although their lands marched for many acres there is no record of fighting between Mackenzies and Frasers. The Camerons do not have an animal crest, but it is recorded that Lochiel in earlier days used to call his clansmen 'children of the dog'.

I was taken across by Calum MacSween to his house and here a very shy dark little girl, eight years old, was presented to me. She was my beloved Lily, to whom this Octave is dedicated in memory of her beloved elder sister Chrissie, whom I should not meet for another year. Chrissie was now near the end of her time at Moray House in Edinburgh and would be given the school on the isle of Scarp this autumn.

Two days after we arrived the Scalpay motor-boat was chartered to take us to the Shiants on a calm and cloudless June day. Yet even with a glassy Minch the overfalls between the Shiants and the coast of Lewis bubbled. They were known in Gaelic mythology as the Stream of the Blue Men, about which even the Admiralty Sailing Directions issue a warning.

Forty years will have passed when these words are printed. Yet I still hear as clearly as I heard on a June midnight the bubbling of that stream as we pass over it in the motor-boat, on our way back to Tarbert. I still see that octogenarian skipper in the stern. I am still listening to the tales of Calum MacSween sitting beside me in the bows as we glide onward up Loch Tarbert through that glimmering moth-grey Hebridean air which is neither dawn nor dusk.

I was writing about the Islands a year or two later:

"To most people the Shiant Islands mean nothing. To some they mean the most acute bout of sea-sickness between Kyle and Stornoway as the MacBrayne steamer wallows in the fierce overfalls that guard them. To a very few they mean a wild corner of fairyland, the memory of which remains for ever in the minds of those who have visited their spellbound cliffs and caves. . . .

"Staffa has become a tourist's tit-bit. One can almost hear the click of turnstiles as they pass through to visit Fingal's Cave; the last fairies of Staffa floated away from it some time ago on a raft made out of cigarette packets with a paper bag for a sail. . . . To drag in Staffa may seem provocative; but thousands visit Staffa for one who visits the Shiant Islands, and the cliffs of both display those basaltic columns which make all other cliffs seem a little tame.

"The columns of Staffa are more regular; but the Shiant columns are considerably more than three times as high, and on one island they tower absolutely sheer five hundred feet above the sea in a sombre bow half a mile long. The bottle-green water at the base of this cliff, the greenish-black glaze of these columns, that lustrous green of the braes and summits which is peculiar to the grass of such a geological formation combine to present a scene of classic grandeur unsurpassed by any of the famed islands of the Aegean.

"A word about that lustrous green. You may see it at the north end of Skye. You may see it in perfection on the slopes of Ben Hiant in Ardnamurchan. Hiant and Shiant are both attempts to express in English the Gaelic *seunta* meaning enchanted or bespelled. To my mind Ben Hiant is the most magical hill in Scotland. I have watched it from Tobermory across the Sound of Mull until it seemed to detach itself from the landscape of Argyll and float like a huge ship of green upon the air. . . . You may see that lustrous green on Canna. You may see it on parts of Eigg. And by what I read of them I believe you would see it in the Faroe Islands, which are the northernmost remains of that volcanic upheaval which ends with the Giant's Causeway.

"Although the Shiant Islands are nominally three, two of them are joined by a grey beach of large rolled pebbles about 100 yards long and 40 yards wide which is never quite covered even in a storm at the height of the spring tides.

"On the map Garbh Eilean (Rough island) and Eilean an Tighe (House island) look like a miniature of the two Americas. At the north end of the beach Garbh Eilean rises almost perpendicular for 400 feet; one's guests are apt to be a little dismayed when invited to ascend this cliff by a narrow path.

"At the other end of the beach, Eilean an Tighe rises about 200 feet, and ultimately much higher; there is a low tract of ground on the west side which is covered with irises, mint, forget-me-nots and many other herbs.

"Here are the remains of an old Columban cell; just beyond are a two-roomed thatched cottage and a couple of bothies dug out of the earth.

"Eilean Mhuire (Mary Island) lies half a mile away eastward; it is sheer all round with only one path up to the top, an undulating plateau of lush grass.

"The whole extent of these islands with a chain of outlying islets and fantastically shaped dark rocks is about 600 acres, but they could hardly be explored thoroughly in a fortnight of hard walking and rugged climbing.

"The bird life is astounding and it is more easily seen there in all its diversity of incident than anywhere I know. The colony of puffins must be the largest in the British Isles and in addition to puffins there are very large colonies of kittiwakes, razor-bills, guillemots, fulmars and great black-backed gulls. Until about fifteen years ago the last eyrie of the white-tailed eagle was to be found on the Shiants. That eyrie was written about by Martin 300 years ago; he observed that the eagles never robbed the ewes of their lambs on their own island, but always flew across to the mainland or to the Long Island for their prey. I wish the great-black-backed gulls would follow that excellent example. One of the eagles was shot by a clergyman collector and that was the end of the sea-eagle in Scotland.

"There was a floral rarity on the island of Jethou, the white pimpernel, which was exterminated by the members of a field club to whom I stupidly gave permission to search for it. There is a great floral rarity on the Shiant Islands; but forewarned I shall not say what it is, and when I find it I shall not say where it is to be found.[1]"

Instead of going back across the Minch by steamer, Calum MacSween escorted us to Gairloch in the Scalpay motor-boat. We spent a night in the Gairloch Hotel, the largest hotel I can remember that was still lighted entirely with oil-lamps.

I may have felt guilty of faint disloyalty to our Jethou birds when I was expatiating to everybody who would listen about the marvellous bird-life of the Shiant Islands. Anyway, when we got back to Jethou I wrote an article about the birds on my island from which I shall

---

[1] That rarity was *Menziesia purpurea*, a member of the heath family, which does not occur again until Portugal. I was never successful in finding it.

quote a few paragraphs because they will postpone for a little while
the difficulty of discussing my own work, still as difficult to-day as it
always has been throughout my life.

"During the winter the oyster-catchers live decoratively in large
groups like the birds in a Japanese painting, but as soon as they mate
they forget all about the beautiful sweeping curves of black and white
they traced across the wintry sky. They become the fussiest and most
undignified birds imaginable; I should hate to be a young oyster-
catcher. The poor children are scolded all the time for the slightest
initiative on their part; the father and mother in turn try to harry
anybody that comes within a hundred yards of the nest, flying
rapidly backwards and forwards with shrill whistles, their long red
beaks appearing redder than usual with exasperation. . . . I have
never heard of anybody who has become friends with an oyster-
catcher, but my own impression is that they are rather intellectual
birds. They never sit looking bored and vapid like the gulls; they
are always strutting about and gossiping to each other.

"The birds I regard as the tutelary creatures of the island are the
wrens. Most of them continue to inhabit the stone walls, but a few
of them have become quite maritime and build their nests in the
lowest clumps of samphire by the sea's edge. There in company with
the rock pipits they search for the minute insects found among the
lichen on the granite. In winter the garden is sometimes visited by
golden-crested wrens which, perhaps owing to the smallness of their
brains, seem perfectly fearless of human beings, round whom they
flutter like butterflies or humming-birds. Some wonderfully delicious
insect must live in the empty gorse-pods of last year, for these tiny
birds will explore them, one after another, through the whole of a
fine morning. . . .

"To return for a moment to the foreshore. I had often noticed
great-tits and long-tailed tits investigating the contents of the
winkles and devouring them with much relish. . . .

"One fact makes bird-life on Jethou remarkable, and that is the
complete absence of house-sparrows; I have never seen a house-
sparrow on the island. This is a blessing, because they are such
offensive little brutes to other small birds. Flocks of greenfinches
arrive instead, one party of which pecked off the sprouts of a
ranunculus bed and pulled to pieces every blossom of the winter-
flowering crocuses. Even the chaffinches cannot resist crocus flowers.
I cannot help sympathizing with the pleasure they must get from
pulling off all the petals and leaving the brilliant stamens to glow

in the wintry air. Few bullfinches visit us; this bird is being so systematically persecuted by fruit-growers in France (whence, of course, we get most of our migrant birds on Jethou) that they become scarcer every season.

"Three years ago the December halcyon was celebrated as it should be by a pair of kingfishers flying out over the tranquil blue sea; but I have seen no sign of them since then. During the winter the thrushes and blackbirds are about equal in numbers; but the thrushes do not stay with us to nest. Nothing seems to cure the blackbirds' wildness. I know every one of them personally, as I might say, but there is not one of them that does not, as soon as it sees me, set up as loud a shrill of alarm as if I were a French sportsman. . . .

"Three pairs of stonechats stay with us all the year round; with the wrens they are the friendliest and most truly native of the birds to my thinking. The whinchats and the wheatears prefer Herm. Last year a buzzard visited us, and on Jethou the splendid fellow looked as large as Sinbad's roc. And then the cuckoos! We shall have at least four pairs next spring, and they will cuckoo all day long, and all night long, when the moon is shining. They will drown the gramophone."

The writing of novels against time and pain in order to preserve my financial integrity and be in a position to devote two years to the completion of a magnum opus was too much for me. When I returned to Jethou I realized that a fixed date for completing *Our Seven Selves* must be abandoned. George Doran had been agreeably surprised by the reception the American critics gave to *Fairy Gold*; I felt I had worked hard enough to keep my contracts to be able to indulge myself in writing a novel I had long wanted to write.

I have told in my fourth Octave how in 1913 Faith and I came to Capri first, and how we happened to arrive when Count Fersen-Adelswaërd was expected back from his exile after a term of imprisonment in France for an offence against a minor. I have told of the grand dinner of welcome given to him by Miss Kate and Miss Sadie Wolcott-Perry, those two wonderful American old maids, that dinner which was to split the island in two irreconcilable factions for the second time over the same subject. Being newcomers, we were able to preserve our neutrality, and I heard from members of both factions the earlier history of Count Fersen. At that date I was not half way through the first volume of *Sinister Street*, but I promised myself to put that history down on paper one day. The tale made such an appeal to my imagination that I dreaded its capture by anybody else, although when all the chief characters were still so very much alive I felt fairly safe, because it would have been impossible to tell the story without completely changing the scene and the players. I realized that the story was still going on, and I had no desire to anticipate with an imagined end the bitter end that fate might provide.

By the time the second volume of *Sinister Street* was finished war had broken out, and my one idea was to get into the middle of it as soon as possible. While I was waiting for a chance of active service I set out to write what might be the last novel I should ever write, and for a brief while I was tempted to tell the Fersen story. Then I decided that *Vestal Fire*, the title for which I had already chosen, was an unsuitable book for what might be a last bequest. I wrote instead *Guy and Pauline*. I corrected the proofs of that at Gallipoli and even then I used to hope I should survive the war and be able to write *Vestal Fire*. When I returned to Capri at the end of 1917 the story was developing so dramatically that I knew I must wait for its end in real life. In any case the publication of Norman Douglas's *South Wind* had made a novel set on a Mediterranean island out of the question for some time to come. So for the next few years I wrote novels that were for me a kind of marking time. However, I did indulge myself by writing my ecclesiastical trilogy which cut down my circulation by two-thirds.

Meanwhile, *Vestal Fire* was postponed even when the death of the principal characters allowed me to tell the story as it happened. This postponement was due to what resembled a beginner's self-consciousness. The copy-cat scratches of many reviewers were faintly irritating but nothing more. I knew that versatility would be counted a vice until I became old enough for it to become a virtue, but I felt that, if my handling of *Vestal Fire* was going to be sniffed at as another attempt to show off like Jack Horner, I might begin to worry about criticism. Then I decided that this was a crucial moment in my career as a writer. Somehow I must make a success of *Vestal Fire*. Toward the end of August I started, and did what I had never done before and have never done since; I made a false start with forty pages which had to be torn up.

There were so many technical problems.

First of all there was the problem of the old ladies themselves. Dared I make them Americans? Should I not by doing so ruin the book's chance of recognition in the United States by a few inconsistencies of speech which would make them not only ridiculous but improbable? I simply could not afford to have those old ladies seem either. If that was the impression they made, the book was lost; it would turn into a mere *chronique scandaleuse*, which was the last thing I wanted it to be. Finally I decided to take the risk, but I doubt if I should have done so unless I had had an American mother and unless in earliest youth the speech of my American relations had been familiar to me. I knew this would not secure me against the likelihood of offending against external probability, but I felt sure that it would at least prevent my offending against internal probability. At last with many qualms I decided not to change the nationality of the two old ladies I called Virginia and Maimie Pepworth-Norton.

The next problem was the cause of the scandal. How was I to avoid shocking my readers without endangering the story? I know that the notion of being shocked by *Sinister Street* or *Vestal Fire* will seem incredible to-day, but 1926 was not to-day. The 'twenties had moved quite a long way from Victorian prudery but it was still considered ill-bred to tell a smutty tale in mixed company. The passionate egalitarianism of to-day does not recognize the existence of mixed company and therefore the good manners of yesterday are regarded as survivals of snobbery and privilege.

As a novelist with a large and mixed public I felt it was my duty to tell a story with as little embarrassment as possible to *all* my readers. Finally I decided to insist, when the opportunity occurred, upon the comic aspect of the scandal even at the risk of suggesting a cynicism I did not feel. I have been amused lately by the label 'satire' affixed to various performances of the B.B.C. in which youth tried to be funny and middle-age tried equally hard to be young. I did not find the week that was quite as effective as Pope or Dryden, as Horace or Juvenal, because it lacked not merely worldly wisdom but also worldly knowledge.

When I made the comic aspect of my theme in *Vestal Fire* predominant I was not intending to satirize homosexuality. I was merely trying to deprive what was called an 'unpleasant' theme of any 'unpleasant' appeal.

There were plenty of other technical problems, not the least of which was how to introduce about forty characters into the first fifty pages without confusing or tiring the reader. I was anxious to avoid getting a picture of Sirene, as I called Capri, from the angle of any individual character, which would have been much the easiest method. I was also anxious, in view of what I knew would have to be the length of the story, not to take up one moment in scene-painting. So I allowed myself no scene that did not provide an immediate background for some character, and I relied upon being able to suggest the natural scene by the accumulated effect of dozens of snapshots. I hoped that my quotations from Latin poets would not be considered showing off, but I intended to use them when I found an opportunity to help the impression of detachment I wished to convey.

The construction of a book with an unusually large number of characters spread over a period of years is always difficult. *Vestal Fire* was divided into three books, each of which in turn was to be divided into eight chapters. I was successful in making the second book only three pages longer than the first, and the third book only three pages longer than the second. This may seem to have a merely arithmetical interest; but since there is no object in dividing a novel into books unless each one is to be relatively complete in itself as within each book each chapter is relatively complete, the least disproportion in these divisions will wreck the architecture of the whole. At the end of the fourth chapter of the second book, which was to be exactly half way through the novel, the crisis of the story must be reached. From that point onward *Vestal Fire* would have to be modulated into another key: whether such modulation had been successful or not could be decided only by the mood of the reader on closing the book. I hoped that the underlying theme of *Vestal Fire* would appear as the tragedy, not the comedy, of futility. I knew that any tragedy of futility must contain more farce than tragedy; I knew that the reading of it would be a waste of time for people without a sense of humour.

Some time later in that summer the expert committee of *The Gramophone* installed a new gramophone with an enormous horn designed by C. Balmain, without doubt the best reproducer of non-electric records yet achieved. Presently the E.M.G. machine would popularize the large horn and remain the machine most esteemed by gramophone devotees for nearly another twenty years.

My new library was near enough to completion for the expert committee to indulge in all kinds of acrobatic acoustics. My smaller study had always been too small for a satisfactory demonstration of such acrobatics.

The visit of these experts, followed by a visit from Christopher Stone with Cecil Pollard, may have inspired me to write apologetically to about three dozen distinguished contemporaries and ask them to contribute to a symposium in the December number to let our own readers know their favourite song, tune, composer and singer. I cannot resist quoting extracts from some of the replies:

When I came back to Jethou after staying with Tim Healy in Dublin I had sent him Oliver Goldsmith's ivory flute which my father had acquired. I was glad to find him writing:

As regards Irish songs, I think, in spite of the modern contempt cultivated for Moore, that he will never be surpassed. True, he had to stretch on the rack Gaelic music in English words. . . . What can beat such lines as begin with:
Oh, who would not welcome that moment returning
When passion first gave a new life to our frame,
And the soul, like the wood that grows precious in burning,
Gave forth all its sweets at love's exquisite flame?
N.B. I am now over seventy-one!

Hamilton Harty wrote from Manchester:

I do not think it would be wise for a conductor to admit that he has any favourite song, composer or singer—so I hope you will excuse me on this occasion.
I am glad of this chance to tell you how much I admired and sympathized with your recent attitude towards those ghoulish folk who are not happy unless they are digging up the very private life of composers like Mozart.

That was an allusion to an exchange of paper darts with Ernest Newman, who had written to the *Sunday Times* of his gratitude to some German microphotographer for restoring the bawdy passages in letters from Mozart to his wife which had been deleted from the script. Newman felt that those passages helped towards an understanding of the Jupiter symphony. I expressed surprise at such a remark coming from a critic of such eminence as Newman, who rather pompously in his column asked me what I objected to. I replied that I objected to hyenas nosing in the entrails of dead lions.

Sir Edward Elgar wrote from Worcestershire:

I really cannot answer either of the questions; I want the best of everything— and of everybody, including Compton Mackenzie, and this series of questions is scarcely that!

Sir James Barrie wrote from Adelphi Terrace:

Kindly overlook my not doing in this little matter as you suggest. It would be no trouble at all and I should do it willingly were it not that I have sworn

Mrs MacSween

Lily MacSween
aged 8

Malcolm MacSween

Norman Douglas and Faith Mackenzie

C.M. at the helm

*off doing anything of the kind anyhow. Please don't think me a curmudgeon. I
daresay I am one but forgive me all the same.*

Noel Coward wrote:

*My favourite song is 'L'heure exquise', my favourite composer is George
Gershwin, my favourite singer is Yvonne Printemps. I am doing this during a
rehearsal so it may sound rather peculiar.*

John Galsworthy wrote, from Grove Lodge, Hampstead:

*I'm not a good hand at Symposiums, but since it's you who asks, here goes.
. . . My favourite composers* $\begin{cases} Bach \\ Chopin \end{cases}$ *dead heat with Glück beaten half a
length. Stravinsky beaten off and Wagner left at the post . . . and so to bed.*

Somerset Maugham wrote from Bryanston Square:

*What a devilish fellow you are to ask a harmless and respectable gentleman
like myself to answer such questions, but here they are*
    Favourite Song—The Prize Song
    Favourite Composer—Wagner
    Favourite Music—The Fire Music
    Favourite Singer—Lotte Lehman
Curses on your head!

Lord Berners wrote from Rome:

*. . . if by 'singer' you mean any kind of singer then the one I prefer is
Little Tich—but on the other hand if you mean merely concert singers please
substitute Clara Butt.*

Walter de la Mare wrote from Taplow:

*. . . Singers are even more difficult to choose between—by me, that is, who
is nothing of an expert. So, much as I admire and delight in many singers,
mine must be an abstraction? He or she would be an artist with a voice so
delicately and sagaciously trained that at hearing it one would not suppose
that it had been trained at all. It would be a voice so responsive to the 'scenery'
of the mind and imagination, making use of it as a beautiful face is; and so
lovely in itself that you would hardly be able to distinguish between it and its
music because the form (the singing) and the contents (the thing sung) would
be so perfectly at poise and at peace together. This sounds exceedingly vague
as well as hopelessly negative, but it is the nearest I can get.*

Bernard Shaw's secretary wrote from Adelphi Terrace:

Mr Shaw asks me to let you know that only people in a deplorably elementary

G

stage of musical culture have favourite tunes and so forth, and that he considers the question a monstrous insult.

Sir John Lavery wrote from Cromwell Place:

How dreadful—I don't like music—when I was quite young I was told that music and poetry were essential to the painter and that he could not possibly be an artist if he did not revel in both. Well, I tried hard for years without success, all the time pretending that I loved and understood them, till I married Hazel—late in life—when I confessed to her the deception I had been practising by having concerts in my studio—attending all sorts of musical festivals and all the time being bored to tears.

Hazel gave the secret away—since when I have had the moral courage to make the above statement.

Max Beerbohm wrote from Rapallo:

What an age since you charmed us with your company here! And what a troublous and tragic Age, too, it has been! However, throughout it, you have been flying from success to success, on athletic pinions. So that's all right. And I have no doubt it's all right you are also editing 'The Gramophone Monthly Review'. Apollo in the house of Admetus. Hercules chez Omphale. A Golden Eagle swooping down from the empyrean and perching on my finger and cooing a 'record' to me in dove-like tones. Such interludes are all in the epic manner. I refuse to be surprised. And I enclose my typewritten contribution to the symposium about Songs, etc—hoping it also is all right. I only stipulate that the thing shall go in exactly as it stands, of course, or not at all. The last sentence of it might conceivably hurt the feelings of some vast Corporation or Company or Interest or something. But without that little sentence the little contribution would have no point. Of course I shouldn't feel the least bit hurt by your suppressing the l.c. altogether. Here it is—all or nothing—for your approval or disapproval.

P.S. If approved, please endorse my appeal to the printers about punctuation; and have a proof sent to me.

In due course I sent a proof of the 'little contribution' to Rapallo and received a second letter from Max on November 9th:

My dear Monty—(if I may do as the world doth and call you so)

I enclose the proof of my words for the Symposium—but only as a matter of form: there are no mistakes in it: many thanks to the printers.

I do not know whether you are in London or on your island—the island from which I received so very kind and delightful a letter. . . . If you regard your post-war books as 'marking time' you are surely in a minority of one. But I am of course intensely interested in hearing that you are going to tackle the

War. Just enough time has elapsed, I fancy, for you to have got the thing in perspective—rounded and manageable—and I am sure you will make a very grand job of it all.

In Octave Two I told of my mother's starting the Actors' Orphanage Garden Party and of getting various distinguished people to name their favourite flower and sign little tabs which were attached to a button hole of that favourite flower and sold at the Garden Party. The only refusal she had was in a pompous little note from Mrs Humphrey Ward.

Among the forty-five distinguished people whom I invited to contribute to our Symposium there was only one pompous little note, and that came from another of what used to be called 'Lady Novelists'. Miss Ethel M. Dell's secretary wrote:

Miss Ethel M. Dell has asked me to acknowledge your letter of the 3rd inst., and to tell you in reply that, owing to the very large number of similar requests she receives, she makes it her invariable rule to refuse them.

That remark of Max Beerbohm's about a book I was planning to write shows what importance *Our Seven Selves* still had in my mind in spite of my preoccupation with *Vestal Fire*.

In April of this year a reporter of the *Daily Mail* had written to ask if it was true that I was planning to write a novel of a million words in seven volumes. "Here is the substance of a rattling good news story, and, if what I've been told is correct, may I ask you to let me have the facts."

A draft of what I wrote to that reporter has survived and here it is:

"The novel is to be in seven volumes and a million words will be its approximate length. For a long time I decided to call the book *Life and Adventure*, but for a year now I have been calling it *Our Seven Selves*, and that is the contract I have made with Mr George Doran who with a boldness that is both refreshing and encouraging to issue in the United States the whole seven volumes together.

"The titles of the various volumes will be:

"1. Alien Corn. 2. The Apple of Discord. 3. The Dark and the Fair. 4. The Heroic Symphony. 5. The Molehill. 6. The Mountain. 7. The Olives of Home.

"The theme of the book is the self-determination of man in relation to (1) his art, craft or profession (2) Women (3) Family (4) Class (5) Country (6) Humanity (7) God.

"The book will begin in the year 1897 and finish in the 1920's. The length of the book is due to the large stage, which extends from

Ireland in the West to Greece in the East, to the length of time covered by the narrative, and to the number of personages and groups involved.

"One or two papers commenting on the announcement of a novel written at such length expressed an opinion that the present generation is disinclined to read long novels. Yet *Sinister Street* has sold more than any of my novels and now, thirteen years after publication, still sells sufficiently well to make a cheap edition not worth while to produce. *Sinister Street* with 375,000 words was less justified for length than *Our Seven Selves*. If a writer has a theme which demands length he is surely right to hope he can 'bring it off' without bothering his head about the fashions of the moment. After all, the fashions of the moment are created by imitators. It was easy enough to imitate *Sinister Street*, but the formula for *Our Seven Selves* may be a little too complicated for immediate imitation.

"I hope to start the actual writing of the book next year and to have it ready for publication by the spring of 1930. Before I can start I must have written enough books to keep me while I am devoting all my time to *Our Seven Selves* and allow me a year's holiday in the South Seas when it is finished. I am supposing at the moment that it will be the last novel of modern life I shall write. After *Our Seven Selves* I plan to write a history of the Crusades in eight volumes to be followed by a History of Polynesia and a History of Scotland. Then I shall start a novel in about thirty volumes beginning in the year 1000 and ending in 1914, a kind of ancestral epic which will amuse my old age. *Our Seven Selves* will be written in Jethou. The daily task will depend on health. That health depends to some extent on not over-working. I have been thinking about *Our Seven Selves* and working at other books incessantly for eight years, so I can hope that with no other books to think about I shall be able to go on working incessantly.

"You ask what was the inspiration of it, and I can only reply 'my experiences during the war'. I was lucky enough to experience active service by sea and by land, to be behind the scenes in diplomacy, to have had a first-hand knowledge of espionage and counter-espionage, and to have had the patience not to rush into print the moment I put off my uniform. I should not have made any announcement of my plans now had I not grown tired of reading obituary notices of my work because I had not been producing *Sinister Streets* every autumn and *Carnivals* every spring since the war came to an end.

"Ever since I went to school, except for the two and a half years of active service, I have been told by school-masters, dons and reviewers that I was not making the most of my gifts, and during those years of war that I was making too much of them.

"I'm afraid none of this will be of much value as a news story but I have answered your questions as well as I can and am grateful for your interest and good wishes."

The problem of publishing *Our Seven Selves* in seven volumes in Great Britain to coincide with Doran's undertaking in America was still unsolved. Cassell's idea of publishing them one after another did not fit in with Doran's plan. Eric Pinker wrote on October 22nd:

I went down yesterday to see Victor Gollancz of Benns, and told him about 'Our Seven Selves'. He was extremely interested, not at all afraid of the project and thinks it would be 'fun to do', which is the attitude we want, and, incidentally, what I expected from Gollancz, of whose abilities I have a high opinion. The trouble, of course, with the scheme is the very large amount of initial outlay which will be involved. Gollancz said he would expect to have to spend not much less than £2,000 in advertisement as he quite agreed that the thing could only be handled in a big way and he expected that the library subscription for the set would be merely nominal so that the demand would have to be built up by advertisement. You see, with an advance of any size—I quoted £6,000—together with the cost of production and advertising, the outlay would be well in the region of £10,000, and this is going to take some getting back. It is a tremendous thing for any publisher. The project inevitably strikes one as bound to be either a big success or a great failure. I offered Gollancz as an inducement 'Vestal Fire' and 'The Ladies of Mitylene'[1] and he asked if it would be possible to read the manuscript of 'Vestal Fire' because if he liked that very much and saw a big sale in it it would greatly encourage him to take on the larger scheme, as he would be prepared to invest in this the prospective profits on the two single books. I said that I thought this would be possible and if Gollancz will come anywhere near our terms for 'Seven Selves' I am in favour of showing him 'Vestal Fire' as it can certainly do no harm. I should like to know when you think you will have finished 'Vestal Fire'. Gollancz is to consider the whole thing carefully and communicate with me again in a few days.

I have no record of what Victor Gollancz decided but no doubt he finally refused *Our Seven Selves*, and who would blame him? Certainly not I.

A letter survives from that autumn dated Tuesday October 26th. Faith was in London and I was writing:

[1] Afterwards called *Extraordinary Women*.

Sylvia's kittens were born on Sunday night. She began at 7.30 and had 4
successfully. Then the fifth was a long time in coming and in her struggles she
must have overlain one of them—a male unfortunately. Then she seemed to
settle down, but about 3 a.m. Honor came in to say that she seemed very bad.
So Nellie and Honor and I sat up with her till nearly five. A very fierce N.W.
gale was blowing, and the sixth, another male, after a terrific struggle was
finally born dead. She's quite all right now with 3 females and 1 male, but I
don't think she likes them as much as the first lot. I think she now realizes
that they grow up and become a nuisance. She is very good, but it was an
anxious two hours because she was in great pain all the time. She couldn't
manage to purr but just twitched her tail in response to our sympathy. Big
staring eyes dull with pain. The gale went on all yesterday. So we had no mail.
To-day is exquisite—cloudless and calm and warm and the garden full of
crocuses. The Cassia was broken by the wind. Some of the squalls must have
reached 60 miles an hour.

I've had an invitation from the Cambridge Union to speak at a debate on
sex prominence in the post-war novel on November 9th. I think I'll accept
because I want to see Eric Pinker before he goes to America but Vestal Fire
still has the difficult finish to write and if I go away in November I'll have to
cancel talking dates in December unless they can swop with November talkers.

An unsigned letter from the secretary of the Women's Union at London
University has reached me after a fortnight's effort by the G.P.O. It was
addressed:

Mr Compton Mackenzie, Savile, Royal Channel Islands, Yatch.

The writer invited by the Cambridge Union to regret the
prominence of sex in the modern novel was J. C. Squire. When I
reached London at the beginning of November with the typescript
of all except the last chapter of *Vestal Fire* I found Jack Squire at the
Savile sporting a pair of mutton-chop whiskers.

"I suppose you've grown those whiskers, Jack, as an appropriate
decoration for this mid-Victorian notion you are going to support at
your old university."

Jack Squire ignored my observation and said it would be a good
idea if we met at Liverpool Street so that we could travel up to
Cambridge together on the date fixed for the debate.

"You'll be a bit lost without me," he said.

I arrived at Liverpool Street in good time for the train at the
closing of a dreary November afternoon; there was no sign of Jack
Squire. In those days Liverpool Street was an infernal station, and as
I waited for my guide I reflected upon the influence Paddington and

Liverpool Street might have had upon the minds of Oxford and Cambridge men. I waited for Jack Squire in vain and finally had to take my seat in the train without him. I settled down to make a few notes for my speech on the back of an envelope on which to concentrate for the rest of the journey, but about ten minutes after we left Liverpool Street the lights went out in the train and I was left to meditate on my speech in the dark.

A peculiarity of the railway-station at Cambridge is that the arrival and departure platform are the same. However, I made my way successfully along its length to be met by the President and other officers of the Cambridge Union. The President was a young man with reddish hair called Devlin[1]; he enquired anxiously for the whereabouts of Mr Squire. I told him what had happened at Liverpool Street and we walked along to the dinner before the debate, the President and officers much perturbed by the absence of Jack Squire. Just when poor Pat Devlin was trying to solve the problem of a speaker to follow the first two, Jack Squire arrived with the coffee.

"Couldn't find a white tie," he explained, "and missed the train looking for one."

To my surprise the mutton-chop whiskers he had been sporting when I saw him a day or two ago at the Savile had vanished.

The House was packed out that night, and—a dashing display of modernity—the Newnham and Girton girls were allowed in to the gallery. They were still many years away from being recognized as undergraduate members of the University.

In due course the opener rose to make his speech and after the usual twenty-five minutes sat down. Then my leader rose.

"Sir, in rising to oppose . . . sir, in rising to oppose . . . sir, in rising to oppose," he stammered.

Ironical applause began, and the President rang his bell to signify that the speaker should sit down. The opposer had been overcome by nerves in rising to face a much more crowded House than any he had yet encountered; even the floor was covered with squatting undergraduates unable to find seats.

Before Jack Squire rose a note was handed to me from the President.

If possible will you speak for 45 minutes. P. Devlin.

To turn a twenty-minutes speech one had thought about beforehand into an extempore speech of three-quarters of an hour and that

[1] Later Lord Devlin.

to a critical undergraduate audience was a bit of a facer but I sent back word to the President that I would do my best.

Jack Squire made a capital speech in which the audience was left with the impression that the only guardians of morality left against the corruption of novelists were the Georgian poets. And then in what might have been the accents of a Prynne denouncing play-actors in his *Histriomastix* he delivered his peroration.

"And now, sir, before I close I must warn you against the speaker who will presently rise to oppose the valuable motion I have had the privilege of supporting this evening. In him you will see the embodi-ment of all the graces, which you may have difficulty in resisting. Do not be beguiled, sir, by the looks and eloquence and wit of my honourable friend opposite. This house has a moral duty to perform to-night."

There is no more dastardly way for a speaker to prejudice an audience than by telling it what wonders the next speaker is going to perform; I realized that somehow I must win the sympathy of the House at once if I was going to keep it for three-quarters of an hour.

"Sir," I said when I rose, "I had understood that the motion before the House this evening deplored the prominence of sex in the modern novel, but my honourable friend opposite in his concluding words seemed to suggest that he was deploring the prominence of sex in the modern novelist. That being so, sir, I feel at liberty to dis-close something about which if my honourable friend had confined himself to the motion on the paper I should have kept silence.

"Sir, this evening my honourable friend had arranged to meet me at Liverpool Street station in order to guide me, a stranger, through a strange land. Sir, when I reached the station my honourable friend was not there. I waited as long as possible but at last I had to pass the ticket-collector and take my seat in the train—alone, without the guidance of my honourable friend opposite, and let me add, Sir, in darkness owing to the failure of the train's lighting arrangements. Sir, where was my honourable friend when I set out upon this dark and lonely journey? Sir, he was concealed somewhere in Liverpool Street station, shaving off the mutton-chop whiskers in which I saw him only two days ago because he knew that he could not support this Victorian motion without the ridicule of an intelligent audience if he was still wearing those moss-grown relics of Victorianism, a pair of mutton-chop whiskers."

After that I was able to keep going for the extra time needed to make up for the absence of a speech from my leader. I thought that possibly I might have been a little too ribald once or twice—we were forty years away from 1965, still in the pre-Chatterley era—and at the end of my speech I switched my voice into the minor key for a moment to apologize if anything in my speech had done any harm to younger people than myself, looking up at the girls in the gallery as I spoke; then quickly I switched back into the major key for a laugh and sat down.

I recall that at the end of a kindly notice of my speech in the *Granta* among the brief criticisms of succeeding speakers was this:

"Mr G. Harding (Queens') is learning to speak quite well."

I wish I could remember what dear Gilbert Harding said, but I know he was deploring the prominence of sex in a minority, for the Union refused to deplore it by well over two hundred votes.

Next morning Jack Squire and I went to breakfast with Pat Devlin at Christ's College, and I recall being a little surprised when Jack Squire asked for beer instead of tea or coffee. I do not recall encountering Charles Snow as an undergraduate in the courts of Christ's College, but I may well have mistaken him for a don.

I was much impressed by Pat Devlin and suggested putting him up for the Savile, to which he was duly elected. He asked me at that breakfast of long ago if I could tell him how I changed my voice into the minor key and back into the major without taking breath. Perhaps he had visions of its effectiveness with an Old Bailey jury. I had to tell him I did not know how it was done; it was just that I was able to do it. A year or two later my father's last remaining sister rang me up after a broadcast and said I had done something with my voice which in her experience she had heard only from her father. I expect my grandfather who died before I was born used that trick when he was playing Touchstone.

When I came back to London Eric Pinker had read *Vestal Fire* and thought it was the best book I had written since our agreement.

"But Cassell's won't look at it," he prophesied.

Rogues and Vagabonds had been held up because Cassell's wanted to serialize it. This they had just managed to arrange for in the *Sunday Chronicle*, but it would mean holding up publication until May. I agreed with Eric Pinker that *Vestal Fire* was bound to be refused by Cassell's, and applauded his notion of sending the book to Charles Evans of Heinemann, who had just accepted Francis Brett Young's *Portrait of Claire* after it had been turned down by Cassell's. Eric Pinker wrote:

Evans has just rung up and is tremendously enthusiastic about Vestal Fire.
He thinks it is far and away the best thing you have ever done and he talked
on for about ten minutes about its wit and treatment and character-drawing
and erudition and so on! He has given the book to another director, and will let
me know his definite decision early next week.

The other director funked it.

Even the gay spirit of the twittering 'twenties was not yet tuned up
to publish a novel which, though it laughed at some aspects of it,
admitted frankly that homosexuality existed.

Eric Pinker now suggested that Constable's should be offered
Vestal Fire, but he had left for America before their answer was
received. Michael Sadleir wrote enthusiastically about *Vestal Fire* to
Ralph Pinker, who was looking after things while Eric was away, but
again the other directors funked it.

About now Newman Flower was taking over Cassell's from the
Berry Brothers, and Ralph Pinker thought that *Vestal Fire* should be
offered to him. He would undoubtedly refuse it, but at least it would
have been offered to him. I agreed.

At Jethou the library and two extra rooms were finished at last.
Looking back at it, I can affirm that no man with the help of a boy of
sixteen ever did a more remarkable building feat in just over a year
than George Macdonald.

The Expert Committee had arranged for us to have radio on the
island, and the *Watch Me's* mast had been set up as our wireless pole.
On Christmas Eve I was writing that I thought the weather would
not allow me to get over to midnight Mass in Guernsey but that I
was looking forward to hearing it on the wireless from Basle, the only
place in Europe from which it was being broadcast.

On Christmas Day we had our first dance in the new library and
the Balmain gramophone with its big horn was at the top of its form.

TO my amazement, Newman Flower wrote to tell me he thought *Vestal Fire* one of the funniest books he had ever read and that Cassell's would go all out on it. The rumour that Flower was going to take over Cassell's from the Berry Brothers would become fact by March. Flower had been serving Cassell's as its literary director for some years but he had always had a difficult job in catering for the magazines. These were now to cease from being a responsibility for Cassell's and exist on their own as the Amalgamated Press.

It was heartening in that January to read:

All departments will now be under my control absolutely. No butting in from anyone. That's why I want to be let loose on 'Vestal Fire'. . . . I own the whole box of tricks—or shall do by March 31st, and what I say in my department will be law. When I go off the deep, as I feel like doing over 'Vestal Fire', something's going to happen. I would like to have told you all this over a cup of tea with a few Siamese around.

I was in bed with a ferocious attack of pain when that letter came; it was a fine sedative.

I have not yet mentioned the great difference made to life in Guernsey by the arrival of the new Lieutenant-Governor, Major-General Sir Charles Sackville-West.[1] The new Government House was a centre of gaiety throughout his term of office. Titwillow, as his nickname was in the army, had been our Military Attaché in Paris. A year or two after coming to Guernsey Charles Sackville-West's brother, Lionel Lord Sackville, died, and he succeeded to the title and to the greatest house in England, Knole. He had been a widower when he had recently married Anne Meredith, an American actress. Anne Sackville-West was anxious to revive the old Guernsey A.D.C. and asked me if I could act in and produce *The School for Scandal* in the week after Easter. With my usual optimism I decided that I should be far enough on with *The Ladies of Mitylene*, as *Extraordinary Women* was still being called, to promise I would tackle *The School for Scandal* at the beginning of April.

Early in February I went to London to make the most of what would all too soon be the last days of the Savile at 107 Piccadilly. There were only two bedrooms for members, both at the top of the

---

[1] The 4th Lord Sackville.

house, and they decided to celebrate the demise of 107 Piccadilly by importing bed-bugs. This put them out of action and members used to stay in a house in Hertford Street. Here I succumbed to a vicious influenza which as usual with me developed into an acute bronchitis. I was delirious for three nights and was looked after by a dear little Irish nurse whose name I have forgotten. Nellie Boyte was sent for from Jethou, but she went down with influenza almost at once and although she was allowed to travel back to Jethou she was laid up there for a fortnight.

Viola Tree with her engaging children had visited Jethou in the summer of that year and had then suggested I should write a secret service play for Gerald du Maurier. She now wrote to ask about this play and I put together a first act. Then Viola had a serious operation and nearly died. Somehow that first act was lost, but it was put to good use by me presently.

Faith's articles about Verdi, Bellini, Donizetti and Rossini had been a great success in *The Gramophone* and I pressed her to follow them up with Puccini, Leoncavallo, Mascagni and Boito, but she was tired of opera-composers and had written a short story which appeared in *The New Statesman*. I felt what she needed was the discipline of writing a book. I had been looking at an old volume I had of Arckenholtz's *Memoires pour servir à l'histoire de Christine, Reine de Suède*, published in 1751.

"She was an extraordinary woman," I commented. "And by Jove, there's my title. I never cared for *Ladies of Mitylene*; I shall call it *Extraordinary Women*."

Faith, to my great pleasure, got seriously drawn to a life of Christina of Sweden, which she worked at for nearly three years and was published in 1931.

Faith always needed somebody or something for whose happiness and success she could feel responsible. Nicolas Nadegine had been a responsibility for the last six or seven years. We had given concerts for him under the auspices of *The Gramophone*, I had persuaded the Parlophone people to record him, and he had had several good operatic engagements, but although he had a magnificent barytone voice it was in a way *vox et praeterea nihil*. He lacked the ability to impress himself on an audience either on the concert platform as himself or on the stage in an opera character. In a word he was not an actor.

I remember John McCormack's saying to me that he knew too well how it ought to be done to go on playing in opera himself.

"I can put myself across as John McCormack to an audience from the concert-platform, but I learned long ago that I could not really put myself across even as Rudolfo in *Bohème*."

I once went with John and Lily McCormack to a performance of *Traviata* at Covent Garden in which Gigli was playing Armand. At the back of the box John kept singing *sotto voce* how Gigli should be singing his arias. There were knocks of protest from the boxes on either side, and at last one of the attendants came in to ask John to keep quiet as people were complaining he was interrupting the performance.

"And yet if I'd gone on and sung in Gigli's place I'd have been just as awkward and idiotic as he was."

Nadegine could not see that his failure to achieve stardom was the failure of his personality. He had to suppose that there were dark plots to prevent his being successful, and Faith was inclined to support him in finding every reason for failure except the right one. About now he married a young Australian, the daughter of a wealthy man, and Faith's responsibility was handed over to a wife. The marriage did not last very long and Nadegine was back again in the shadows of some play by Chekhov, where he would remain for another thirty years. All our Russian friends agreed that he was a good, even a great, poet but the book of verse he dedicated to Faith and myself, although it appealed deeply to the Russians in exile, was naturally frowned upon by the Communists.

About the same time as Nadegine got married Isabella Caracciolo married an English official on the Gold Coast. She too was a great loss to Faith.

I was particularly glad that Faith was able to preoccupy herself with Queen Christina of Sweden because my financial future was looking grim. The three-years' agreement I had made with Eric Pinker had come to an end and by the terms we had made I was over £6,000 down. This meant that I would have to work very hard for the next three years at least to pay back Pinker by the end of the time. Of course, a film might come to the rescue, but I could only count on books at the rate of two a year and £1,500 a year at most for myself, out of which I should have to keep up my £10,000 endowment policy at over £600 a year in which the bank had first charge against my overdraft and Pinker second charge. As I remember, difficulties were raised by the Westminster against that second charge, which considering that Pinker also banked with the Westminster seemed a little absurd. However, thanks to Ridley's unremitting help, this was finally accepted. I have already tried to

pay a grateful tribute to that bank manager in High Street, Oxford.
Looking back now on those difficult years of the 'twenties, I salute
once more his memory.

There was an agitation in the popular Press that spring about the
amount of income-tax lost to the revenue through authors living on
the Riviera, millions according to the popular Press! In fact the sum
total, apart from Somerset Maugham and W. J. Locke, would hardly
have added up to £10,000. Winston Churchill allowed himself to be
taken in by the preposterous sums credited to authors on the
Riviera, or what was regrettably more probable, seized the chance
of a little cheap popularity for the Chancellor of the Exchequer.
Anyway, in his Budget speech he announced his determination to
deal with such tax evasion by making every publisher deduct
income-tax from the author's royalties before they were paid to him.
A more flagrant, indeed flagitious piece of unfair discrimination by a
Chancellor of the Exchequer has never been imposed.

At this time Churchill believed himself to be the farmer's boy; he
had not realized what a ruthless farmer Stanley Baldwin was going
to be. He was to take the unpopular measures like putting the country
back on gold in which he did not himself believe, and when it suited
Farmer Baldwin he would be got rid of. Churchill had better claims
to be a member of a National Government than any politician of any
party. Yet he was excluded from the 'National' Government of 1931,
for which Baldwin would find excuses, and from the 'National'
Government of 1935, for which the nation itself would pay dearly.

I recall a story from Bob Boothby[1] who had become Winston
Churchill's Parliamentary Private Secretary in 1926. One day
Lloyd George, who was then at a low ebb politically, asked to see
the Chancellor of the Exchequer.

"I suppose I'll have to see him," Churchill told Bob Boothby.

So Lloyd George was ushered into the Chancellor's room and
Boothby left the two great men together. Half an hour later, after
Lloyd George's departure, Bob went in and found the Chancellor
sitting by the fire, that glazed look in his blue eyes which made them
seem almost like porcelain.

"Bob," he said. "A relationship has been established in this room
—the relationship of a master and a servant. And *I* was the servant."

The genius of Winston Churchill had always recognized the
genius of Lloyd George, who himself had always recognized the
genius of Winston Churchill.

[1] Lord Boothby.

The relationships of politicians to one another are a puzzle to the layman. I would never attempt to make a politician the central figure of a novel; their mental approach to life eludes me.

I recall going to see Philip Cunliffe-Lister to consult him about something to do with gramophone records; at that date he was President of the Board of Trade.

"Why are you authors always so down on politicians?" he asked.

I replied jokingly,

"I think it must be because you don't give us enough knighthoods, Philip. The only artists that ever appear in the Honours' List are actors or organists."

Being a politician, the President of the Board of Trade took this explanation of mine seriously.

"That's interesting, Monty. What literary chap do you suggest for a knighthood?"

As a novelist I thought I should be on the safe side by suggesting a critic.

"What about Walkley, the dramatic critic of *The Times*?"

"I'll speak to Stanley about him," said the President of the Board of Trade, making a note of Arthur Bingham Walkley.

I was never given the pleasure of boasting to critics that I was responsible for one of them being knighted, because A. B. Walkley died before the New Year's list of honours was published.

Those two stories have taken my mind off my financial situation. I must return to it unwillingly.

It was going to be difficult enough to get through the next three years, untaxed; if taxed it would be impossible to maintain Jethou. I wrote to the Society of Authors to ask when they would protest against this unfair discrimination in the Budget, only to find they were going to do nothing at all. Algernon Thring, who was then the Secretary, was a firm believer in quietism. Finally I consulted Victor Carey, who wrote to their Lordships of the Treasury for advice. Was I to carry on with my improvement of Crown property or not? Their Lordships, with a realism that gave me more confidence in the financial future of Great Britain than I had been able to feel for some time, suggested that if I sold my copyrights in future no deduction from income-tax could be made by the purchasers.

This income-tax business had been going on all through that spring and summer. I find the draft of a letter to Newman Flower on July 4th:

"Does the clause compelling you to collect income-tax specify the

Channel Islands? At present the whole question between the Channel Islands and the Imperial Government is *sub judice*, and until some arrangement has been reached the Imperial Government has no right to beg the question in this way. As my landlords are the Treasury I can hardly be accused of being ungetatable."

So from 1927 until I was domiciled in Scotland in 1931 I sold the copyright of every book I wrote. In Scotland, however, I found that income-tax was chargeable on sales of copyright, or in other words that things that were equal to the same thing were *not* equal to one another.

I took advantage of their Lordships' advice about income-tax to ask if my lease of Jethou at £100 a year could be changed from twenty-one years to life and one year over. This was granted.

I have told in Octave Three of Arthur Bourchier's coming to see the O.U.D.S. performance of *The Merchant of Venice* at Oxford in the summer term of 1903 and of his offering me a seven-years' contract to appear as his *jeune premier* on a salary starting at £500 a year and rising gradually to £2,000 a year. I had never met him since, and I was astonished to receive a letter from him in this February which has not emerged from my papers. The gist of it was:

"Many years ago, more years than I care to remember, I made you an offer I never made any young man before, and I doubt if any young man ever had such an offer. As things have turned out for you you were right to refuse my offer, but in memory of that offer would it not be nice if when I come back from this tour in South Africa for which I am leaving shortly I found you had written a play for me?"

I must have written to say I would come and see him in February when I went to London, where obviously I had made a date to see him and had to excuse myself on account of that infernal illness. I find the following note written from the Strand Theatre, Aldwych on February 11th:

I am so sorry and also for the cause. Yes, do let us meet when I return. It would be too splendid also if I could snare a play from you!

But I never saw Arthur Bourchier again; he died on that tour in South Africa.

The Guernsey production of *The School for Scandal* was a great success. Anne Sackville-West was a very good Lady Teazle, and Sibyl Beaumont was an admirable Lady Sneerwell; she was as good a Lady Sneerwell as I ever saw.

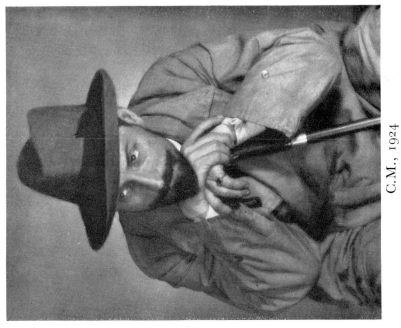

C.M., 1924

Amateur Dramatics, 1927
C.M. and Lady Sackville

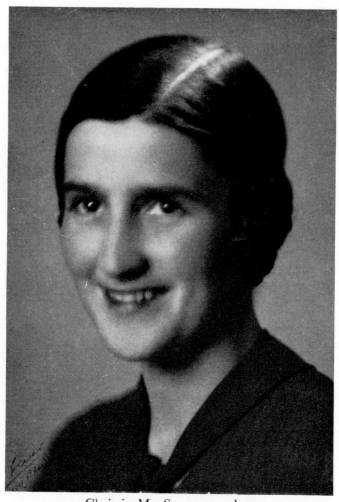

Chrissie MacSween, aged 30

By an enjoyable coincidence I had just written those words when our *facteur* arrived with the post in which was a letter from Dame Sibyl Hathaway, D.B.E., the Dame of Sark, who had become a double dame.

Seigneurie De Sark
23rd June

Dearest Monty,

Lovely to hear from you. I was faintly hoping you would be in London. The investiture is on 8th July and it would have been grand to see you.

Your giant Echiums still flourish here—and my Embothrium is now 30 feet high and a blaze of scarlet.

Yours ever
Sibyl

Those echiums first went to Sark from Jethou and it may have been I who suggested that the Dame should plant an *Embothrium coccineum*.

Christopher and Felicité Chinnery came to stay with us in time for the last night of *The School for Scandal*, which was celebrated by a jovial party at Government House.

Sidelights on the activities of the Guernsey A.D.C. are provided by extracts from a letter to me by a performer in another production.

I recall a lively Annual General Meeting at which the Dean complained of our rehearsing on Sundays. Do you remember your memorable reply? As far as I can remember, you said "I regret very much that Mr Dean's parishioners have been shocked at our rehearsing on Sunday. As a Catholic I am always astonished at the sensitivity of the English on this point, when they cheerfully flock in their thousands to see a football match on Good Friday." And for good measure, "So far none of the Church charities to which we have contributed have refused our donation." Very naughty, but very funny.

One last glimpse of you at the dress rehearsal of 'Madame sans Geêne'. We of the cast sat spellbound in the stalls as you instructed Marshal Lefebre in his part. You will remember that owing to a temporary affliction you had to do it entirely in mime—a performance I have never forgotten. The young Captain of the Duke of Cornwall's Light Infantry who played the part is now Lieut-General Sir William Oliver.

While we were in Guernsey the bluebells had come into flower in the ancient chestnut wood, to be succeeded presently by *Cineraria stellata*, which Basil Leng had planted. Those who have only seen the latter in a greenhouse can have no idea of its beauty as a blue sea of flowers in the shade of leaves.

H

Rogues and Vagabonds appeared as a book in that May. The reviews were good and bad. The bad ones complained as usual that I was not giving the world another *Sinister Street* or *Carnival* or *Sylvia Scarlett*, or indeed any other book except my *Parson's Progress*, which they hoped I would never repeat.

Favourable and unfavourable reviews both supposed I was trying to write a fairy story, but the fairy tale part of *Rogues and Vagabonds* was the true story of Rosie Boote who sang 'Maisie is a daisy' at the Gaiety and became Marchioness of Headfort.

Two letters about *Rogues and Vagabonds* gave me more pleasure than the most laudatory reviews:

> Bandrum
> Carnock
> Fife
> *16th May, 1927*

Dear Mr Compton Mackenzie

Though I am sure you are bored with letters about your books I feel I must write and tell you what joy of a very rare kind you have given to a small family on a Scotch hilltop where there are not many rogues and vagabonds in the flesh, though we are of that ilk in the spirit.

Bless you for that bairn Letitia, so real a bairn, so enchanting—surely she must be your own. She behaves like a child, talks like one, is altogether adorable.

I fear you will never 'better' Rogues and Vagabonds—it is so truly human, the work of genius in the most lovable quality.

Bless you once again. You may know my name as the purveyor of harmless fiction for many years. Much joy have I had in it and keeping a loyal and affectionate public for forty-five years. It's the heart that does it—same as you demonstrate in your last and most beautiful story.

This requires no answer or acknowledgement—it is merely a very sincere thank you.

> *A. Burnett Smith*
> '*Annie S. Swan*'

It was my privilege five or six years later to meet Annie S. Swan at a dinner of the Glasgow and Lanarkshire Association in London of which Sir Ian Hamilton was President and at which Annie S. Swan and I were guests. In my speech I said how proud I was to meet for the first time a woman whose books had brought such pleasure to countless lonely crofts all over the Highlands and Islands for fifty years and more, and in the name of those countless Highlanders and Islanders I took it upon myself to thank her. When Mrs

Burnett Smith made her speech she said how deeply moved she had
been by what I said and, bursting into tears, sat down.

"You're a nice chap for a fellow Lord Rector to go out to dinner
with," said Sir Ian to me.

The other letter came from:

Les Pergolas
Hardelot
Pas de Calais
France
June 21st

My dear Mr Compton Mackenzie

*We the undersigned feel that we owe you a debt of gratitude for the pleasure
derived from reading your delightful* Rogues and Vagabonds, *which book
we brought away with us to this place where we have come to spend some weeks
of quiet (not to say completely empty of everything but sand) convalescence for
one of our number. I (Berta Ruck speaking) read this book aloud every
evening until it was to our regret finished. Humour and drama alike enchanted
us—and a wistful glance back at conditions that are no more and the pleasure
of reading about a side of life described by someone who knows it!*

Yours sincerely and gratefully

Berta Ruck
June Head
Arthur Oliver

Berta Ruck was the wife of Oliver Onions and herself the authoress
of many popular novels. Ray Lankester used to get great pleasure
out of her books when he was no longer able to move about. I have
never been able to understand why Oliver Onions did not receive
the critical recognition his work deserved. He went on writing good
novels and short stories until he was getting on for ninety. His range
was great. He wrote some remarkable tales of the eighteenth century,
some equally remarkable ghost stories, a masterpiece of morbid
psychology, *In Accordance with the Evidence*, a devastating view of
journalism in *Good Boy Seldom* and in his old age some impeccable
historical novels. The failure of critics to recognize a major novelist
like Oliver Onions does not encourage respect for critics. It is amusing to recall from that signature 'Arthur Oliver' that Onions as a
surname was felt to be a handicap to the rising generation.

In the summer of 1927 the Savile had to forsake 107 Piccadilly and
move into the late Lord Harcourt's house at 69 Brook Street. The
ceiling of what had once been the large main drawing-room was
painted with nymphs and cupids—on seeing which Max Beerbohm

commented "Ah, Lulu Quinze, I perceive". Harcourt had always been called Lulu Harcourt.

Ivor Back and William Orpen disliked that ceiling and it was turned by them into the café au lait ceiling of to-day. Some of us wanted the Harcourt dining-room to be the billiards-room, but the bridge players, who had long resented their small room high up at 107 Piccadilly, secured it for themselves and would not be driven out, even although some of us used to profane their jealous solemnity by playing Old Maid. As I remember, it was not until after the Second War that we finally got them upstairs into the old drawing-room. The ante-room of the card room, known as the Sandpit, became the centre of the Club's life and took the place of the billiards-room at 107 Piccadilly.

Bill Orpen was on the verge of resigning that summer because the committee had twice held up the election of Sydney Dark as a member. Sydney Dark had been joint editor of *John O'London's* before he became editor of the *Church Times*, and if only for his gifts as a raconteur was an obviously suitable member. Bill Orpen's long upper lip looked longer than ever as he asked me if I would threaten to resign unless Sydney Dark was elected. I managed to calm him, and presently the committee elected Sydney Dark, who was immediately a great Savilian success. He once afforded me a sight I never expect to see again. He had dozed off in one of the armchairs in the Sandpit with a lighted cigarette. Suddenly he leapt up with fumes coming from his mouth; that lighted cigarette had set fire to his false teeth. This is not just one more Savile story; I saw those fumes with my own eyes and I heard Sydney Dark's shout of dismay as he leapt up and hauled the denture out of his mouth.

It may have been in the middle of the Savile move that the B.B.C. suggested my doing a weekly programme of gramophone records. I did not feel I could travel up every week from the Channel Islands and suggested that Christopher Stone should be asked, the only stipulation I made being that he should be announced as the London Editor of Compton Mackenzie's paper *The Gramophone*. I recall going along to 58 Frith Street and telling Christopher what I had arranged for him to do. He protested, but I insisted that he could not let us down and in the end he agreed. He was a terrific success, although he was in such a state of jitters that he put records on the wrong way round. However, the public response was warm and immediate. It was such a relief to hear something different from what was then known as the B.B.C. voice.

I do not think I exaggerate when I say that for the next twenty years Christopher Stone was the best loved individual talker in B.B.C. programmes.

The reception of *Vestal Fire* by the critics when it was published that autumn was as usual mixed. I shall quote the youthful Cyril Connolly in the *New Statesman* on November 12th, but I shall charitably abstain from quoting what Norman Douglas wrote to me in a letter about that review.

"*Vestal Fire* is a novel about Capri. That is to say it is dialogue occasionally interrupted by a thread of plot and appealing to a small public of cynical and scholarly people and the larger one of those on the island itself. Both these publics were given a masterpiece in Mr Douglas's *South Wind*, and to write a book that enters into such vain and obvious competition with the latter is to merit deserved and speedy misfortune. The explanation must be that Mr Mackenzie is suddenly desirous of re-entering the literary world and has written this book as a testimonial that will placate the few and decimate the habitual readers of his books. Possibly he has been so long on Capri that he requires 400 pages in which to settle up his accumulation of scores. To produce a witty and unpleasant chronicle of clique life is good exercise for a romantic author; to season it with racy academic jokes is good discipline for a popular one. Unfortunately Mr Mackenzie, though consistently amusing, is not quite hard-bitten enough to convey the dry malice, the electrical gossip, and the glow of disillusion that we have come to expect from the Capri novel. His endless quotations from Martial and the Latin elegiac poets are usually apt but never striking; in short, they add nothing to the reader's emotion except the feeling that they are there on show. The theme of the book is the infinite time it takes an American colony to discover that a man, if he is a French Count, young and rich, artistic, handsome and polite, can still be an intolerable bore. Even so, this conclusion is not deduced from his words but gradually built up in the knowledge that he has been in prison, is not really a Count, is given over to all the exotic vices and is afraid to join up in the War. As a sequel to *South Wind* it is as feeble as sequels are, as a new departure for Mr Mackenzie, it is bracing and rather hopeful."

The riper Gerald Gould wrote in the *Observer*:

"The real beauty of the book consists in this—that though the whole story of decay and drugs and death is cast in a comedy vein and much of the rich detail is funny, there is no cynicism and little satire; on the contrary there is an extraordinary tenderness, as sunny

as Sirene's noon. The presentation of fact is merciless; the characterization is merciful. And the blend of scholarship and worldly
wisdom is astonishing."

Perhaps the money-grubbers who were busy turning Capri into
the Isle of Capree complained at Fascist headquarters. Presently *Vestal
Fire* was banned from Italy by Mussolini's order on five grounds:

(1) Making fun of the carabinieri.
(2) Making remarks derogatory to the State.
(3) Mentioning the unmentionable.
(4) Injuring the réclame of Capri.
(5) Contra bonos mores.

I cannot remember when I finished *Extraordinary Women*; what I
recall was the disagreeable shock of hearing from Newman Flower
that he was not prepared to risk publishing it, and a week or two
later that George Doran was equally shy. The future of *Extraordinary
Women* was solved by Martin Secker's arranging to publish a limited
edition of two thousand at a guinea. My agreement with Pinker made
it necessary for me to give Cassell's a spring book. So I undertook to
have a novel for them delivered by the end of February. The
financial situation was saved by the *Sunday Pictorial's* engaging me to
write a weekly review of gramophone records for the last three
months of 1927. Luckily these were so successful that when the three
months came to an end the *Sunday Pictorial* again gave me a yearly
contract, which lasted until the *Daily Mail* took me on as literary
critic in the autumn of 1931. Besides that weekly job for the *Sunday
Pictorial* I was writing monthly essays for *Vanity Fair*, some of which
were reprinted in a volume of essays called *Unconsidered Trifles*.

The writing of *Extraordinary Women* had tired me. Looking back, I
should say it was the most exhausting book I ever wrote. The
subtitle was *Theme and Variations* and I wondered if composers used
to feel as tired when they were trying to work out another variation
upon a theme. I felt I was entitled to a week or two in Scotland.
Lady Elspeth Campbell and I were planning a set of gramophone
records for teaching Gaelic and I went up to consult Father John
MacMillan at St Munn's, Ballachulish.

I have painted a portrait of Father John MacMillan as Father
James Macalister in *Whisky Galore* and other novels.

Maighstir Iain was a Gaelic bard of the olden time from the
Catholic island of Barra, and his great desire was to return there as a
parish priest. Soon after the war he had gone to Canada with a

number of emigrants from the Catholic Highlands and Islands. There he had a great fight with the Canadian authorities, who he felt had not kept their side of the bargain and were inflicting unnecessary hardship upon the immigrants. In the end, though not going as far as Henry II, they managed to get rid of a 'turbulent' priest.

Ballachulish was an Episcopalian stronghold and, as I remember, both Papists and Presbyterians, being minorities, were in alliance against the Episcopalians, an unique state of affairs in Scotland. Father John impressed upon me that whenever an opportunity presented itself I should let it be known how deeply and dearly he longed to be a parish priest in his native Barra.

I think it was in this autumn that I first met Angus Campbell, the Captain of Dunstaffnage, in George Macleod's bookshop in Oban. His father and the previous Duke of Argyll had had an expensive lawsuit to decide who was the Keeper of Dunstaffnage, which was finally settled by the Duke's remaining Keeper and Angus's father becoming Captain of Dunstaffnage.

A similar solution had been reached when Mackintosh of Moy and Cluny MacPherson contended for the chiefship of Clan Chattan. Mackintosh was recognized as Chief and Cluny became the Captain of Clan Chattan.

Angus Dunstaffnage spent one night every year in the partially ruined castle but lived in the village of Connel. He had been one of the British prisoners-of-war who had been sentenced to a period of solitary confinement by the Germans as a reprisal for Winston Churchill's announcement that German submarine officers would be given specially rigorous treatment. Afterwards he was sent to a prisoner-of-war camp for Russians, for whom he felt a life-long affection. My friend Raymond Wavell-Paxton, who had been Assistant Military Attaché in Vienna before the Great War started, was another of those condemned to solitary confinement. A year or two after this summer I was accosted in the Station Hotel, Inverness.

"Hullo, Monty."

I wondered who it was.

"You don't recognize me? It's Raymond Wavell."

He had been so changed by that infernal confinement that I did not know one of my most intimate Oxford friends, whose portrait I gave in Octave Three.

There is no doubt that the ordeal those officers suffered marked them for life. Angus Dunstaffnage's entry in *Who Was Who* 1951-1960 proclaimed him to be 20th hereditary Captain, Chief of Clan Aonghas an Duine; Hereditary Keeper of Royal Forest of Dalness; Steward of Upper Lochow; Knight of the Order of Malta; Member Royal Bodyguard of Scotland; Privy Chamberlain of the Sword and Cape to the Pope; Vice-Lieutenant and Hon. Sheriff-Substitute of the County of Argyll. It does not mention his regiment or service in the Great War; that was an experience he wished to obliterate, and never once in the course of an intimate friendship which lasted from that day in 1927 until he died in 1958 did Angus speak to me of that experience.

His house at Connel was in my mind when I described Kilwhillie's house in my Highland comedies. And it was Angus Dunstaffnage's habit of burying a new kilt in a bog for a year to season it which suggested that habit for Kilwhillie. There, however, the resemblance ends, for Kilwhillie himself is a creature entirely of my own fancy.

Dunstaffnage's house at Connel remained as it had been in mid-Victorian times. One slept in feather beds under eiderdowns really stuffed with the down of eider ducks. Alas, it was burnt to the ground in the early 'fifties, part of that ill-fortune which dogged Angus Dunstaffnage throughout his life.

That visit to Father John MacMillan gave me my first view of Glencoe on an autumn day of heavy cloud. The *làraichean*, foundation stones of the houses of the massacred Macdonalds, still visible in that melancholy glen, affected me deeply.

I was enjoying myself so much with Father John's innumerable stories that I put off leaving Ballachulish until I simply had to catch the Sunday night train from Glasgow to London where I had some talking engagement. So after Mass it was decided that Johnnie MacConnacher should drive me. All the way we passed closed inns and hotels with a notice Six Days Licence and by the time we reached Glasgow we had an appetite and a thirst. I took Johnnie to my favourite Malmaison Restaurant in the Central Hotel and after studying the menu I decided to start with Bisque Homard.

"Are you enjoying your soup, Johnnie?" I asked.

"It's very good soup, Mr Mackenzie. It's very like tomato soup."

After the Bisque Homard I decided that a mixed grill would be the best dish for Johnnie and ordered a couple. When we had finished I asked Johnnie what cheese he would like.

"Och, I don't think I'd be liking cheese at all. Could I not be having what we're after having over again?"

The maître d'hôtel and head-waiter tried their best not to look surprised when Johnnie settled down to his second mixed grill with obvious enjoyment while I toyed with some Stilton.

I had a tiring week in London before going back to Jethou, where I was almost immediately laid out by one of my bad goes.

At this date Dean Inge was writing every week for the *Evening Standard* and once or twice had sniffed down that thin red-tipped nose of his at popular novelists. At the end of that November he wrote an article headed 'What Some Famous People Did *Not* Say' in the course of which I spotted one or two misquotations of his own. For a week I set out to chase any others I might find and wrote a letter to the editor of the *Evening Standard*:

"Sir, Dean Inge in his article on 'what some famous people did not say' is mistaken in attributing '*Quem Deus vult perdere, prius dementat*' to a misquotation or corruption of Publilius Syrus. The original is a fragment of Euripides quoted by Athenagoras, the authenticity of which there is no reason, I believe, to doubt.

"Joshua Barnes (1654-1712) was responsible for the solecism by translating the fragment as '*Quem Jupiter vult*' etc. 'Barnes', says the Dictionary of National Biography, 'was a man of wide reading, but his scholarship was inexact. He had a good memory, but weak judgment.'

"There are other inaccuracies in the Dean's article. 'It is worse than a crime; it is a blunder,' was first said neither by Talleyrand nor Fouché but by a more loyal Bonapartist—Boulay de la Meurthe. 'La garde meurt et ne se rend pas' was attributed to Murat also, so that Cambron's disclaimer only answers for himself. It was the kind of remark Murat might credibly have made.

"Cowper wrote 'the cups that cheer but not inebriate' not in the singular as the Dean misquotes him with the mob. He also misquotes Chaucer who wrote 'yet in our asshen olde is fyr-y-wreke'. 'Cold' makes nonsense as well as an ugly line, and 'yreken' never existed. Y-reke means 'raked together'.

"I do not know when Goldsmith wrote 'We have given hostages to fortune', but if he ever did, he was anticipated by Bacon in 'Of Marriage and Single Life'. 'He that hath a wife and children hath given hostages to fortune'.

"The Dean is probably right in refusing to accept Theodoret's statement that Julian the Apostate cried out at the point of death, 'Thou hast conquered, O Galilean'. The accompanying miracle makes one suspicious of the ecclesiastic, and nobody could wish to embarrass with one superfluous miracle a decanal mind already too much oppressed by the demands of orthodoxy. But why not be content with Montaigne's and Voltaire's refutation of Theodoret?

Why attribute to Julian a Calvinistic distinction between the Catholic Church and Christianity?"

The gloomy Dean, as the popular Press called him, was a formidable adversary to tackle and I was quite prepared for a broadside in his next article. Apparently he had to accept my corrections; there was no reply.

I think it was in this December that an addle-pated jury awarded £2,000 damages to Artemus Jones, K.C., because some author had unwittingly used his name by writing about little Artemus Jones at Ostend with a lady who was not his wife. So far from having suffered a loss of £2,000 by those words Mr Artemus Jones became Sir Thomas Artemus Jones very soon after this and a County Court Judge. Then followed the award of damages to somebody called Lewis Seymour on equally absurd grounds. Solicitors began to rub their hands in anticipation of settling libel cases out of court to their own advantage.

On December 7th I wrote to the Editor of the *Morning Post*. My letter was headed

AUTHORS' RISKS OF BLACKMAIL

"Sir, Last year I received a letter from a firm of commission agents, suggesting that I should settle an outstanding account of over £40. Inquiry showed that somebody had been betting with them in my name. Not being anxious to be posted as a defaulter, I interviewed the Turf Guardian Society, and asked what could be done about it with the aid of the police. I was told that nothing could be done. The Law did not recognize a man's right to his own name on the Turf.

"But any obscure individual who threatens an author with legal proceedings for the admittedly unintentional use of his name may expect the support of a jury and the encouragement of a judge.

"Yet the Law does not allow the wretched author any copyright in the names of his own books. Mr Matheson Lang called a play put together from an Italian original with a title of its own, 'Carnival'. It would have been idle for me to go to law, because Mr Lang would have demonstrated that his play was not a colourable imitation either of my novel or of my play by the same title. And anyway, what author would go to law if he can help it, knowing, as he does, that extracts from his work will be read aloud in Court by a lawyer? What material damages could compensate him for such havoc of his reputation as a writer?

"There used to be an admirable way of settling this kind of

dispute, and that was the duel. But we were deprived of such a direct and rapid solution by the lawyers, who put a price on a man's honour and offered him their services to obtain it. Lawyers always have encouraged and they always will encourage people to quarrel in an orderly way. Their tyranny is threatened at the moment by doctors; but we shall soon have an alliance between the two, and the rights of the individual will recede even further into that obscurity where already they are hardly visible.

"Restore the duel. Let authors and husbands protect themselves. Leave the Law Courts to women. They are realists and will make a better job of the Law. Even with the present hermaphrodite juries an author will have fairer play than he did. Most men are nominalists—we found that out in the war—and you cannot expect a juryman, whose only link with reality is his own name printed above his shop-front, not to respect names. The most familiar quotation in the English language is 'A rose by any other name' etc. Why? Because it administers a mental shock to every male who hears it for the first time.

"As I finish this letter I turn on the wireless and hear an exhausted uncle in the Children's Hour gasping at the end of an unusually long list of birthday wishes. Thus are the young people of to-day encouraged to suppose that their mere names have a magical potency.

"Many happy returns to little Artemus Jones of Rotherhithe and to little Lewis Seymour at Newcastle-under-Lyme."

Just before Christmas Dr Davidson, the Archbishop of Canterbury, introduced the Measure to sanction a revised prayer-book to the House of Lords, which, in spite of some No Popery ranting by Lord Curzon, approved of it by a big majority. The House of Commons was less broad-minded, and allowed itself to be swayed by the emotional balderdash of Joynson-Hicks, who took the House back into the seventeenth century with a gimcrack eloquence that would have been incomprehensible to the century itself. The Attorney-General, Sir Douglas Hogg, tossed a pearl of legal ambiguity to the members. "The rejection of the Measure will be a disaster, but its acceptance will be an even greater disaster." Enough members gobbled up this pearl to reject the Measure by thirty-three votes. One of the most influential puffs of hot air came from a Presbyterian, Rosslyn Mitchell, whose flowers of speech had nothing to do with the case.

A few days after this we had a gardening tragedy on Jethou. Just before dusk one afternoon I suggested to Keegan that it might be wise to put in the frame fifty seedlings we had raised from the rare white *Amaryllis belladonna*.

"I've a feeling we're going to have a frost to-night," I told him.

That night there was a vicious frost and every single one of those white Belladonnas was killed. That was a drear December of heavy frosts alternating with savage N.E. gales. The Channel Islands had experienced no such December for years. I lost a sad lot of my sub-tropical shrubs and that blue cloud of *Cineraria stellata* would never again mist the ground beneath those gnarled chestnut-trees. It was indeed a damnable December, and January continued to be infernal. To add to our depression Michael conceived a hatred for his sons, whom he set out to kill. In the end he had to be given away and went to live a long and happy life on the Borders until it was ended by his being shot by some trigger-happy keeper. I was laid out through Christmas and the New Year, but somehow managed to start *Extremes Meet* before my forty-fifth birthday.

FORTY-FIVE YEARS OLD: 1928

IN my last Octave I told the story of a young subaltern of mine in
Syra called Wilfred Macartney, who was sent to the island of
Cerigo after I had managed to secure its temporary independence
instead of its surrender to the Royalists. I had not seen him since I
left the Aegean in 1917, but he had served in the field in the Ump-
teenth battalion of the Royal Scots, been wounded, been taken
prisoner and made a daring escape.

After the fiasco of the Arcos raid in May of the previous year that
disastrous Tory Government of 1924 tried to produce red bogies in
order to recover some of their lost face with the electorate. Macartney, who had joined the Communist Party, felt he must do something to show what a treasure he was to them. Through a young
German, he got in touch with a Russian agent and procured for him
a catalogue of some aeroplane firm which could have been obtained
without help from Macartney. The sleuths of M.I.5 got on Macartney's trail and after the deplorable evidence of their incompetent
direction in the Arcos raid offered Macartney as a sop to the
Government to justify it in the eyes of the public for the mess it was
making of foreign affairs. Macartney was arrested and tried before
Lord Hewart, the Lord Chief Justice, at the Old Bailey. To impress
on the electorate the danger to its future from the machinations of
Russian spies, the Attorney-General, Sir Douglas Hogg, led for the
prosecution, Macartney being defended by my old friend St John
Hutchinson. The Lord Chief Justice evidently felt as much under
obligation to Mr Baldwin and the rest of them as Judge Jeffreys felt
to King James II and VII; he sentenced Macartney to ten years'
penal servitude with two years' hard labour. His German associate
was given the same sentence and died in prison.

I was shocked and wrote the following letter to the *New Statesman*:

"THE 'RUSSIAN SPY' CASE

"Sir,

I have no idea what your editorial attitude will be toward the
Macartney case, but I hope you will allow me to say something on
behalf of the unhappy young man himself. In 1917 he was serving
with me in the Aegean, and I now learn that he was only seventeen
when he was sent to me from Egypt with two other officers to
administer a censorship of posts and telegraphs for which job he was

unfit, having no word of any language except English. I gave him instead some rough and tumble work among the islands, and finally he was stationed as port control officer in Zea to keep an eye on the traffic between there and Laurium during one of the periodic blockades of Greece. I notice in the Press that this job has been magnified into a governorship. Such a statement testifies at once to Macartney's megalomania and the imbecile credulity of the police. He was always liable to get a little above himself, but, though I often had to talk to him rudely about foolish pranks, I had a respect for his pluck and loyalty. I have not seen him or heard of him since. I had no idea that this young man who had been wounded in France and given a commission from the ranks was really nothing more than a schoolboy.

"I do not propose to occupy your space by criticizing in detail the many sinister aspects of this case. They must be obvious to every honest man with a grain of common sense. But I must protest against the vindictive sentence passed on both these spies and I make that protest not out of sentiment, but because it is obvious that in these days spies may become an inconvenience, but can never become a real danger. In fact, they are bogies. It would scarcely be more criminally absurd to condemn a man to penal servitude for ten years and hard labour for two years because he had frightened Sir Douglas Hogg with a turnip and a sheet. I am not a member of the Communist Party, but if anything could make me become one it would be the thought of this wretched young fool (young knave if you like, but still young and long ago ruined for humdrum life by the precocious excitement of the war) condemned to this monstrous doom. This kind of judicial hysteria has a disturbing affinity with witch-burning, Chartist hunting, and other cruel panics of the unhappy past.

Yours etc

Compton Mackenzie"

At the same time I wrote to St John Hutchinson:

January 20th

My dear Hutchie,

I have been dreadfully upset by the sentence passed on this wretched fellow Macartney, and I have been wondering if there was anything that could be done in the matter. I enclose a copy of the letter I have sent to the New Statesman. *I felt it useless to attempt to get such a letter into* The Times.

A pressman was sent to see me from the Daily News *to ask what I know about Macartney, and I spoke to him very strongly about the case. You had of course a difficult job in defending him, because the only real defence was to say that he was a half-wit, and that is not recognized as a form of insanity. A few more cases like this and we shall have the Law Courts back in the condition they were in the Chartist times.*

Let me know if I can do anything beyond writing abuse of this despicable Government.

Yours ever

Monty

To the *Daily News* reporter who got a column out of his interview with me on Jethou the afternoon after I heard the news on the wireless I was as rude as I could be about the Government.

Fifteen months later Macartney's mother was dying and Joynson-Hicks, the Home Secretary, refused permission for the convict to see her. This naturally enraged me again. Lord Justice Scrutton in some remarks allowing an appeal against one of the Lord Chief Justice's sentences criticized his handling of the case. I sent this letter to the *New Statesman*:

"March 15th 1929

"Sir,

After reading with what is called 'gloomy satisfaction' the remarks of Lord Justice Scrutton on the Lord Chief Justice's capacity for prejudice I venture to call attention once more to the cruel sentence of two years' hard labour and ten years' penal servitude which in January 1928 he passed on Macartney for attempted spying. We have had several instances in this country of judges who have continued to function for some time after a suspicion had arisen that their mental faculties were declining, and I suggest that an examination of the cases conducted through the last year or so by the Lord Chief Justice will leave in the minds of many a doubt of his fitness to remain in the responsible position he now holds."

This letter was returned to me by Clifford Sharp, that brilliant editor, with the following comments in his own hand at the bottom of it:

My dear Compton Mackenzie

Twelve months ago I was hauled before the L.C.J. for contempt of court and had to pay £500. I really cannot risk it again before 1930.

Besides, your suggestion is wrong. I know him well. He is pushing, prejudiced, brutal, and utterly unprincipled. *But he is still young and his mental powers are by no means declining. He is one of the quickest and cleverest devils I have ever known, witty too, but possessing no other redeeming feature.*

Yours ever

Clifford Sharp

Of course I was wrong about Hewart's brains. He was still the best after-dinner speaker in the country. Now in my mind's eye I see him sitting in that corner of the Garrick Club under the staircase like a spider into whose parlour only a privileged few of the members ventured to walk.

That first act of the play I was proposing to write for Gerald du Maurier proved not to be such a waste of time as I had feared. When the refusal both of Cassell's and Doubleday Doran to publish *Extraordinary Women* made it financially imperative for me to produce a novel for the spring the theme of *Extremes Meet*, which I had worked out as a play with a time-span of only two days, suggested itself as the most suitable for a 100,000 word novel that would have to be ready for press by the end of February at latest.

The effort of constructing a novel was likely to bring on another of those goes of pain which would make it impossible to finish in the time allowed. The construction of a book, although it may only have involved twelve hours of concentrated thinking, usually ended in one of those painful attacks of nervous exhaustion. If I failed to deliver a book by the end of February it would mean that the publication of *Extraordinary Women* would be held up both in Britain and America because Cassell's and Doubleday Doran would object to its appearing in the same publishing season as their own book. At this moment I was still £4,000 down on my agreement with Pinker and the bank was still making difficulties about a second charge on my insurance policy. With much generosity Newman Flower volunteered to guarantee my overdraft and this made it doubly necessary for me to fulfil my side of the bargain.

Somehow I managed to finish *Extremes Meet* by the end of February, and it gave me immense pleasure to dedicate it to J. Heron Lepper, the chief editor at Cassell's, "who had steered so many of my galleys safely to port". J. Heron Lepper had seen to press all my books since *The Heavenly Ladder*, and I owe to his memory infinite thanks for the trouble he took not merely over misprints but to give me heartening encouragement. I abstain from printing any of his letters to me because they might seem a display of self-praise and yet

I cannot help regretting this; such letters would be an example of publishing standards forty years ago that for various reasons do not exist to-day.

J. Heron Lepper himself was a cripple, too much of a cripple even to be able to pay me the visit to Jethou which I should have so dearly welcomed. I see now that modest, great-hearted man crouched over the desk in his little room at La Belle Sauvage and I humbly salute his memory. My gratitude for what he did for me in those difficult years of the 'twenties can never be adequately expressed. How pleased J. Heron Lepper would have been in 1927 if he had known that *Extremes Meet*, with that dedication, would be reprinted in two cheap editions nearly forty years later.

The reviews of *Extremes Meet* when it was published at the end of May were almost uniformly favourable, but I realized how little all but one or two of the reviewers appreciated the scope of my Intelligence work in 1916 and 1917, which provided the material for the novel. Most of them supposed I was again indulging what they called my Dickensian ability to produce grotesques of character who never really existed in the flesh. Tribute was paid to my comic invention, but it was usually suggested that such comic invention was at the expense of realism. Several reviewers pointed out how much truer to life was W. S. Maugham's *Ashenden*. Maugham's work for Intelligence during the war had consisted of acting as a kind of inter-mediary to gather the information of agents he met in Switzerland and communicating that information to Indian Intelligence head-quarters in London. My experience and Maugham's were com-pletely different. He handled his own material in the best Maugham manner; he could not possibly have handled mine.

I began to wonder whether my prospective novel *Our Seven Selves* in seven volumes would prove to be worth the effort it would mean. I did not make up my mind yet, but I began to play with the notion of writing my war memories instead of using them for fiction. I was beginning to get impatient of the form pacifist propaganda was taking. I did not feel that the world would avoid another war because some people had found it muddy and lousy.

When the fountain at the Horse Guards, raised in memory of the glorious dead of the Royal Naval Division, was unveiled by Winston Churchill there were sneers at the sonnet of Rupert Brooke graved upon it. I wrote an article in *G.K.'s Weekly*:

" 'Their memory is thus linked for ever with the Royal Navy whose child they were, of whose traditions they were so proud, and

I

whose long annals, rich with romantic and splendid feats of arms, contain no brighter page than theirs.'

"That noble sentence from Mr Winston Churchill's address will probably strike as mere rhetoric in the ears of the devitalized young intellectuals by whom Rupert Brooke's sonnet is no longer regarded as poetry. The war was not many months old before the humanitarian press was inveighing against the romantics who were to arise after it was over and glorify the beastly thing. They have not yet appeared. They lie in Flanders, those romantics. Their dust is mingled with the tawny soil of Helles. The mighty cone of Athos observes their tombs. They went early to the fight, those romantics; conscription does not breed martial apologists. So far the art inspired by the war has mainly followed the course that humanitarians can approve. We have had two successful plays, in one of which an officer followed the example of King David, in the other of which the point of view of the coward was presented with sympathy and considerable insight. We have had a clever volume of short stories, in which the author (C. E. Montague), a distinguished intellectual, seemed to have been profoundly disillusioned by his experiment of exchanging the pen for the sword, and we have had the poets, few of whom ever succeeded in giving form to any emotion deeper and wider than a fleeting mood of disgust or homesickness. Assuredly the humanitarians have reason to congratulate themselves. There is no sign at present of any attempt to romanticize war, which does not mean, however, that humanity is a single step nearer to the achievement of perpetual peace. The greatest political ideal hitherto evolved by the imagination of man was the condominium of the Emperor and the Pope. Imperial ambition and Papal futility combined to destroy it. What the world failed to obtain from the co-operation of two picked men will hardly be obtained from the association of bureaucrats known as the League of Nations, by the constitution of which the world has been made safe for hypocrisy.

"War will never come to an end for practical reasons, and one may be allowed to feel no regret for this, since if Humanity cease from war because it has become too expensive or too destructive or too unpleasant for the non-combatant population, nothing would have been gained that was worth while, and indeed much would have been lost. So long as the seeds of strife sprout and flower and seed again in every human heart, it is idle to expect mankind to forsake for moral reasons the vast and hideous harvest of war. The devil is sick; he has donned the cowl, or rather he assists with notebook and pencil at the important assemblies of the League of Nations, while Italy bullies Greece. . . .

"The real lesson to be gained from the last war, as it seems to me, is that never again shall we wage war as we waged it in Flanders and France. Yet, the bitterest supporter of the Western school of tactics was the humanitarian *Nation*, which shed as many crocodile's tears as would have set the Nile in flood over the waste of the world's youth, rather than forget its vendetta against Mr Lloyd George and admit that the Eastern school of strategy was right. Better the bloody mess of Passchendaele than the romantic side-show; better that thousands of conscripts should be slain than that those romantic volunteers should have taken Constantinople.

"In reading through once again the sonnet of Rupert Brooke that is carved upon the mermaid fountain, we may find it, ten years after his death, untouched by time. He lies for ever where Achilles but sojourned, in Scyros; and whatever may happen to the rest of his verse, those sonnets of war will last as long as the crags of that austere island in which his body waits. To pretend that Rupert Brooke is not a figure on which the imaginative mind may dwell with greater exaltation than on some pale and trembling junket of a creature whose melting point becomes the centre of interest in a book or a play is mere wantonness."

What I wrote in 1928 I do not feel inclined to qualify today.

It was some time this year that a story by D. H. Lawrence appeared in the *London Mercury* called *The Man who Loved Islands*. I told Charles Evans of Heinemann's that if he included it in a forthcoming collection of Lawrence short stories I should injunct it.

"But it's not meant to be Monty," Lawrence moaned. I replied that I was well aware of that but that if Lawrence used my background of a Channel Island and an island in the Hebrides for one of his preposterous Lawrentian figures the public would suppose that it was a portrait. In any case Lawrence needed a lesson in botany. He had written too beautifully about flowers to be easily forgiven for covering a granite island in the Channel with cowslips; he should know that cowslips favour lime. I was in fact getting tired of Lawrence's caricatures of people against photographic backgrounds.

When *Lady Chatterley's Lover* was privately printed some time in 1928 I received a letter from two young men who asked me if I would let them have £200 to buy a gypsy caravan and go round England, preaching the way of life revealed by D. H. Lawrence; they were also asking Mr Aldous Huxley to let them have £200. I wondered why young men should expect me or Huxley to finance propaganda for something which, as James Joyce said, needed no propaganda.

Francis Brett Young wrote to tell me that Lawrence was ill and that my injunction of his story was making him worse. So I withdrew the injunction and the lunatic story may be read to-day.

At this date medical opinion was inclined to ascribe any kind of rheumatic trouble to pyorrhoea of the gums; the slipped disc had not come into fashion. So at the end of March all my teeth were taken out. A fortnight later I was writing to let Faith know in Paris that I did not find false teeth the least handicap to speaking and that all I had to bother about was the pace at which my nails grew, now that I could no longer keep them in check by biting them. I was due to go to Scotland at the beginning of May, and during that April I worked hard to get a month of *Sunday Pictorial* gramophone reviews in hand and five *Vanity Fair* articles. On top of that a new British film company was proposing to do a film about University life which they wanted me to write. I wasted too much time over this, and in the end, two years later, they made a mess of *Carnival* instead.

The day after my teeth all vanished I received a letter from J. B. Macdiarmid, the Labour and Home Rule candidate for the Western Isles:

We all agree that to a man of your calibre who is still young a great and beneficent career is open to you to play in Scottish Story. Your being a R.C. and by place of birth an Englishman are not any real disabilities for such a part. Gladstone was an Anglo-Scot. You being of Highland extraction and a Hebridean laird beats out the objections you make. What Scotland needs to-day are leaders. I hope you will agree to stand for a Scots constituency at the approaching election. Mr Ben Shaw, Secretary of the Scottish Labour Council, expresses to me the earnest hope that you will come forward. He has two or three suitable constituencies still unprovided with candidates.

I felt it might be my duty to contest a seat so hopeless that there would not be the slightest chance of my winning it, but I decided to postpone any definite answer until I went to Glasgow.

At this date a law student at the University, J. B. MacCormick, had parted company with the Labour Party and founded the Glasgow University Nationalist Association with the intention of putting up R. B. Cunninghame Graham as their candidate in the Rectorial election next October. This remarkable young man, seconded by James Valentine, another remarkable young man, had been able to convince various seniors like Lewis Spence and   .

Muirhead that if the National movement was to make real headway it was vital to amalgamate the various Home Rule associations already in existence into what should be called the National Party of Scotland. A conference was held in Glasgow at the beginning of May at which this amalgamation became an accomplished fact. I was appointed a member of the Council, and John MacCormick asked me to make the announcement of Cunninghame Graham's candidature for the Rectorship in the Glasgow University Union. This was likely to be a bit of an ordeal, especially as it would be the first time my false teeth were tested by a public speech. There were two or three minutes of noisy clamour as was to be expected when I stepped forward but then the audience settled down and listened quietly enough to what I had to say.

Cunninghame Graham wrote from London:

Many thanks. It was indeed good of you. I would not face those 'Ephesians' for anything, not that I mind a rough meeting or opposition, but Glasgow students go to make a row, quite apart from what they may think.

"C'est trop barbare"!

I'm glad you think so well of the position.

I met at the Glasgow conference Christopher Grieve (Hugh MacDiarmid) whose poem *A Drunk Man Looks at the Thistle* I had read last year. Did I write to tell Grieve it was a poem of creative genius? I do not remember. Anyway, of that first meeting with him in Glasgow I wrote to Faith:

I found Grieve the poet very remarkable—a little like D. H. Lawrence, but with a harder intellect and, I think, a richer genius. I hope that between us we shall be able to steer the movement out of any kind of parochialism.

Grieve had started a Scottish branch of the P.E.N. Club of which he was Secretary, and, let it be added, an extraordinarily lively and energetic Secretary. There was a dinner at the St Enoch's Hotel, Glasgow, at which that wise, modest, lovable and full-bearded poet Gordon Bottomley was the guest of honour. We sat down at 6.30 p.m. in dinner-jackets on a warm sunny evening in a room with magenta walls. I can hardly believe that the impeccable St Enoch's of to-day ever had such a hideous interior as it had in 1928.

One of the guests at that dinner was a slim, good-looking young man who was introduced to me as the head of the newly recon-stituted B.B.C. organization in Scotland, the headquarters of which were in Blythswood Square, Glasgow. This was David Cleghorn

Thomson, not long down from Balliol College, Oxford, the son of a well-known and much loved Edinburgh doctor. Of him more later.

Grieve invited me to go up and stay with him for a day or two in Montrose, where he was editing the local paper—the *Montrose Gazette*. He and his wife Peggy had a small son not yet a year old.

The passionate plans of Christopher Grieve and myself for the future were temporarily interrupted by my having one of my bad goes of pain. Grieve had been a medical orderly at Salonika in the war and announced his familiarity with giving injections. Neil Gunn, whose novel *The Grey Coast* I had read with admiration, had just arrived to stay with the Grieves in Montrose, where at the Episcopal church he and I were to be godfathers of the Grieve baby at his baptism. Neil Gunn was standing by when Christopher put the needle into my arm. As it went in, the tall and distinguished figure of Neil Gunn went down on the floor full length in a dead faint caused by the sight of a minute drop of blood. When he became conscious Grieve was able to assure him that lots of men nearly collapsed when being given an injection.

From Montrose I went for the first time to Iona, where I met J. B. Macdiarmid and told him definitely that I was not prepared to contest a seat for Labour because Home Rule was obviously not going to be a main plank on their platform at the next General Election. Ian Mackenzie, whose mother ran the hotel, had the grazing of Staffa and the Dutchman's Cap in partnership with John MacInnes. Staffa was certainly impressive but not so impressive as my own Shiants.

From Iona I drove across Mull to Tobermory whence by way of Oban I went to spend Whitsuntide with the Duke of Argyll and his sister Lady Elspeth Campbell at Inveraray Castle.

By this time Lady Elspeth and I were preoccupied with getting a set of Gaelic records made on the lines of the Linguaphone method. We had tried to persuade the Linguaphone people to take this on, but they felt they had done enough for Gaelic with their Irish course. In the end, after endless humming and hawing because everybody suggested a different speaker as the right one for the job, they were made by the Rev. Alistair Maclean, the Church of Scotland minister at Daviot and father of the author of *H.M.S. Ulysses* and other popular tales of naval life, at this date a schoolboy.

I recall that when I wrote to Lady Elspeth proposing Whitsuntide for my visit, she wrote back that as her brother was away she did not know when Whitsuntide was. Lady Elspeth was firmly Church of

Scotland; the Duke was as firmly Anglo-Catholic.

I had not met 'Niall D' since he was Mr Niall Diarmid Campbell and one of the lay pillars of the Anglo-Catholic revival, about which I wrote a good deal in my Second Octave. He was now over fifty, a good deal plumper than he was when I had first met him in 1899 but with a face on which the years had not etched a line. He had a fantastic memory of the days of his youth. He had once spent part of a Long Vacation with a reading party on Sark, and as soon as I arrived at the Castle he began to ask me about various shopkeepers on Sark whom he had not seen for over thirty years. The Duke and his sister carried on conversation without either of them paying the faintest attention to the other and as we walked round the gardens of the Castle both of them would be inviting me to look at a different rhododendron. The only time they both showed me the same thing was when we reached that exquisitely designed and decorated cannon which had been salvaged from the Armada ship sunk in Tobermory Bay.

The Duke must often have contemplated being received into the Roman Church, but even when his uncle, the previous Duke, made Iona over to the Church of Scotland he remained faithful to the Episcopal Church of Scotland, which he regarded as the heir of St Columba. The Society of St John the Evangelist, known to undergraduates in my day as the Cowley Dads, had built a house of retreat on Iona and it had been the intention of 'Niall D' to hand over to them the Cathedral as soon as he succeeded to the Dukedom. I do not think 'Niall D' ever quite got over that bitter disappointment. He remained absorbed in what used to be called Ritualism for many years, but fond though he was of talking over the prelates and priests and Anglo-Catholic laymen of the past with me he could not approve of my Nationalist activities, and when some time after this I suggested his giving me a lease of a house on Mull he refused.

I longed to ask Lady Elspeth if she remembered playing the piano in her chemise, a habit Osgood Mackenzie of Inverness mentioned at Compiègne in 1903 as one to be discouraged. I nearly did ask her after a story she told me about her father, Lord Archibald Campbell. She and he were walking on a summer's day over Tiree, one of the islands belonging to the Duchy of Argyll when Lord Archibald was suddenly taken short. At the nearest crofter's house inquiries were made about a water-closet for his lordship's needs. The crofter, a splendid patriarchal specimen, threw wide his arms in a gesture of boundless hospitality:

"The whole island is a water-closet, my lord," he declared.

Some years later I saw in Eoligarry House on Barra a photograph of Elspeth Campbell in her early twenties. I have seldom seen as lovely a face. Now in 1928 she was in her fifty-fifth year with a massive figure, but her eyes were as bright and her ankles as slim as once upon a time. The Crown Prince of Germany had wanted to marry her, and considering that her aunt Princess Louise was also the aunt of the Emperor such a match should not have roused agitation at Potsdam.

"But though I liked him very much I never wanted to marry him," Lady Elspeth assured me. "I never wanted to marry anybody."

She was, indeed, wedded to Inveraray but she did not live in the Castle all the time; she had a house of her own in Inveraray with a huge Aeolian organ.

Neil Maclean and his wife Jenny Currie were guests at the Castle when I was there. Neil Maclean was at this date head of the Aberdeen station of what was then known as Northern Regional by the B.B.C. He had a fine tenor voice to which the gramophone records of the period failed to do justice; the records made by his wife were more successful.

The Great Hall at Inveraray Castle was a perfect setting for the Gaelic songs which Neil Maclean and Jenny Currie sang almost continuously after dinner. I have described it in my picture of the Great Hall at Glenbogle Castle in *The Monarch of the Glen*—the claymores, Lochaber axes, stags' heads and ancestral portraits on the walls. The Duke himself was not a devotee of Gaelic songs and after being interrupted a couple of times in reminiscences of that Anglo-Catholic society we both knew so well he would retire from the singing.

On the third day of my visit Lady Elspeth told me that Sir Harold and Lady Bowden were coming to stay. I cannot remember what she wanted to get out of them or get them to do, but I was warned to make myself agreeable. I told Lady Elspeth that it would not be difficult because Sir Harold had been helpful to my mother when she had her repertory theatre in Nottingham.

The Bowdens arrived in a brown Rolls-Royce with a pigskin pyramid of suitcases and a lot of gold about. I had a success with Sir Harold by telling him I thought Nottingham was bound to become more and more important as a city. His face lighted up.

"Ah, you realize that. We think that one day it will be the chief city of the Midlands. It has so much that Birmingham lacks."

The Bowdens were staying only for a night but Lady Elspeth was not prepared to let them off Gaelic songs. After dinner Sir Harold retired with the Duke; Lady Bowden, looking rather depressed, sat tinkling the half-dozen jewelled bracelets on each of her arms while Neil Maclean filled the Great Hall with his songs.

At last in a pause Lady Elspeth told me she was going to try for a salmon to-morrow.

"I saw a beauty under the bridge this morning."

"Bridge? Did somebody suggest bridge?" Lady Bowden exclaimed in hopeful anticipation.

One afternoon Dunstaffnage, George Campbell of Succoth and Miss Olive Campbell of Inverneil came to tea. Miss Inverneil, as she was always called, had been crippled by a hunting accident and had a sarcastic tongue but obviously a lively mind. Her nephew John Lorne Campbell, two or three years later, would become one of my most intimate friends. I admired the brogues that Dunstaffnage and George Campbell were wearing but finally decided that the ones I liked better were Dunstaffnage's. I asked him the name of his bootmaker and was told it was Sinclair of Nile Street, Glasgow.

"Do you mind if I ask him to make me a pair like yours?"

"Of course not," Dunstaffnage said. "I'm glad you like them."

I made up my mind to visit that bootshop on my way back. We shall hear more of those brogues in the next Octave.

When I look back now to that visit to Inveraray I remember most vividly being woken every morning at 8 o'clock by the Duke's piper with the sad melody *Mhuinntir a'ghlinne so*, and lying awake after the piping was silent in a big four-post bed, looking at the mid-Victorian wall-paper along the top of which was a wide frieze of flamingoes wandering along among reeds, their necks arched at various angles. With those flamingoes I wandered back into Scottish history and the past of my race.

I wrote for *The Pictish Review* of Ruaraidh Erskine of Marr the following words. Readers may think it was just another flamingo stretching out his neck.

"Mr Grieve has done well to state the need for a Scottish idea. A merely territorial nationalism must inevitably wither soon or late, and the position of Scotland on the map has long ago weakened hers. Our territorial idea was gratified and satisfied at Bannockburn Mr Healy once said to me, 'You Scots had a Bannockburn. We never had a Bannockburn in Ireland.' The lack of such a victory has now given to Ireland the leadership of the Celtic world. If Bannockburn successfully affirmed a territorial idea, Culloden thwarted something greater—a spiritual idea; that it did not quench that spiritual idea altogether is due to the 'romantics' of whom contemporary nationalists are too scornful . . . for many years a sentimental Jacobitism is the emotion that has kept alive the idea of Scotland as a nation, and it is now the duty of the nationalist leaders to see that such fervour is given an opportunity of practical expression. The time for keepsakes has gone. So be it. Then give those who cherished them something to fight for.

"Yes, Mr Grieve has done well to state the need for a Scottish idea and he will, I hope, forgive me for insisting that his Scottish idea is precisely that for which Culloden was fought. I will admit that the men out in '45 imagined that they were fighting for a dynasty and that not one of them would have known what Dostoievsky was driving at. Nevertheless, the true inspiration of their enterprise was as much an impulse to protest against the dehumanization of humanity as any vision of the future that wrote its lightning across the murky horizon of a Russian mind. The darkness falling upon Drummossie Moor that fatal spring night obliterated the Scottish idea. No lightning could disturb the mind of a people so comfortably positive that a great victory had been won for common sense. Yet the Scottish idea had survived until Culloden notwithstanding the cold breath of Calvinism blowing for ever upon it with the Devil's icy ardour. Calvinism has less power to chill nowadays; most of its influence has been replaced by the materialism for which it made straight the path. Even the Devil has no respect for Calvinism any longer; he is not so much out of touch with reality as the English House of Commons.

"But Mr Grieve does not need to be told by me what Calvinism has done for Scotland. The real question he has raised in my mind is whether it will be wiser to concentrate all our passion upon political independence and let the renaissance of the arts take care of itself, or whether it would be wiser to nourish the artistic renaissance and assume that it will fire us with the desire for political independence. After meditating on Mr Grieve's words I have reached a conclusion in my own mind that the arts must take care of themselves and that every intelligent Scot, wherever he may be, must devote himself practically to the desire for political independence. All the dreams that haunt us—the salvation of Gaelic, the revival of Braid Scots, a Gaelic University in Inverness, the repopulation of the glens, a Celtic federation of independent but interdependent states, and a hundred things will only embody themselves when we have a Scottish Free State under the Crown.

"That the great majority of the Scottish people has no desire to be free is lamentably true. Such a melancholy fact becomes less disheartening when we reflect that the great majority of the human race has no desire to be free. A growing complacency in servitude is the most conspicuous effect of the machine upon the mind of man. The individual American has more comfort than any other human being; he has at the same time less mental freedom. . . . We must take warning by the course of Irish Nationalism and we must aim from the start at nothing less than the independence which Ireland now enjoys. There must be no measure of Home Rule. There must be no taking of bribes from any English political party. It must be all or nothing. . . . Fuse thought with action and recreate a nation. I have enough faith in Mr Grieve's poetic genius to believe that it might effect even as much as this."

I went to Glasgow for a Council meeting of the National Party and was a little worried because it seemed to me that those who were offering themselves as candidates at the next General Election were already beginning to climb up on to that fence so grateful to the backsides of parliamentary candidates. It was a relief to be setting out for the Islands; I went by way of Mallaig, for I was anxious to see the Prince Charlie country, even if it would only be from the train. I recall being woken at five of a glorious morning in the month of June by the boots or under night-porter of the Central Hotel, who helped me with my packing; when I was going to tip him he said he would much rather have a signed copy of *Vestal Fire* which he had read and enjoyed.

Of that journey I wrote to Faith:

The journey to Mallaig was the most exquisite railway-journey I have taken anywhere. The weather was perfect—the lighting of Loch Long in the flower of the morning, the trees in perfection, the golden cloud shadows marvellous. I must remember the date so as to time it for our journey next year. The sun must rise at the right moment. I left Glasgow at 5.55 a.m.

As perfect companions for such a journey I had Gordon Bottomley and his wife in the compartment.

Bottomley was one of the first enthusiastic supporters of *The Gramophone* and of the National Gramophonic Society, which, by the way, recorded this year a promising young conductor called John

Barbirolli with a small orchestra, the first orchestral recordings the N.G.S. had attempted. Gordon Bottomley had written to me once or twice; one of his letters, of March 25th, 1925, has survived. I quote a few extracts from a very long screed:

I am an almost antiquated 'gramophil' by now, ill-health having impelled me in that direction at a time when it must have seemed hardly worth while to most people and when a single faced 12" disc with scraps of the Variations from the Kreutzer (quite well played by Szigeti) seemed worth its weight in Treasury-notes, only there were none then! In those days I used to wish I could do what you have done (but I was too far away and too ill for that to be possible); and that makes me competent to appreciate the change you have caused in less than two years. Before the war we had to seek the best records in Germany: but now England is decidedly the best record-producing country, and that is greatly owing to you.

And personally I feel considerably indebted to you for the time and trouble and money which the reviews and reports in 'The Gramophone' save me, in comparison with the old days when one had to buy records in the dark.

There followed two pages about music he was hoping to have recorded which ended,

I have a lusty appetite for things no Company ever seems to think of—from Mendelssohn's 'Melusine' to Sibelius's 'Swan of Tuonela' and Debussy's 'Nocturnes'—listening by the way for Berlioz's 'Symphonie Fantastique' and the orchestral sections of his 'Romeo'. . . .

All this by way of a footnote to my letter; but I never really told you how pleased I was to hear from you. I am not much accustomed to Awards and Medals, and to know that you have noted and approved the Roy. Lit. Society's award to me in your far-off island anchorage touched and gratified me. It is by far the nicest thing that has ever happened to me—and perhaps the most acceptable thing that can happen to an English writer—carrying with it, as it does, the encomium and approval of one's contemporary workers in literature; and I value your endorsement of their vote because it comes from a fellow craftsman, and so distinguished a one; and the praise of one's fellows is most worth having of all.

And I know my encomiast. My wife and I have been your debtors for Jenny and Ireen; for Pauline and Guy and Plasher's Mead, the boat at midnight; and for many others, but most of all perhaps for Sylvia Scarlett's delightful youth: and we are happy in this opportunity to thank you.

For me and for Bottomley it was a moment of deep emotion when the train swept round the viaduct and we saw the monument to

Prince Charles Edward at the head of Loch Shiel, raised by a Macdonald on the spot where the banner was raised to the exultant
shouts of the Camerons and Macdonalds gathered there on that
August morning in 1745. I was grateful to be in the company of two
people able to understand that. The Bottomleys left the train at
Arisaig; I did not see him again for over twenty years. That was
when I was writing a book for the National Trust called *I Took A
Journey* and on my way through the Lake District was able to visit
him at Silverdale by Carnforth. He lived in a small house called The
Shieling in the middle of a thick wood where he and his wife were
already living when Gordon Bottomley wrote me that letter. What
might have seemed a gloomy habitation was irradiated by what I
can only call the saintliness of that man, who in his seventy-fifth year
had not long lost his wife and was now alone. He himself died a
month or two after I visited him, living there in solitude with his poetry
and his music on the edge of death's mystery.

I was by myself in the compartment after the Bottomleys left the
train at Arisaig and, full of dreams as I was, I almost believed I was
seeing an apparition when a piper in kilt and shirt appeared in the
middle of the moorland and the sound of what seemed a ghostly
pibroch floated through the open window of the compartment.

In the *Plover* at Mallaig I was glad to meet again Captain
'Squeaky' Robertson, of whom I should one day paint an inadequate
portrait as Captain MacKechnie in *Whisky Galore*. He insisted that
he had read all my books, and I was tactful enough not to ask him
which he had enjoyed most, for I did not believe he had read one of
them. On board when we sailed was what I knew must be the
Roman Catholic Bishop of Argyll and the Isles with a small dark
priest in attendance. I debated whether I should make myself
known to the Bishop but felt he might think it was an intrusion and
abstained. When the *Plover* reached Eigg the Bishop was taken off
in a boat to perform some pastoral duty and I got into conversation
with the small dark priest, who assured me that Bishop Martin
would have been glad to meet me. The small dark priest was Donald
Campbell[1] who was on his way to Loch Boisdale and from there to
Castlebay, of which he was to be the parish priest in succession to
Mgr. Cameron.

We went on to call at Rum and the vivid green island of Canna,
where a herring catch was in progress. After we left Canna the wind
got up and we had a lively tossing as far as Loch Boisdale, where I

[1] The late Archbishop of Glasgow.

met for the first time Canon Joseph Gillies, the Dean of the Isles. The *Plover* did not leave South Uist until 10.30 p.m., but I managed to sleep fairly well in a very rough sea and what is more eat a good breakfast before we reached Tarbert next morning at eight. There on the pier, waiting to greet me, was Calum MacSween, and after I had had to eat a second breakfast at the hotel he came along to take me down to Caberfeidh to meet his wife.

As we came in I saw in the doorway of the kitchen a girl in a blue frock with a red belt. Her dark hair was parted in the middle and coiled over her ears in the fashion known at that date in the Highlands as 'earphones'. Her eyes were so dark as to seem black above her red rose cheeks.

In that moment of meeting I knew that this girl must become a part of my life.

"This is Chrissie," said her father. "She's home for the holidays from her school in Scarp."

I saw standing in the doorway of the parlour opposite that shy little dark girl who in the previous winter had been nearly drowned when returning to Scarp and who, with an ability to know her own mind that she has retained to this day, had refused to go back to school in Scarp after she came home for the Easter holidays.

Then I was introduced to Mrs MacSween who with her abounding sense of humour would be the best audience I should ever have for my stories. She and Martin Secker both used to weep with laughter when they told or when they listened to tales, and that sense of the ridiculous would be inherited by Lily, that little dark girl whose face was buried in her pinafore with shyness.

Though I was two *Sunday Pictorial* reviews in hand, there was a large pile of unanswered letters and promises of articles for this, that and the other paper; but I was so happy that I could think of nothing except my happiness. At the same time I was glad to hear that Nellie Boyte was sufficiently recovered to make the journey to Harris in another two days. Then came a letter from Hilda Matheson, one of the Mathesons who sold Lewis to Lord Leverhulme, to ask if I would do a talk about the Hebrides for the B.B.C. I have told about my first broadcast of gramophone records in 1924 and of my being asked to do a weekly programme in 1927, for which I suggested Christopher Stone. I was firmly under the impression that the first talk I gave was about Siamese cats; and had actually started to write about it when I found scribbled in pencil a talk called *The Enchanted Isles* with a B.B.C. notice signed by Hilda Matheson to say that the talk would be given at 10.35 p.m. on July 12th, 1928. That talk had vanished from my memory and even now I should have believed that I never gave it if I had not found about two dozen letters from listeners, all heart-warming and many of them saying how annoyed they were by my having to stop too soon for the nightly dance-music programme. The talk about Siamese cats was not given until September of this year.

Hilda Matheson was an outstanding personality and what she did for the B.B.C. in those early days was of inestimable value. Her early death was a very severe loss.

That month in Harris was a magical experience and I feel that some of its magic may have been expressed in that talk I gave in London on my way back to Jethou. I was in a state of what might be called spiritual exaltation. Critics of these Octaves of mine often suggest that I indulge too much in polite evasion, and one or two of the younger critics have complained that I do not pay enough attention to the inner life. My experience of people who talk about their inner lives is that they are too often talking because they cannot make up their minds what they want to do next. For me, as I read it again, that talk I gave on the radio brings back the memory of happiness. So I shall indulge the memory of that happiness by printing that talk of mine long ago. It is true that I do find it extremely difficult to talk about my feelings or about my work. A possible explanation of my having completely forgotten that talk may be that I felt I had given too much of myself away.

"I wonder why more people do not go the Hebrides. Even were I at this moment sailing among the isles of Greece instead of sweltering as I am in London I should still be heartsick for them. I should still be wondering how it was possible for any human creature to be so idiotic as to travel 12 hours in a steamer and then 17 hours in a train for the purpose of severing himself from those mountains and immense sands, from those cliffs and caves and rolling dunes of flowery grass, from that soft grey midnight which evokes the insubstantial landscape of a dream and gives to the most savage rocks the fluttering likeness of a moth's wings. There are many Hebridean islands of which I should like to tell you to-night; and if I were talking from Harris or Lewis or Uist or Skye I should not hesitate to do so, because I should be talking in a land where time has little significance and where few would complain if I held up the dance-music for another hour instead of fifteen minutes, but having been idiotic enough to make that long journey from the North and having become a slave of the clock again I shall only have time to speak of my own Hebridean islands.

"The Shiant Islands are not large. On the usual map of Scotland they look as if somebody had left three specks of black pepper in the middle of that uncomfortable stretch of sea between the Outer Isles and the mainland which is called the Minch and which has probably had more triumphs over the weakness of the human body than any other stretch of sea of similar size in the world. I was not trying to give my talk a coloured frontispiece when I called it 'The Enchanted Isles'. The epithet sounds too good to be true, but that is what 'Shiant' means. Perhaps ages and ages ago somebody baffled by the charm of these islands gave them this name in despair, like myself, of being able to communicate even faintly their incommunicable charm. Or perhaps the name is an echo of the ancient legend of the Blue Men who haunt the dangerous tidal rips and overfalls that guard the islands on either side. One of these nowadays is called the Stream of the Barking Dogs from the noise the waves make in their anger. Anyway, whatever the origin of the name, nobody who has stood on the highest point of the islands 540 feet above the dark green sea that washes the base of these stupendous cliffs and looked westward to the blue hills of Harris, or northward to the Atlantic rolling in between the Butt of Lewis and Cape Wrath, or eastward to where the mountain line of Sutherland and Ross runs indigo-dark along the horizon like a jagged saw, or southward to the fantastic luminous huddle of Skye and the misted peaks of Uist—nobody who had stood thus, swung between earth and heaven, could deny the magic of these islands.

"Let me take you to them with me for a few minutes. We must start from Tarbert in Harris where the herring-boat *Daffodil* is waiting for us by the pier. The first four or five miles will be in calm water, past the rocky shore of Harris to port and past the various small islands to starboard until we reach the island of Scalpay and see the white house where Prince Charles Edward stayed until he was forced to leave because the minister Macaulay, the great-grandfather of the historian, was the only man in the Highlands with enough greed to covet the £30,000 reward offered by the Hanoverian Government. It gives me satisfaction to boast that he was foiled by Mistress Mackenzie of Kildun.

"Back into the Minch now with a fine following breeze from the southwest. The great sail is hoisted. The *Daffodil* leaps forward and the miles slip behind her in a froth of foam. From here we can see

only two of the Shiant Islands. The bigger and higher one to the left
is Garbh Eilean or Rough Island; the other Eilean an Tighe or
House Island. Actually these two are joined by a beach of sea-
rounded grey stones but from here they appear separate. When we
were within a mile the islands appeared framed in a perfect rainbow
—a sight to fill one with awe at such beauty. We pass a fringe of
outlying islets and rocks, dark and strange, the slopes of which
make the most elaborate décor of a Russian ballet look suburban.
There is one in particular—a huge old lady, a hundred feet high,
who in crinoline and poke-bonnet stands for ever, in tempest or
calm, with a marketing-basket on her arm. We reach the northern
face of Garbh Eilean—a mighty crescent of sheer black cliffs from
four to five hundred feet high which darken with their shadow the
water. The basaltic columns, some of them eight or nine feet in
diameter, are covered with kittiwakes, razor-bills and guillemots
which at this distance have the appearance of a cloud of white
butterflies. The third island, named after the Blessed Virgin, on
which in whose honour there was once a chapel, is now in full view.
Imagine a rolling meadow of rich grass on top of sheer cliffs about
200 feet high and you have some idea of Island Mary—75 acres of
emerald grass and velvety purple orchises. I think of those orchises
and thinking of them I'm afraid I really find London rather a
ridiculous place.

"I dare say many of my listeners have an idea of the Hebrides as
bleak and colourless and windswept. I wish they could see the flowers
on my islands—tracts of yellow irises with forget-me-nots and king-
cups and ragged-robins, honeysuckle and dog-roses in crevices of the
rocks, campion in every shade of pink and crimson as vigorous as
garden stocks, silver-weed and milkwort and thyme and heather,
bog-asphodel and cotton-grass, bog-violets and red rattle and—but
that's enough.

"You are ashore now, and I expect you are thinking 'confound
all those flowers, where am I going to sleep to-night?' Come with me.
You see that diminutive hut thatched with reeds, mind your head.
The door is only four feet high. You had better sit down at once, or
the smoke will make your eyes smart. It's rather dark inside because
the only light comes from the hole in the thatch which is letting out
the smoke. Gradually, however, your eyes get used to the dimness
and you find yourself in a dwelling-place that has grown as it were
out of the island like one of its own flowers. It is as genuine a product
of environment as Robinson Crusoe's residence. It makes you a little

K

impatient even of a tent. Every bit of wood used in the construction
has been washed ashore on the island beaches—even the planks
covered with rushes on which you are going to sleep. The bothy was
built by fishermen that come here every year in winter for two or
three weeks at a stretch to catch lobsters. You might disdain your
quarters at first, but after you've climbed all over the islands you
will be glad enough to lie down and sleep with the firelight flickering
on the sooty thatch, watching the blue cloud of smoke above your
head and the pearl-grey Hebridean night through the only aperture.
You begin to think yourself a child again, living in one of those jolly
places which the illustrators of fairy-books love to draw, but in
which few of them ever have been lucky enough to live. And perhaps
I might mention that you'd better not leave such things as leather-
bags lying about—the rats might chew them up. They are very
enterprising—our rats. Still, in spite of the rats if I go on talking
about this bothy I shall pack up and go back by the 7.30 train to-
morrow evening, which would upset those absurd things called
business appointments. You see, I can't stand at any door in London,
nor even in the Channel Islands, and watch not thirty yards away
an eider duck with her duckling swim in the sea at twilight, I can't
be an object of curiosity to an intelligent slant-eyed seal. I can't
wonder if I shall presently see a whale, and then actually see one
routing about lazily in the water for herrings. The Aquarium at the
Zoo is a wonderful place and many a fine sight can I see there; but I
can't watch the two black fins of a basking shark like two black sails.
I can't sit on a green brae and count fifteen great creamy dappled
Atlantic seals on the rocks below. I can't walk through a tract of iris
in full golden bloom to go and lie in the sun on a mattress of sea-
pinks and watch on the face of a cliff 300 feet high a thousand
thousand birds not one of which allows my presence to disturb it.
There on one narrow ledge you will see seven guillemots in a row
with their backs to the sea looking like seven little Eton boys turned
to the wall in disgrace. Each of them has an egg and not one of them
dares turn round and enjoy the view for fear of kicking the egg off the
ledge. Close to me is a fulmar petrel with cold disdainful eye. If I
went too near she might spurt a jet of horribly smelling oil in my
face. Just below her is a kittiwake—prettiest and daintiest of all the
gulls. Mr Kittiwake flies up and says 'My dear, you've been sitting
on those eggs all day. Do for goodness sake go and take a short fly
round. I'll sit on them while you're gone.' 'No thank you, dear,' says
Mrs Kittiwake. 'I'd rather stay where I am.' 'Nonsense,' says the

considerate husband. 'Get off.' And then he pulls at her wing with his beak and there is a short argument between them. But Mr Kittiwake pulls her off the nest in the end and settles down on it himself while his wife takes a short afternoon flight. A sheeny cormorant alights close by me and croaks in rather an agitated tone. I look at her and see two newly hatched young ones like a pair of black slugs in a crevice of the rocks, and knowing that the cormorant is rather more shy than some of the other birds I wander off to a brae which looks like a great green sponge because thousands and thousands of puffins have been making their burrows here. At the entrance of each sits a bird not unlike Mr Pickwick and inside sits his lady on a solitary white egg. The puffins arrive each year on the last Sunday in April and spend 24 hours on the island clearing out the burrows. Then away they all go again for ten days into the Atlantic for the honeymoon, and then one morning they are all back again without a quarrel over their houses which are all waiting swept and garnished for their solitary white eggs to be laid—myriads and myriads of puffins. Lots of the husbands sit about all day at the entrances of their burrows but others fly round and round the islands like a swarm of flies round a chandelier. It is fascinating to watch them when they are feeding their young, arriving with half a dozen sprats packed in their big orange beaks—head and tail as neatly as sardines in a tin. How do they manage it? How do they know how to catch the fish in the right order?

"There are plenty of other kinds of birds nesting on these islands—snipe, wheatears, larks and pipits. I have counted 300 great-blackbacked gulls sunning themselves on motionless wings above a green valley. The peregrine falcon has his nest here, and the raven—but that is enough to broadcast, for alas, there is a pestilent race of apparently human beings called collectors, and since if I caught one of them on my islands I should without remorse push him off the cliff it is as well that I should not tempt any of them to run such a risk by visiting them for rarities.

"I wonder if I have given you any kind of a picture of these enchanted islands. I fear not. I think that all I have done is to make myself more heartsick than ever for that moth-grey night which is glimmering over there at this moment."

It is difficult for me to withdraw myself from the mood of that talk and remember that a month later the suppression of Radclyffe Hall's novel about lesbianism *The Well of Loneliness* would set Secker and myself wondering what was going to happen about *Extraordinary*

Women, due to be published on September 1st. I realize that the reason for Newman Flower's refusal of *Extraordinary Women* may have been the fact that he had turned down *The Well of Loneliness* after having had quite a success with Radclyffe Hall's previous novel, *Adam's Breed*.

The attack on *The Well of Loneliness* was launched by James Douglas, the Editor of the *Sunday Express*, who declared that he would sooner give a healthy boy or girl a dose of prussic acid than a copy of Miss Radclyffe Hall's book. As the *Clarion* said, "Could fatuity go further? Who is asking to give a boy or girl that book? What boy or girl would be likely to read it? And if a boy or girl did read it what would they find of an exciting and inflammatory character?"

Jonathan Cape was frightened by the cheap rhetoric of a literary scavenger and sent the book to the Home Secretary, Sir W. Joynson-Hicks, to express an opinion. 'Jix' himself, or one of his leather-bottoms at the Home Office, was shocked; Cape was advised to withdraw *The Well of Loneliness*.

I told Secker that if *Extraordinary Women* was prosecuted I should handle the defence myself without the help of solicitor or counsel. However, the Home Office officials were wise enough not to prosecute. I recall asking one of them why they had refrained.

"It *was* discussed but finally we decided not to prosecute."

"What a pity," I commented. "You robbed the public of many good laughs. I should have enjoyed cross-examining you."

"Yes, that's what we rather felt."

The failure of the Home Office to prosecute *Extraordinary Women* upset some of the Labour people; in the *Daily Herald* and elsewhere they kept urging the Home Secretary to explain why he had suppressed an earnest and serious book like *The Well of Loneliness* and not taken proceedings against *Extraordinary Women*, which treated the theme with 'cynical flippancy'. The *Glasgow Herald* suggested an answer:

"It is a daring conception and one that plainly lends itself to fierce vituperation on the part of readers and critics who fail to observe that it is a farcical tour de force, and that its gorgeous prose and exquisite rhythm are the fitting garb of a truly Dionysian piece of folly."

But I must quote a contradictory opinion. Raymond Mortimer wrote:

"With luck we may expect another brace of novels by Mr Compton Mackenzie before Christmas. For 'Extraordinary Women' is the third [in fact it was only the second] of his books to be published in a year. In the circumstances it would be unreasonable to look for a very high level of writing or invention. But the dullness of his August novel [September] passes all bounds. . . . Mr Mackenzie is undoubtedly neither uneducated nor inexperienced. Having had the enterprise to deal with a subject unexplored by English novelists he might have produced an interesting book. But all I can see in 'Extraordinary Women' is an expression of male pique and wounded vanity. I should add in case anyone is misled by the high price at which the novel is published, that it is in no way pornographic."

Daffodil himself could not have expressed more elegantly one point of view.

Extraordinary Women was published in the United States by the Vanguard Press and received plenty of intelligent reviews. The two thousand copies at a guinea published by Secker were quickly out of print and in the following year the book was reissued at 3s. 6d. I thought it would be only fair to those who had forked out a guinea for the original edition that a few pages should be omitted from the cheap edition. In October the B.B.C. announced an hour's debate between James Douglas and myself about the censorship of books, with Desmond MacCarthy as Chairman. James Douglas funked it. A few hours before the debate was to go on the air he was conveniently too ill to appear. In 1953 *Extraordinary Women* was issued by Macdonald's with the cut passages restored, and it was amusing to read in the *Daily Express* "What a joy it has been this week to re-read that exceedingly naughty book, EXTRAORDINARY WOMEN."

Some time in the spring of 1928 I had written an article about Siamese cats which had led to my being proposed as President of the Siamese Cat Club, and when one afternoon in that September Lance Sieveking came into the Frith Street office and asked why I did not do another talk on the radio I suggested a talk about Siamese cats. This was put up to Lionel Fielden, who was the director of talks. He wondered whether listeners would be much interested in Siamese cats and suggested another talk about islands. In the end a compromise was reached and the talk "Siamese Cats and Some Islands" was settled for September 26th.

"I am feeling guilty at this moment," I began, "because I have always considered it unpardonable for anybody to talk about his pets, and I am only sustained by a conviction that the Siamese cat is just the pet that lots of people are wanting. I am not trying to gain the sympathy of prejudiced listeners when I say that it combines all that is best in cats and dogs, because I am not prepared as a fanatical lover of cats to admit that the cat requires to borrow any virtues from the dog. Still, the personal devotion of the dog to its master is one of its glories, and even more attractive to my mind is the personal devotion of the Siamese cat not to its master but to what I think is a better relationship, to its friend. . . .

"The Siamese cat is an animal of most definite personal likes and dislikes, and unless it likes you naturally no amount of coaxing or bribery on your part will ever win its affection. . . ."

Then I went on to talk of Pauline in Capri and of Bing, the Siamese kitten I had in Syra in 1917.

"When I lived on islands that were shared with other people I had to be content with one Siamese at a time, but now that I live on an island of my own I am able to keep eleven Siamese cats, every one of which has a marked personality of its own. Jethou is only fifty acres, a small green hump beside such a neighbour as Guernsey, but yet with most of the things on it that human beings or cats can want. There is a garden where I shall have as many flowers out at Christmas as many gardens are proud to display now. There is a library with nearly ten thousand books and a very big collection of gramophone records. There is a wireless which nearly always seems to behave itself. . . . There is a wood of all sorts of ancient trees at the foot of which the garden goes tumbling down in terraces to the sea. . . . There are sands which set off the Siamese cats to perfection when they walk on them like miniature lions in the desert. There are prawns in rocky pools, and Siamese cats think that nothing is so good to eat as even the discarded tail of a prawn. . . .

"I suppose I ought to mention some of the faults of the Siamese cats before I stop. They are very jealous, and suffer acutely from it. They are very greedy. They think that Samarkand rugs were only woven to be scratched to pieces by their own sharp claws. They have no idea of doing without something they want; if they haven't something they want, they make a noise till they get it. But what are these faults compared with their virtues—with their sense of humour, their fidelity, their dauntless courage (unless they think they've seen a ghost when they will tear away in all directions like so many animated bottle-brushes), their playfulness (they will retrieve a ball of paper as many times as you will throw it for them), their conversational powers (if you have Siamese cats you *must* talk to them a lot), their awareness of themselves (each one of my Siamese cats knows its own name and one after another will respond with a twitch of the tail as I speak to each in turn), their love of people rather than place, their honesty (by which I mean they'll take a lobster off the table in front of you), their continuous passionate interest in all that is going on around them, and their depth of affection, which they are able to show in so many exquisite ways."

At the end of my talk I said that any listener who had been interested by it might like to know that the fifth annual championship show of the Siamese Cat Club would be held at the Philbeach Gardens Hall, Earls Court, next day.

I recall asking the presiding announcer in the small studio if there was a reason for putting the clock at the back of the speaker so that in turning round quickly to see how he was for time he might crick his neck.

The announcer replied that he did not think there was any technical reason for placing the clock where it was.

"Well, wouldn't it be a good idea if the clock was in sight of the chap who's talking?"

The announcer agreed warmly and said he would suggest asking the engineers about it. The engineers must have taken the suggestion kindly, because soon the clocks in the studios were in sight of the man at the microphone.

About a year after this I was asked to compère a programme of old Alhambra ballet music. At that date the compère was put in the middle of the orchestra, from which he had to emerge at the right moment, descend a couple of steps and bend down over a microphone hardly eighteen inches above the floor.

"And now," I would say to my unseen audience, "I'm going to ask you to imagine that you are sitting in the middle of those comfortable stalls at the old Alhambra, some of you smoking the cigars we used to smoke when we could afford cigars before the penal tax on tobacco," and each time I had to conjure up the luxurious pre-war past it was made much more difficult by having to bend over nearly to the floor.

"I suppose there's a technical reason," I asked when the hour's programme was over, "for the microphone to be eighteen inches from the floor?"

The producer did not think so.

"Then surely if the mike were on a level with the compère's mouth it would make it easier for him," I suggested.

This was noted a good idea, and future compères could thank me for a happy suggestion.

When the Siamese Cat Show was opened on the day after my broadcast the power of the microphone was brought home to me. Normally the Show, which had started in 1924, would not have attracted many more than a couple of hundred—if as many in the course of the day. On September 26th, 1928, the Parish Hall of St Cuthbert's Church was continuously packed out, and there were crowds in Philbeach Gardens, waiting to get in.

Mrs Wade, the Secretary, wrote to say that I should be President for life, and as I write these words thirty-seven years after that September I am proud still to be President of the Siamese Cat Club. Mrs Wade did superlative work in building up the Club, and the early death of that lovable woman, Phyl Wade, was a sad loss for her friends, whether they were people or cats. To my pleasure I found that one of the Vice-Presidents was to be Louis Wain, whose picture of cats swinging round a giant's stride had been one of my protections against the nightly terrors of my early childhood. I see it now under the gaslight of nearly eighty years ago.

I had to leave the Show before it closed because I was due at the Mòd in Inverness where I was to take the chair at one of the two final concerts. I believe it was the late Sir Alexander MacEwen, who was then Provost of Inverness, who was responsible for the invitation. Lady Elspeth Campbell arrived with Dunstaffnage in attendance, to stay at the Station Hotel where I also was staying. I recall two moments. The first was when she and Lord Ashbourne met for the first time on the steps of the Town Hall, Lord Ashbourne in a saffron Irish kilt, Lady Elspeth in her dress of the Campbell tartan. He addressed her in Irish Gaelic; she replied in Scots Gaelic. To the obvious surprise of the onlookers each apparently understood what the other was saying; nobody conversant with Irish or Scots Gaelic had ever immediately understood what either Lord Ashbourne or Lady Elspeth was saying.

The other moment was more dramatic. Lady Elspeth at her most dignified self as the sister of MacCailean Mòr, the Gaelic name for the Duke of Argyll, was standing with Dunstaffnage and myself in attendance to receive various people presented to her. With her also was Grant of Rothiemurchus,[1] a valiant and popular Colonel of Lovat's Scouts who had just been made Sheriff-Substitute of Inverness, Elgin and Nairn, which he would remain for another thirty years; he was a contemporary of mine at Magdalen. In due course the female leader of some Dublin artistic association was presented

[1] Colonel P. Grant of Rothiemurchus, C.B., M.C.

and as she shook hands with Lady Elspeth asked in would-be friendly accents,

"And are you Scotch?"

Dunstaffnage, Rothiemurchus and I reeled.

"I am the sister of MacCailean Mòr," Lady Elspeth proclaimed in what was intended to be a tone that would obliterate the lady from Dublin.

"Yes, I thought you might be Scotch," she said. "And I wanted to tell you how very much we are enjoying our first visit to Scotland."

The two final concerts on the last night of the Mòd were held in the Wesleyan Hall, over which Sir Archibald Sinclair presided, and in the Central Picture Theatre, over which I presided. I was infernally nervous, as might be expected. I was a fluent enough speaker on subjects I knew something about, but I felt that I was such a novice in Gaelic that I might make some howler. Father John MacMillan had tried to teach me an opening sentence in Gaelic but I funked it. However, the audience of 1,200 was so kind that I forgot my nervousness after the first minute or two. I was much encouraged by Maclean of Ardgour, next to whom I was sitting. He and his wife had four delightful small daughters and when Ardgour died barely two years after this Mrs Maclean tried to bring the lairdship of great antiquity to her eldest daughter. It was only after many years of litigation that the claim to the arms and chieftainship was finally granted.

I went on from Inverness to Kyle of Lochalsh and thence to Tarbert. A letter of October 5th to Faith from the Harris hotel says:

Just a scrawl, this being the 51st letter I've written to-day. This broadcasting is a bit of a business with other things too. I still have 17 letters to answer about Siamese cats! The enclosed note is from Johnnie, the younger MacSween boy who's at Inverness Academy. Don't you think it's very sweet? He's about 16 and came in to help me pack at the hotel in Inverness.

By this time the MacSween family had really become an integral part of my life and I was overjoyed when Mrs MacSween gave her consent to her daughter Chrissie's giving up her job as school-teacher on the island of Scarp at Christmas and coming down with me to Jethou when I should arrive to fetch her in January. I had known that Calum MacSween was in favour of her sharing the work of secretary with Nellie Boyte, but Calum was a great deal more impulsive than Barabel, his wife. She was indeed an infallible judge of character. I salute her memory with deep gratitude.

In spite of its remoteness the island of Scarp still had a school of some twenty pupils with a high level of intelligence. It was situated on the west of Harris at the end of fourteen miles of road. The end of that road provides one of the most beautiful land and seascapes in the British Islands, with the hills of Harris and Uig in Lewis, the island of Scarp on the other side of a channel which can be ferocious sometimes, and southward beyond the tiny township of Hushinish the Atlantic. Some six miles west of Scarp, a minute dot in the ocean, is the island of Gàisgeir where in early October the great grey Atlantic seals go ashore to breed. I had expressed a wish to see this phenomenon, and on a calm blue morning Calum MacSween and I reached Hushinish to wait for the small boat from Scarp that would take us out to Gàisgeir. I recall sitting in a cottage and hearing its owner tell me how during the winter storms an otter used to come in from the sea and sit beside the peat-fire to warm itself before going out again into the blast.

The Atlantic seal presumably became a seal at a much later stage in evolution than the common black seal, which breeds in spring and the young of which take to the water as naturally as fish. Not so the young of the grey seal. They, like the otter, have to be taught to swim. I recall as a piece of luck being able to watch for a couple of hours a pair of otters teaching their young to swim by the natural arch on the west side of the island of Taransay: it was a poetry of motion beyond the achievement of any choreographer.

The Atlantic seals, having chosen the unpropitious autumn for breeding, need a variety of adjuncts to provide a suitable place. They must find an island with a way up out of the roaring Atlantic and a way down into it for the baby seals on the lee-side. They must find an island with a number of pools and lochans of graduated depth and size for the babies to spend six weeks or so in learning how to live through the fierce Atlantic winter. They must find an island remote from the destructive hand of man, and an island with grassy slopes on which to suckle their young. All these necessities Gàisgeir provides in the space of some thirty acres; what those who wish to visit the Atlantic seals on Gàisgeir must find is a day in October sufficiently calm to enable them to land.

We had a glorious day, but even so the swell was heavy enough to make the task of scrambling ashore by the steep slippery rocks on the east side of the island—the one accessible spot—a heart-quickening

business for a novice. As our boat drew near we saw the great
monsters galumphing down the slopes and plunging headlong into
the sea, there to bob up and watch with anxious heads our approach.
There must have been over a couple of hundred of them that did not
wait for us to land. When we got ashore and reached the grassy
slopes on the top we found that all the devoted mothers had remained
to guard their babies. The babies are silvery white when born and
this fur comes away like thistledown when one strokes them, so that
it is a useless crime to massacre these innocents with the notion of
preserving that lovely silver fur. They are so far from being sea
animals at this age that one poor little chap in trying to escape from
us actually drowned himself in a puddle not six inches deep. We had
the unique experience as far as I know of seeing the birth of a seal
before our very eyes, and I regret to say that the first act of this new-
born creature was to eye us with horror in its mad-looking globular
eyes and utter strange snorts of fear and anger. The expression in the
eyes of those baby seals could never be forgotten by anybody who has
seen it. They are the eyes that one might fancy a changeling must
have, with a sinister fairy look. I reflect now when I read of the
barbarous massacre of baby seals to gratify the salmon trade how
well we humans deserve that snort of fear and anger.

Immediately after the birth two giant bulls plunged down into the
small loch and began such a fight as made one think oneself back
in the age of the great saurians. Blood spurted on the banks, so small
was the space they had in which to fight; finally one of them charged
out of the water and went galumphing up the opposite slope, where
he remained in an attitude of ineffable dejection while his conqueror
went galumphing up and down the lochan like a performing sea-lion
in a circus. The lady who had been the cause of this desperate duel
had by this time quietly returned to her task of suckling the baby,
entirely indifferent to the attractions either of the vanquishing or the
vanquished suitor.

We had hardly more than half an hour to spare in which to wander
upon what seemed an antediluvian world. We noticed that the few
sheep which had been put down to grass on this lonely islet seemed
as much bewildered by the strange life of the seals as we were ourselves. Westward the ocean was thundering against the broad steps
of rock up which the seals had come. Southward the islands in the
Sound of Harris stood up like shapes of blue smoke in the crystalline
air. Eastward the superb line of the bens of Harris gradually ran
down to the long low evenness of Lewis, broken here and there by

yellow beaches and white breakers. The sky was still azure as June, but the wind was rising and unless we wanted to spend the winter on Gàisgeir we had to be away. We paused to take a last look at the incredible scene, and to watch one young seal that had passed its swimming test wriggling its way down the narrow burn on the steep east side, by which path all the young ones in turn would go down to their great mother the sea, away from that green islet which was all that they still needed of the earth that for so many thousands of years had been their mother before they evolved into amphibious creatures.

It had been a heart-quickening job to land; it quickened the heart still faster to make that jump down into the boat again. However, the idea of spending even a night with those mad-eyed creatures, would have made people less active than ourselves determined to risk anything to avoid it. It was deep twilight before we reached Scarp again after innumerable tacks; and the Atlantic was roaring and tumbling angrily between Scarp and Harris. The seals were not likely to be disturbed again this year.

On October 13th I was writing to Faith:

Delighted to hear that you're off to Italy, but I wish I had had a legible address in Rome in the wire. . . . I'm kept in all day, working at letters, proofs, reviews and articles. A dog's life. Chrissie got over from Scarp for the week-end and is far enough on with her speed writing to take down a lot of letters which she wrote out for me, but that was a drop in the bucket. I am having my autumn cold and am glad to get it over before speaking in Glasgow etc. But it's pestilential for work, as my head is like lead and my throat very sore. . . . Calum MacSween told me to-day it was reported in the village that the ghost of Lord Leverhulme had been seen sitting in an armchair in the house of a man who had swindled him!

Give my love to people in Italy and have a good time.

Calum MacSween had some business to do about sheep and while he was in Dingwall I visited Cromarty, being entertained by the Provost. My ancestor the Reverend Bernard Mackenzie was the Episcopalian priest in Cromarty until he was thrown out in 1690 after Dutch William usurped the Throne.

Cromarty had a lively life during the war but by now it was very quiet again. The house of my ancestors was still standing but had become a large barn. Over the door was a sandstone coat of arms, the details of which had been blotted out by time. The Provost was anxious to present me with this shield but, feeling it would inevitably be broken in removal, I declined the present.

Perhaps what made me realize more sharply than anything the remoteness of Cromarty from the world of to-day was that the barber was still charging only three-halfpence for a shave.

That night Calum MacSween and I went down to Glasgow, where I was due to preside at the annual gathering of the Gairloch and Loch Broom Association at one of the Glasgow halls. As we sat down to dinner at 6.30 I asked the Chairman what topic would appeal when I made my speech.

"Och, any topic at all except the great solan goose. Mr Seton Gordon talked about the great solan goose at last year's gathering."

Just before I was going to rise to speak I noticed a smallish man in a dark blue suit sitting on the platform. It was Sir Harry Lauder.

"Why aren't you in the kilt?" I asked.

He shook his head.

"What I can wear on the stage of a music hall I would not wear at a real Highland gathering."

I was moved by such sensitivity.

In my speech I told the audience what a privilege it was for me as a Roman Catholic to be talking to a gathering of Free Presbyterians because in our case extremes met since we both refused to compromise over our fundamental beliefs.

Later on one of the members said to me,

"Well, that's the first time I ever heard a Roman Catholic tell the people of Gairloch they were on a level with the Papists and get applauded for telling them so."

G. K. Chesterton and Hilaire Belloc had been unable to keep their promise to speak at the University Union for Cunninghame Graham; rather against my will I agreed to speak for the second time in favour of his candidature. To my surprise I was given a quiet hearing; my hopes that Cunninghame Graham would make a good showing rose, and I went off to join him at the Caledonian Hotel in Edinburgh where he was staying to await the result of the election. I might mention here that the candidates in a Rectorial election never make a personal appearance on any platform. I told Cunninghame Graham how much optimism there was in Glasgow about our putting up a good show. We should almost certainly beat Rosslyn Mitchell, the Labour Candidate; a few optimists like myself believed that he would poll almost as many votes as Sir Herbert Samuel, the Liberal candidate. The fourth candidate was Baldwin.

"You think we shall beat the Labour man?"

"I'm certain of that."

"Poor Labour," Cunninghame Graham sighed in courtly sympathy, for with William Morris, John Burns, Keir Hardie and others he had been a leader of the Labour movement once upon a time.

Next day the telegram from Glasgow arrived just as people were coming into the lounge at the Caledonian for afternoon tea. My heart was beating as Cunninghame Graham held the envelope in his hand for a moment, and then opened it with the gesture of a Georgian macaroni tossing back his ruffles and flirting with a lace handkerchief. He read the telegram and handed it to me.

"Only sixty-six votes behind Baldwin," he murmured, "well, in the circumstances I think that is as good as a victory, better indeed because I shall escape the bore of having to prepare and deliver a Rectorial Address."

I was so elated by the news that I sent my bonnet whirling up to the roof of the Caledonian's lounge, and it barely missed obliterating an old Edinburgh lady's tea when it came down.

Don Roberto, as I shall call him henceforth, preserved as much of his graceful nonchalance as he could, but on each cheekbone there was a flush of happy achievement; in all his long adventurous life h e could not have enjoyed many moments as sweet as this.

That evening there was a meeting of the National Party at Edinburgh in the Usher Hall which, owing to the news from Glasgow, was much fuller than any of us had expected. I spoke with a good deal of passion, trusting to the response of the audience to spur me into eloquence. As Don Roberto and I went off the platform together he said,

"Yes, you'll be able to do that till you're sixty. After sixty you'll have to prepare your speeches and know exactly beforehand what you're going to say. Otherwise you may have a sudden black out."

I am still unable to prepare a speech and still trust to the inspiration of the moment, but I never step on to a platform or rise at a dinner-table to make a speech without that warning from Edinburgh still in my ears, and without an apprehension that suddenly in the middle of my speech I shall find myself unable to say another word, and that, retiring in mortification from the public view, I shall be confronted by the stern form of Don Roberto and hear him say 'I told you so'.

A couple of nights later he and I appeared on the platform at St Andrew's Hall, Glasgow, with the late Duke of Montrose, Christopher Grieve, and young John MacCormick. The atmosphere of that huge gathering was tense. No meeting held in Scotland since has had

3,500 people seeming to breathe in the air of a national resurgence. That a group of young students should have been able to amalgamate the various associations in Scotland, each in its own way preaching the gospel of Home Rule, into a single body called the National Party of Scotland was a miracle.

"Man, it was great," Calum MacSween said to me. "Och, I was nearly getting up on my feet and shouting out loud I was so excited."

When the huge gathering broke up Don Roberto and I went off to have supper together at the St Enoch's Hotel. There was nobody in the dining-room except ourselves, and the waiter was not over-enthusiastic about clearing a table already laid for breakfast to provide us with cold chicken and ham.

Under the emotion of the evening, which, however well he might conceal his own susceptibility to it, had deeply stirred him, the old man, for he was now in his seventy-seventh year, began to see at the tables round us the ghosts of his fellow adventurers in politics in the past. He pointed to one of them.

"I remember sitting at that table one evening with John Burns just before the Trafalgar Square meeting in November, '87."

That meeting, owing to the foolish instructions to his constables by Sir Charles Warren, the Chief Commissioner of Police, had led to a riot. The Tory government, then in power, frightened of Mr Gladstone, frightened of Parnell, and very frightened indeed of the unemployed, had tried to stop public meetings; on Sunday, November 13th, 1887, the police knocked about not only the demonstrators but many peaceful onlookers. Cunninghame Graham, leading a party into the arena, had been badly cut about the head by a truncheon; although a Member of Parliament, he was arrested, and had to serve about two months in Pentonville gaol with John Burns.

"And I used to sit at that table with Keir Hardie in the old days, when he and I were pleased if we could get an audience of two nurse-girls and a boy under a lamp-post. And that table over there in the corner. . . . Parnell and I sat there in . . . I've forgotten the date."

Don Roberto went on to mention the names of several other bygone agitators, patriots and reformers; I divined that he was asking himself if the great meeting at the St Andrew's Hall that evening was a sign that his country was awake. He shrugged his shoulders and murmured something in Spanish.

I have never understood why Don Roberto was regarded as such an extremist. He was willing to contemplate a separation between

Scotland and England at least as complete as that between Ireland and England when the Irish Free State was created, but he did not desire so complete a separation and always hoped that Home Rule would not be denied too long, as it was to Ireland. He had a logical Latin mind, for claimant though he was to the two ancient Earldoms of Glencairn and Menteith, and with the blood of how many romantic figures of the Scottish past in his veins, he always seemed more Spaniard than Scot. He had in fact a Spanish maternal grandmother with whom he spent much of his boyhood at Ryde. He looked at the future of Scotland with that logical Latin mind, and faced up to the fact that unless Europe could preserve the independence of her small nations Europe was doomed. General de Gaulle would express for Cunninghame Graham his own point of view most nearly of contemporary European statesmen.

It was that logical Latin mind which enabled him to write such good English prose. His knowledge of Spanish adorned his prose as it adorned that of W. H. Hudson. I commend to young writers now under the influence of contemporary deliquescent North American prose an extensive study of W. H. Hudson and Cunninghame Graham.

We may call Don Roberto a happier knight-errant than Don Quixote, for although he did not live to see his dreams for Scotland near to fulfilment he was spared much disillusionment. He wrote to me once about Prince Charles Edward:

Povero Carluccio! He should have died after he got back to Paris—perhaps murdered by a Hanoverian agent, or run away with by his horse and drowned in the Loire. Best of all killed by lightning, or he might have been killed fighting against the Turks.

As Don Roberto looked back to see the ghosts of the past in the St Enoch's hotel on that October evening in 1928 I now look back to see him in Rotten Row, riding his white steed with the Mexican saddle.

On November 2nd I was writing to Faith from a gloomy temperance hotel in Dundee:

Here I am, waiting to make the last speech of seven consecutive nights' speaking. The Rectorial election was a triumph. Baldwin 1014, C.G. 978, Samuel (Lib) 396, Rosslyn Mitchell (Soc) 226. C.G. had a majority of 211 among the men but the women supported Baldwin.

I went on to tell about the meetings in Edinburgh and Glasgow:

It was as if the country has been shaken. The Morning Post had a leader, warning the Empire that some hot-headed and irresponsible intellectuals fomented by Sinn Fein are out to break up the Union.

I've been asked by the Edinburgh University Nationalists to stand for the Rectorship next year but I've refused. After C.G.'s triumph it would be unwise to risk a heavy defeat. I am refusing also to contest any of the Edinburgh or Glasgow constituencies. . . . Newman Flower and Lepper both write enthusiastically about The Three Couriers.

I cannot believe that I had been able to finish *The Three Couriers* by the beginning of November and think this must have been an instalment of it. Yet it was finished by the end of the year and was published in February 1929.

We had a meeting at Perth before that meeting in Dundee and in spite of the confidence about the future expressed in that letter that confidence had been shaken by the meeting in Perth on the previous night. As I watched a thinnish audience listen apathetically to one of the most eloquent speeches I ever heard Grieve make I began to wonder if the country had really been shaken. For the first time I began to wonder if the policy adopted at the last Council meeting of contesting parliamentary seats was a wise one yet awhile.

I went south two or three days later and a letter written to Harris on October 31st forwarded to Jethou and from Jethou to the Savile Club took about a week to reach me. It was from Eric Maschwitz who was the editor of the *Radio Times*:

Dear Mr Mackenzie,

I have always admired and constantly re-read your novels. Of them 'Carnival' still remains my favourite. As a small boy, I read it on the day of the publication and was, if I remember rightly, sent to bed for doing so. (I was not surprised. He was only eleven and a half.)

A group of us here were discussing 'Carnival' the other day and decided with enthusiasm that the story of Jenny could be made into a delightful radio play in the new microphone manner of read narrative interspersed with acted dialogue and music. There is so much atmosphere in the story that could be captured by the microphone—and music could play such a great part in the development of it. I should like to have your permission to attempt this dramatization. You need not worry, I think, that I should spoil the delicate beauty of your story, for I have had 'Carnival' in my blood for fifteen years.
Yours sincerely
Eric Maschwitz

L

Under the pseudonym of Holt Marvell, Eric put together a version of *Carnival* which if it had been made use of by the two talkies that succeeded the silent film made of it in America during the war might have spelt success instead of comparative failure for those who put them on and complete failure for the author of the book.

Carnival was a bold experiment for the B.B.C. because the general feeling still was that broadcast plays should not last more than half an hour. *Carnival* was planned to play for two hours and ten minutes. Val Gielgud had just become head of drama and his enthusiastic support of Eric and myself was invaluable. I recall a lunch at the Mont Blanc in Soho when at Eric's suggestion I was picking out the popular songs of around 1910 for the studio scene. Those popular songs were undoubtedly the chief reason for the hitherto unequalled success *Carnival* enjoyed as a radio play, and it may be added that the B.B.C. have made a feature of music hall songs of once upon a time ever since. *Carnival* cut to an hour and half would be revived eight times and it would be chosen as the play to celebrate the 25th year of the B.B.C. repertory, so splendidly maintained by Val Gielgud.

Of the actors, I recall best the performance of Hermione Gingold, who was a brilliantly lifelike Maudie Chapman; I think I am right in saying it was her first good opportunity to show what a great comedian she was, and is.

I recall too giving a demonstration to Harmon Grisewood, who was playing Maurice Avery, in the Dieudonné restaurant, of how to talk to a girl about love. Elsa Lanchester had been cast for Jenny Pearl but her place had been taken at the last moment by Lilian Harrison, who had a great success. I also recall asking the girls who were playing the Cockney parts not to add their own notions of how Cockneys spoke.

"If you will just say my lines and note the punctuation you will all sound Cockney," I assured them, rather to their indignation at first.

Mummerset has long been a joke in the theatre for the attempts of actors to convey what they believe to be the rural speech of the West of England. I find equally remote from realism the attempts of actors to convey English speech north of the Trent, which may be called Hankypankyshire because it is unable to distinguish between Lancashire, Yorkshire and the Northern Midlands. To Mummerset and Hankypankyshire may be added the Mockney with which a B.B.C. actress playing a parlour-maid in some Pinero revival imagined was the way parlour-maids used to speak once upon a time.

Above the last words of the play when Jenny Pearl had been shot
by her husband we wanted to hear the seagulls screaming and the
recorders set out with a microphone to the Embankment, only to
find it impossible to keep out the noise of the L.C.C. trams. Then
they tried St James's Park where there were always plenty of seagulls
in winter. There was a brief contretemps when one of the pelicans
came waddling up to the microphone on its stand and seemed to be
wondering whether it was edible; a press cameraman got a good
photograph of that pelican, which appeared in one of the evening
papers.

When the recorders came back with their seagulls, the screaming
was perfectly reproduced; unfortunately above the noise of the gulls
the hooting of taxicabs was reproduced with equal perfection.

Eric Maschwitz and Peter Creswell, the admirable producer,
regretfully abandoned the seagulls as a closing effect for the play.
Val Gielgud has told how a young effects boy took some elastic and
a piece of wood from his pocket and to everyone's amazement produced the noise of seagulls. That effects boy was George Inns, the
future producer of 'The Black and White Minstrels'.

The record of those synthetic seagulls became a stand-by for years,
and was the regular opening for 'Desert Island Discs' week in, week out.

I see Val Gielgud now as I write these words, seated at the new
effects—I almost call it 'organ', so many stops had it, with which he
was controlling the sounds in the various studios that were illustrat-
ing the dialogue.

I was reading the narrative that linked the scenes away in some
remote studio at Savoy Hill. In those days there was no way of letting
the narrator hear the performance. So I had to sit in silence and
solitude for two hours and ten minutes with nothing to indicate that
life on earth was still going on except the green light which signified
my cue to read the narrative. I would be saying to myself that Val
Gielgud must have forgotten it was now my cue, so long did the
intervals always seem.

Those first two performances of *Carnival* took place on January 8th
and 9th of 1929, and I received over four hundred letters from
listeners. It was repeated in the autumn.

Before I leave this forty-sixth year of mine there are one or two
relics of it I want to preserve.

One is of reading in A Londoner's Diary of the *Evening Standard*
some well-justified remarks about the use of 'literally'.

I sent the following letter to the Editor:

Sir,

An amusement of mine for many years has been collecting 'literallys'. I caught a beauty some time ago in A Londoner's Diary when a distinguished Admiral was said to have literally won his spurs at the Battle of Jutland. And only last week I caught another beauty in an account of the Peltzen case where a foot-note said that Armand Peltzen 'as a matter of fact had literally gone to pieces after his arrest'.

But is 'A Londoner' right in thinking that 'literally' is a mistake for 'figuratively'? He is too kind to the culprits. Are they not looking for one of those wretched augmentatives which, like inflated ticks, batten on the language?

As I write these words I hear on the Wireless from Mr P. F. Warner that W. G. Grace 'literally' killed the fast bowlers of the last century', which must have kept his brother, E.M., the coroner fairly busy.

This letter prompted half a dozen newspapers to produce amusing examples of 'literallys', but what gave me much pleasure was a letter from Sir Herbert Samuel to tell me that he too was a collector of 'literallys' and enclosing some beauties. Among them was one from his time as High Commissioner in Palestine when a British officer who had had to deal with some difficult Arabs told Sir Herbert Samuel that after he had admonished them they went out of the room 'with their tails literally between their legs'. In my acknowledgment of Sir Herbert Samuel's letter I said I was sure that British officer must have been Wyndham Deedes.[1] And it was.

For the next thirty years and more Lord Samuel and I would exchange 'literallys' at intervals, although it was not my privilege to meet that great man until a year or two before his death.

My favourite 'literally' of all must wait to be recorded until my next Octave.

I had read with admiration Rosamond Lehmann's first novel *Dusty Answer* and was annoyed to find Hugh Walpole, in a survey of the year's books for recommendation to what he called a Midland friend, making some derogatory remarks about *Dusty Answer* in which he said he could not imagine its lasting far into the future.

I wrote to the Editor of *T.P.'s and Cassell's Weekly:*

Sir,

I really must protest against my friend Hugh Walpole's remarks about 'Dusty Answer'. If that Midland friend of his lives anywhere near the heart of

[1] The late Brig.-Gen. Sir Wyndham Deedes, C.M.G., D.S.O.

Shakespeare's country, and has an ear and an eye for English beauty, he had better pay more attention than Mr Walpole advises to Miss Rosamond Lehmann. What is the use of looking at a lovely spray of apple-blossom and wondering whether the apples will keep over Christmas? I confess I am growing thoroughly impatient of the contemporary habit of trying to anticipate popular guides to English literature a hundred years hence. Nobody in England has any clearer notion than the man in the moon what will be the future of any living English author, and all attempts at prophecy are on a par with the efforts of a fortune-teller on the road to Epsom. . . . I will add that I have not the good fortune to know personally Miss Lehmann. Such a disclaimer is necessary in these days when literary criticism and social intercourse are so often indistinguishable.

I am sorry to write in this exasperated style, and I hope my old friend will forgive me, but I feel exasperated, and it is no good pretending to be polite.

Hugh Walpole replied:

I have read with great interest Mr Compton Mackenzie's letter. I would like to thank him for the courteous tone of it. He says that he is exasperated. He is as charming when he is exasperated as when he isn't, which is more than can be said for many authors.

His exasperation comes from my prophetic pontificating. I agree with him that there is nothing more tiresome.

When I wrote those notes on a few novels of 1927, I intended my opinions to be never dogmatic, always personal, with all the limitations that that implies. So many novels one hasn't read, so hemmed in one must be by personal taste and fancy!

But as to prophecy, is it not part of the estimation of every work of art to consider whether it has some quality of permanence, or even quasi-permanence? Futile, of course, as Mr Mackenzie says, but nevertheless an essential part of criticism? . . .

Several reviewers of *My Life and Times* have got it into their heads that I gibe at Hugh Walpole. I wish they could grasp that I am trying throughout these years to present my contemporaries as they appeared to me at the time. There is no point in recording eighty years of a crowded life from octogenarian remoteness.

It is true that I laughed at some of Hugh Walpole's early absurdities, as they seemed to me at the time, but I always remember with affection the people at whom I have laughed and I was glad to read in Rupert Hart-Davis's remarkable biography that my letter congratulating him on his knighthood gave him as much pleasure as any of the numbers he received.

I can be acquitted of even trying to draw an unkind portrait of him in any novel and so given him the acute pain he suffered from Maugham's caricature of him in that overpraised book *Cakes and Ale*.

I think I must have written to Rosamond Lehmann after these letters and expressed a desire to meet the author of what I thought was much the best evocation of girlhood on the edge of womanhood I had read. At any rate not long before she married Wogan Philipps she came to dine with me at the Gargoyle. We have often laughed since at the memory of that first meeting because she had what I do not hesitate to call the heaviest cold in the head any beautiful young woman ever had. Nevertheless, that dinner at the Gargoyle began a friendship which has been one of the privileges and pleasures of my life.

Early in this year 1928 I wrote an article about Jane Austen with particular reference to *Emma*. I find on reading it nearly forty years later, that what I said then about Jane Austen's approach to the novel represents my own approach to it in the great majority of the forty odd novels I have written, and this December seems an appropriate date to reprint some of that article because it will help to explain why I abandoned my plan to write *Our Seven Selves* and substituted for that huge novel my factual memories of the Great War after writing *Extremes Meet* and *The Three Couriers*. The reviews of both were with few exceptions complimentary but I realized that my method of presenting character and action would lead too many readers to suppose that I was indulging my own powers of comic invention at the expense of truth, because they lacked a sense of drama in reading my dialogue and therefore a capacity for dramatic expression was beyond them.

Here are some extracts of what I wrote about Jane Austen:

"'Miss Austen always demands two qualities from her readers, and never does she demand them more insistently than in *Emma*. They must have a sense of humour and a capacity in themselves for dramatic expression. The lack of these does not hinder admiration, but it will prevent any passionate enjoyment.

"There are equally great novelists who need for their enjoyment an absence of humour and a complete incapacity in the reader for dramatic expression. Such an one is Charlotte Brontë. The books of such writers refuse to be read aloud. That does not detract a whit from their greatness; but the devotees of such inwardly revealing literature are warned against supposing that the outwardly revealing kind of novel which asks to be read aloud is superficial. There are many people who can enjoy a play when acted, but who cannot read a play either to themselves or aloud. And there are the people who, when they read *Emma*, find Miss Bates as much of a bore as she was meant to appear, but which through the delicious wit of her creator she is not. *Emma* is essentially a comedy which we must act for ourselves. These are, indeed, many pages when the narration flows along like a limpid brook but such pages will be wasted on a reader who cannot be dramatizing the characters for himself. So perfectly does each one present himself in dialogue that whenever we hear about him in the narrative we are under the impression that we are hearing him talk, and it is easy to deceive oneself into remembering scenes which, when we turn the pages to refresh our memories, prove to be no more than the briefest statement of a very unimportant incident.

"I believe I am right in saying that nowhere in the whole of Miss Austen's works can there be found a scene in which men take part without a woman's presence. That means she is too meticulously aware of her limitations to run the risk of destroying the illusion of her men's actuality by letting us hear them talk among themselves. Would that a thousand women novelists since had imitated that fine discretion. The result of such discretion is that Miss Austen's men are more credible than almost any other female writer's. We accept Frank Churchill's attractiveness for women while aware that we should probably have agreed with Mr Knightley in thinking him a spoilt puppy. But Miss Austen does not venture to show us Frank Churchill and Mr Knightley alone together. She leaves their conversation for us to imagine. If the reader be a man he will have no difficulty in doing so; if she be a woman, it will not interest her.

"Throughout *Emma* there is not a single instance when the reader pauses to question the probability or possibility of her tale. What does happen happens as it would in a good comedy. Miss Austen allows us to know her people only through their speech and action before an audience, though to Emma herself she does allow the privilege of soliloquising. She gives us as much opportunity of knowledge as we should have in actual life; but no more. She does as much as Shakespeare or Molière; but not more. And there will always be a happy multitude who will consider this is quite enough.

.   .   .   .   .

"The novels of Jane Austen have been compared to several small and beautiful things, but never so far as I know to the reflection of life in one of those round slightly convex Dutch mirrors of her own date. That is how I see them: as a diminished and detached, a tranquil and crystalline life, where concentration lends an extra vividness to the colour of the fabric, an added lustre to the simplest ornament, and where the curve of the glass touches with playful caricature the movement of humanity within. If I find myself in a room with such a mirror the luminous spectacle of the light therein reflected is to me more exciting than the light it reflects.

"It is no paradox to claim that of all Miss Austen's exciting books *Emma* is the most exciting. I must have read it at least a dozen times, but it has taken me three days to make these few ill-composed observations, because I kept putting down my pen to turn over and over again the enchanting pages.

"Yet hear what Miss Brontë has to say so beautifully and so blindly:

'I have likewise read one of Miss Austen's works—Emma—read it with interest and with just the degree of admiration which Miss Austen would have thought sensible and suitable. Anything like warmth or enthusiasm, anything energetic, poignant, heartfelt, is utterly out of place in commending these works: all such demonstrations the authoress would have met with a well-bred sneer, would have calmly scorned as outré and extravagant. She does her business of delineating the surface of the lives of genteel English people curiously well. There is a Chinese fidelity, and miniature delicacy, in the painting. She supplies her reader by nothing vehement, disturbs him by nothing profound. The passions are perfectly unknown to her; she rejects even a speaking acquaintance with that stormy sisterhood. Even to the feelings she vouchsafes no more than an occasional graceful but distant recognition—too frequent converse with them would ruffle the smooth elegance of her progress. Her business is not half so much with the human heart as with the human eyes, mouth, hands, and feet. What sees keenly, speaks aptly, moves flexibly, it suits her to study; but what throbs fast and full though hidden, what the blood rushes through, what is the unseen seat of life and the sentient target of death—this Miss Austen ignores. She no more, with her mind's eye, beholds the heart of her race than each man, with bodily vision, sees the heart in his heaving breast. Jane Austen was a complete and most sensible lady, but a very incomplete and rather insensible (*not senseless*) woman. If this is heresy, I cannot help it.'

"Far be it from me to sneer at that stormy spirit, but criticism like this makes me turn to the opening pages of *Jane Eyre* and ask myself if there may not have been something to be said on behalf of Mrs Reed. It is impossible to claim for Jane Fairfax the tragic grandeur of Jane Eyre. Nor would her creator have ventured for a moment to make such a claim. But Jane Fairfax is not less moving. She is presented to us with the delicate externality of early Mozart, not with the direct appeal of later Beethoven. But neither Mozart nor Miss Austen ignores the 'unseen seat of life'. It is as much implied by them as sometimes it is just a little too much insisted upon by Beethoven and Miss Brontë. We cannot claim more for poor foolish little Harriet Smith than pathos, but there is pathos in the spoiling of her match with Robert Martin, quite enough to make a reader omit all the misunderstanding and read on with, perhaps, a too unsophisticated eagerness toward a happy ending.

"Was Miss Austen such an incomplete and insensitive a woman?

"There is one sentence in *Persuasion* which alone refutes such a charge:

" 'All the privilege I claim for my own sex (it is not a very enviable one, you need not covet it) is that of loving longest, when existence or when hope is gone.'

"I do not find anywhere in any of the Brontës so simple and so brief and yet so poignant a revelation of what Balzac called the shadow and the silence of a wounded heart."

Let me repeat that I am not attempting to judge between the artistic value of the Austen and the Brontë method in presenting life through the medium of the novel. Some novelists become their characters; the characters of other novelists become those who created them. The former are the more tolerant. They can admire their opposites without enjoying them, but the latter find it difficult to admire and impossible to enjoy the former.

In an earlier century Fielding became his characters and only obtruded himself in those brief prefaces to every chapter which all except professors of Eng. Lit. can afford to skip to-day. On the other hand all Richardson's characters are emanations of Richardson himself—Sir Charles Grandison, Pamela, or even Clarissa Harlowe. Incomprehensibly to me, Dr Johnson esteemed Richardson far above Fielding, though, to be sure, he did once observe to Boswell that you could hang yourself for impatience if you read him for the story. The admiration Rousseau and Macaulay had for Richardson is easier to understand, but to-day the characters of Richardson are lifeless because they existed only in his imagination with help from friends to give them the correct externals of their period, and this deluded contemporary readers into believing that they were real people.

Yet if at this moment I were to open *Tom Jones* to search for a reference I should have to read on because I should be back in the world in which Fielding lived and absorbed in the stories of the real people around me. Partridge's remark to Tom Jones about Garrick, that "you wouldn't know he was acting", quoted earlier in this Octave, reveals Fielding's attitude to art.

Anybody could see that Richardson was writing, and in the future anybody would be able to see that the Brontës were writing, that George Meredith was writing or later still that Joseph Conrad and Henry James were writing. This is not said in any spirit of detraction but to try to explain to myself why at the age of eighty-two I find the novels of Jane Austen as lively a joy as ever whereas the Brontës are for me unreadable. Yet at seventeen I was bored by *Emma* and could read *Jane Eyre* with passionate absorption. In my twenties the only novel of Conrad I could read with enjoyment was *The Secret Agent*, which at that date was regarded by Conradians as Conrad's only mistake. I was relieved when Henry James once alluded to Conrad as that 'interminable old man of the sea' because that was what he seemed to me at a time when the highbrows and egg-heads of the period seemed to be supposing that Conrad's approach to the novel had made the use of natural dialogue an old-fashioned intrusion. I used to insist in argument that Conrad was compelled to abandon natural dialogue because he was unable to write it, at any rate in English.

When Charlotte Brontë sneered at Jane Austen's inability to behold the hearts of her characters in her preoccupation with their externals she was in fact revealing her own inability to understand simple people through their speech. The emotional egoist is incapable of putting himself in the place of somebody else. Charlotte Brontë could not become any of her characters; all of them had to live in a Brontë world. This is equally true of D. H. Lawrence, and to a great extent of E. M. Forster.

It was the realization of how many are incapable of grasping dramatic expression outside the theatre or the cinema, to which is now added television, which made me abandon the project of *Our Seven Selves*. It may be remembered that my original conception of *Sinister Street* as the prologue to a *comédie humaine* I intended to call

The Theatre of Youth was also abandoned. The reason for that was the Great War which would inevitably become a monotonous *deus ex machinâ* for what was Youth before that war.

With my conception of *Our Seven Selves* continuously at the back of my mind I could not help regarding the books I had been writing on Herm and Jethou during the last few years as marking time, but that they were written with any idea of maintaining my circulation I must deny. My ecclesiastical trilogy was a tourniquet for my circulation. Nevertheless, for financial reasons I had to write two books a year. Fertility is always regarded with suspicion by critics because, with a very few distinguished exceptions, the critic is aware of his own inability to create. I once heard a Professor of Eng. Lit. arguing in the Third Programme of the B.B.C. that to-day criticism was more important than creation.

I made the novels I wrote in those hard-pressed years as good as I could make them, and it is heartening to find many of them being reprinted even in hardback editions forty years on. All of them were written when I was out of sympathy with the mood of the moment and every one was completely different from its predecessor. This led to the critics supposing that I was attempting various experiments in an effort to recapture the spirit of my pre-war books. In early middle-age the versatile writer, or indeed versatility of any kind, is still suspect. One must reach at least seventy before it is applauded.

So when *Extremes Meet* was published and I found that I was being patted on the back for having written a successful thriller, I felt that the only way to use my war experiences was by putting them down on paper as a true story. The reception of *The Three Couriers* would convince me how right I had been to abandon *Our Seven Selves*. I might hope to avail myself of my dramatic ability in relating that complicated tale of intrigue lasting without a break for two years without being suspected of trying to compete with thrillers. Perhaps I felt I owed it to myself to make it clear that my experience was the result of my own creative passion and that the organization I built up in Greece was from my point of view as much a creative work of art as my Sunday school in Cornwall, my adventures with irises, and my enthusiasm for the gramophone. I did not want it to be regarded as mere material for fiction.

FORTY-SIX YEARS OLD: 1929

⟫◦⟨⟩◦⟪

AFTER the broadcast of *Carnival* I went with Nellie Boyte up to Inverness, where I was due to give a lecture in the Town Hall, which in those days at any rate was one of the most difficult halls for a speaker on account of the tall windows on either side. I do not know how most speakers I hear to-day would fare in trying to hold the attention of an audience without the help of a microphone; indeed, I could add to that speculation by wondering how most of to-day's actors would have fared in the theatres of once upon a time. I seldom see a bad performance on television, however ill-constructed and incomplete the play, but on the very rare occasions I visit a theatre nowadays I seldom see a perfect performance.

We went on from Inverness to Kyle of Lochalsh, where Calum MacSween was to meet us with his daughter. Then we all went over to Skye, where I was to preside at some Gaelic gathering in Portree. For two years I had had my eye on Flodigarry, the home of Flora Macdonald, as a possible place for my home in Scotland. Last year it had come into the market without my hearing of it until too late; it had been bought by Mr Simpson, the owner of the Royal Hotel in Portree, for the ridiculous price of £1,560. Besides the house, which included a billiards-room and billiards-table, there was a farmhouse with a hundred acres of land. My notion was to instal the MacSweens in the farmhouse and use the land as a resting-place for the sheep from the Shiants on their way to the sales; the transport of them to the north of Skye would be as easy as any.

We explored Flodigarry on my forty-sixth birthday, one of those all too short days of wintry sunshine when the Western Highlands and Islands seem to possess a supernatural beauty beneath the pale blue January sky. I was writing to Faith:

I saw the Shiants from the north end of Skye under a light of paradise, and Harris gold and silver and grape-blue beyond. Really a radiant vision of beauty. . . . I've written an article on Dickens wired for by the Radio Times; 6,000 words of Gramophone, and dictated masses of letters. Chrissie and Nellie getting on very well together. Columbia has wired for my translation of Traviata for their forthcoming album. So I must get busy on that.

The view from Flodigarry across the channel between Skye and the mainland is in my mind's eye still, a mighty frieze of mountains.

Before it was time to drive back to Portree I went out with Chrissie to the lawn beyond the house and to my joy saw the new moon over my right shoulder.

"I think I'm going to get Flodigarry," I told her.

But the good fortune that the moon promised me was not the acquirement of Flodigarry; it was the dark-eyed girl beside me who would be always beside me until her death thirty-five years hence.

I offered the new owner of Flodigarry £3,000; he asked £6,500. Even if I could have afforded it I was not prepared to indulge any man's profiteering to that extent. So the notion of living at Flodigarry was abandoned. As always when I fail to get something I have set my heart on I discovered many reasons why it could have been a mistake to buy Flodigarry; among them was a crack in the wall of the billiards-room.

A day or two after my birthday Nellie Boyte, Chrissie and myself went to Edinburgh, where I had taken rooms in the Caledonian Hotel to help in the campaign for the North Midlothian Election for which the National Party of Scotland had put up Lewis Spence.

I did not feel at all sanguine about the result and, although in the excitement of Cunninghame Graham's assault upon such a Tory stronghold as Stanley Baldwin I had supported the notion of contesting seats at the next General Election, I was by now convinced that it was premature to do this, and I advocated instead that the National Party should campaign to persuade supporters of Home Rule to abstain from voting. We should then be able to claim that every elector who did not vote would have voted for a Nationalist if he had been standing. None of the other three parties would be able to be sure of the strength of the demand for Home Rule. Already both the Liberals and the Socialists were expressing their support for Home Rule, but of course without committing themselves to making it one of the main planks of their platform. I pointed out further that we should be able to indulge in pipe-bands and patriotic rallies which were denied to candidates by electoral regulations.

As the campaign progressed I became more and more convinced that the result of the poll would be a cold douche for the National Party. I recall a meeting to be addressed by Grieve and myself at which the audience consisted of a solitary man. To be sure, it had been announced by mistake for a different hall, but that was only one more example of the muddle our organization was in. A young man called David Keir, who in future Octaves will reappear as an intimate friend of mine, just down from a successful career at the

University, had managed to get hold of the Duke of Montrose and persuade him to support his candidature as a Liberal, and somehow convinced him that if the Liberals got into power they would immediately bring in a Home Rule Bill. Undoubtedly the Liberals were beginning to dream of recovering their political position with the help of Home Rule. I was offered by Lloyd George's chief organizer in Scotland any constituency in the Highlands, all expenses paid, if I would sway the National Party to Liberalism. At the same time the Labour organizers suggested that if I would persuade the Nationalists to abandon their proposal to contest Camlachie and West Renfrewshire at the General Election they would support me as a Nationalist candidate for Ross and Cromarty.

More and more did I regret the decision to fight North Midlothian and not less bitterly the muddled way in which it was being conducted. At the end of that January the only wry satisfaction I had was of having been right. The seat was won by the Socialists; the Nationalist candidate with a little over eight hundred votes forfeited his deposit; young David Keir secured well over three thousand votes for the Liberals.

It may have been on my way back to Jethou that I attended a dinner at the Savile given by Leonard Rees, the editor of the *Sunday Times* since 1901. It was Rees's custom to give a dinner occasionally to an elder statesman; the dinner on this occasion was to Austen Chamberlain. The ritual for such dinners was for the elder statesman to sit at the 'high' table with his host and half a dozen senior members of the Club. At right angles to the 'high' table were two more tables seating six a side of less senior members and other guests of Rees. Halfway through dinner at a signal from the host all the members seated on the inside of the 'high' table changed places with those seated inside at the other tables. This was to give the members an opportunity to meet all the guests.

On this evening before we went in to dinner Rees told me not to change places with the others.

"I have put you opposite 'Tony' Eden. I think you'll be impressed by him."

At this date Lord Avon was Parliamentary Private Secretary to Sir Austen Chamberlain. During the dessert we were presented one after another to the Secretary of State for Foreign Affairs, and I recall thinking, as he sat there next to Leonard Rees, that he was more like a waxen image of himself in Madame Tussaud's than flesh and blood.

When the guests had departed, Rees, who was forty years older than the P.P.S., asked me what impression 'Tony' Eden had made upon me.

"He seems rather an anxious young man," I said. "He talked very little at dinner and after dinner he seemed to be wondering all the time whose babble he ought to be listening to."

"*We* think he's the future hope of the Party," Rees said. "We're building him up as our future Prime Minister. We think he has everything."

"You know much more about politics than I do. The only young Tory I can dimly see as a future Prime Minister is Bob Boothby.[1] And of course he isn't really a Tory at all."

I was due to debate Scottish Nationalism with Bob Boothby over the microphone at the end of February but had to default because I was laid up with a bad attack of bronchitis and pleurisy. The meeting of Bob and myself had been looked forward to because as Hilda Matheson put it, "You are neither of you afraid of the microphone."

My place was taken by George Malcolm Thomson, for whom the ebullient Bob was not a fair match. I recall listening to the debate from my bed in Jethou and, in spite of a vile cough, spitting ripostes at Bob, who was booming away at George Thomson like the headmaster in a school-story at some errant pupil.

The reception given to *The Three Couriers* made me glad I had started *Gallipoli Memories* as soon as I got back from Scotland.

In *The Three Couriers* I had drawn a portrait of J. M. N. Jeffries as Carteret the correspondent of the *Daily Mail* in Athens:

". . . of the many correspondents with whom one side of his work had brought him into touch Waterlow had always found Carteret the most straightforward, the most intelligent, and the most sympathetic. Carteret himself did not look at all like a correspondent. He looked like some delicate gentle creature out of the pages of Lewis Carroll, as diffident and as timorous as the fawn that accompanied Alice across one of the squares on the other side of the looking-glass. He talked like some shy and intellectual undergraduate who had been brought up with a quantity of sisters. And of all the many correspondents in that white blazing city he was almost the only one who never tried to serve himself or his paper, the *Daily Mail*, at the expense of other people, and who by some strange freak of poetic justice never failed to supply his paper with the best authentic news

[1] Lord Boothby.

available and who never ran away even from the ugliest situation."

I was tremendously pleased to get a letter from Jeffries less than a month after the publication of *The Three Couriers* because I knew then that the book had recaptured the life of those hectic years in Greece and the Aegean. He wrote from Port-of-Spain in the West Indies:

Thank you for 'the portrait of a gentleman'. You were always kindly to me; I never knew you depart from kindliness even when heat and hate and Greece had pointed every human soul against its neighbour in that feverish summer of 1916. I marvel at your understanding. You understood silence, I see, and other kindred ways. It has been a luxury to read you: how great a luxury I doubt if even you know. . . .

Your book brings back so much to me. . . . I don't know why it should particularly but one minor memory obtrudes itself—you calling in the extremes of exasperation to Tucker, Macartney, etc from the steps of the Hermopolis wharf when they twice fouled the gig of the S.N.O. . . .

Do you remember your revolution as privately owned by you as any deer-park? What days! What times!

J. M. N. Jeffries was a sad loss to good journalism. R. I. P. Stony-hurst can be proud of an *alumnus*.

That confounded bronchitis held up work on *Gallipoli Memories*, but I was able to dictate enough stuff for *The Gramophone* and the *Sunday Pictorial* to have an intensive fortnight on *Gallipoli Memories* when at last I was able to start it again. Then Faith succumbed to one of those mysterious gasping fits, and seemed so bad that I sent for Dr Carey, who came over from Guernsey in spite of the bad weather.

"There's nothing functional wrong with your wife," he assured me.

"You mean it's hysteria?"

No general practitioner likes to commit himself to pronounce such a verdict, but when he had left the island I looked up hysteria in Quain's Dictionary and there I found that the *globus hystericus* was a recognized symptom of hysteria. I told Faith half jokingly about the *globus hystericus* and from that moment she never had another of those gasping fits, or at any rate none for me to hear.

Faith was writing to my mother on February 29th:

I had a bad nerve attack which had its funny side, though I did think I was dying. Monty was able to assure me it was pure hysteria, that I was simulating (not deliberately of course, he explained) certain things that seemed functional.

I was so amused by this that I came round very easily and for three days I haven't had another attack of this horrible gasping. But it makes me a little nervous. I hate making an ass of myself.

Then as if that weren't enough for the household for one day, Monty must go and fall into the library fire—saving himself with his right hand which holding his pouch (fortunately) was plunged into the heart of the blaze.

Burn dressings were applied and after an hour or so of agony he did some more work. His hand is healing well now, but he's still only convalescent after the bronchitis and pleurisy. I needn't say he is working night and day and keeps both secretaries busy. Chrissie MacSween is a great success and gets on well with Nellie. Very intelligent, with a trained mind.

On March 8th Faith was writing to my mother:

Monty succumbed to sciatica after finishing the first part of his Gallipoli reminiscences. It's not surprising; his whole heart and soul were in it and I've never seen him so passionately engrossed since Sinister Street. *He's been marvellously free from pain this year but having worked all the time he had 'flu, bronchitis and pleurisy, dictating articles for* Vanity Fair *and* Gramophone *he has never had time to convalesce as ordinary people do. So this attack isn't surprising.*

That article in the *Radio Times* about Dickens recalls the most annoying cut any editor made in an article of mine.

I wound up the article with these words:

"Those portraits which lots of dull people have called caricatures were not caricatures at all, but are as realistic as a portrait of the Dutch *genre* school . . . I am old enough to remember when London was full of people out of Dickens. I had a Dickensian nurse of my own, an eccentric old woman who used to send me out to take long walks by myself in Kensington when I was six years old. At the same time I was reading 'Dombey and Son' and thinking to myself how very like Paul Dombey's nurse my own nurse was. My knowledge of queer characters has been gained like that of Dickens. At that date when I was reading Smollet and Fielding, particularly Smollet, who was Dicken's own favourite author. But I enjoyed one great advantage over Dickens. I was able at this age to read Charles Dickens himself."

And the sub-editor cut "I was able at this age to read Charles Dickens himself".

By Easter which came in March this year I was two-fifths of the way through *Gallipoli Memories* and was much encouraged by the reception Eric Maschwitz and Val Gielgud gave to it when I read them what I had written during the ten days they spent on Jethou. It was then that I was seized with the notion of publishing a weekly paper which was to be called *Vox* and devoted to radio criticism. I had visions of doing for broadcasting what I had been successful in doing for the gramophone. At this date the Press was still trying all it could to denigrate what it considered a dangerous rival. Intelligent criticism was ignored but the smallest contretemps at Savoy Hill was given the maximum publicity. The more we talked about it in that Easter week the more imperative it came to seem that *Vox* should be given lungs. But where was the capital coming from to launch a weekly paper?

The answer came from 'Togo' Maclaurin, whose kind and delightful parents were living in Guernsey. Togo was not long down from an Oxford of Oxford bags, and his Oxford bags were the baggiest I ever saw. Contemporary with that fashion for trouser-legs almost as wide as petticoats was the game of 'beaver'. He who spotted a beard and called 'beaver' first scored a point. Togo had a passion for gramophone records and we had taken him on the staff of *The Gramophone*. When he heard of my notion to bring out a weekly review of broadcasting, Togo and a friend of his, John Barrow, persuaded their fathers and an uncle to put up the capital to form a company to publish *Vox*, of which Togo Maclaurin and Jack Barrow were to be managing directors, while I was to be editor.

The editorial office of *The Gramophone* was to be moved from 58 Frith Street to share with *Vox* the much ampler quarters of 10A Soho Square. Christopher Stone never liked the idea of *Vox*, but he agreed to the move and also to *The Gramophone's* investing £1,000 of the £10,000 of capital for the new venture. Faith was much in favour of *Vox* because my editorship would entail our having a flat in London.

I was booked for two or three broadcasts in April and when we went to London we were lucky enough to find the right flat in Dryden Chambers, that relic of the early 'nineties in Oxford Street. It was on the top floor, which meant climbing a hundred stone steps, there being no lift, but it was as quiet as the country, with a view out over roof tops; with four rooms and a kitchen it was the right size. The sitting-room was given black walls, a black carpet, a golden ceiling and red lacquer for the door, mantelpiece and any other woodwork. The bedrooms were papered with Chinese scenes.

One of the broadcasts for which I was booked was a debate under the auspices of the British Drama League in their headquarters at

8 Adelphi Terrace. Miss Naomi Royde-Smith was to move that 'the Broadcast Play is not a satisfactory form of Art', which I was to oppose.

Geoffrey Whitworth, the Secretary, was writing:

"All, I believe, is getting in order for the Debate on Friday, April 19th, and already the Library is putting on some queer attachments of wires and cables. Will you give me the pleasure of your company at dinner before the Debate at the Garrick Club punctually at 6.45. I say punctually because the Debate is timed to begin at 8 o'clock, and as you know the B.B.C. demand the utmost exactitude in the keeping of their appointments. I am asking Miss Royde-Smith and Major Vernon, who is to preside at the Debate, to dinner also, so that there will be an opportunity for a little stage management."

In those days women guests at the Garrick Club were rushed through the lobby to a dreary dining-room the windows of which looked out on a white-washed wall. An air of profanation clung about their admission to this male sanctum. Geoffrey Whitworth's hope of a 'little stage management' was frustrated by Miss Royde-Smith, whose only idea of it was the sound of her own voice and the twirling of her own fingers. Her ignorance of the technique of broadcasting was complete, and she kept calling on young Woodley to agree with her silliest arguments. Van Druten, the author of *Young Woodley*, a very successful play of the previous year, splashed about so enthusiastically in her shallows that once or twice I rapped the table in contradicting them both. This produced an urgent telephone call from Savoy Hill to say that I must not thump the table so loudly because listeners would think it was an explosion. Yet I was only tapping the table with a finger.

That reminds me of another protest by the B.B.C. engineers against table-rapping. In the autumn of this year my sister Fay and I were asked to give a Shakespeare reading on Sunday afternoon after the Bach cantatas which were then the regular Sunday afternoon entertainment for listeners (with the result that most of them tuned in to Luxemburg to listen to lighter music).

We were to read the murder scene from *Macbeth*, the nunnery and the mad scenes from *Hamlet*, a scene between Rosalind and Orlando from *As You Like It* and the death scene from *Antony and Cleopatra*. We found in the studio one copy of Shakespeare's works in the smallest print and one microphone at which we had to sit huddled together. At the run through before we went on the air I rapped on the table as the cue for Macbeth to say:

What is that knocking?
How is't with me, when every noise appals?

And again I rapped when Lady Macbeth says:

I hear a knocking
At the south entry:

This second rap brought in Stuart Hibberd looking as emotionally upset as Macbeth himself.

"The engineers say you're shaking the whole building," he said. "I think it will be better if you just say 'knocking heard'."

"That's ridiculous. I'm not going to say 'knocking heard' and then

Wake Duncan with thy knocking! I would thou couldst.

"No, Hibberd, isn't there something I can knock on without shaking the building?"

Stuart Hibberd retired and must have used all the gold in his voice to persuade the engineers to let me knock on a small cardboard waste-paper basket. He held it up and tapped it gently.

"Will that be all right?"

"It doesn't sound to me much like a knocking at the south entry, but if the engineers are happy I am."

Hibberd offered me the waste-paper basket.

"No, no, Hibberd. *I'm* not going to do the knocking. You must do it. I'll give you the cue each time, by lifting my left hand."

I can still see the expression of almost agonized expectation on dear Stuart Hibberd's face as he gently taps that cardboard waste-paper basket to the cue of my raised left hand.

I said a few words to introduce each scene; in half an hour to the second as Cleopatra says

And there is nothing left remarkable
Beneath the visiting moon.

the reading came to an end.

We each got ten guineas for that half-hour, and I remember being told by somebody that this was twice as much as the usual fee for poetry reading.

Eric Maschwitz under his pen-name of Holt Marvell had made a broadcast play of *The Prisoner of Zenda* and asked me to listen to it in Jethou and send a frank criticism of it to *The Listener*. I reproduce some of what I wrote because it shows a stage in the development of broadcast drama for which Val Gielgud deserves so much of the credit.

"*The Prisoner of Zenda* is just over, and I have now read it as a book, seen it as a play, watched it as a film, and heard it as a radio drama. I ask myself whether if I had not already possessed a good knowledge of Ruritania I should have been able to follow this evening's entertainment without a single pucker of doubt; I fear I must answer with a decided negative. Mr Holt Marvell must not be blamed for this. His work was something like a Marvell of ingenuity . . . but this new policy of suppressing the names of the actors and the characters is, to speak bluntly, stupid. Nothing is gained by its except a small amount of space in the *Radio Times*. . . . Somebody once said that if a dramatist wanted an audience to understand his play he should tell them something is going to happen, show it happening, and then tell them it has happened. To this simple rule Mr Holt Marvell adhered, but his adherence was nullified this evening by the fact that many of his audience did not know for a long time to whom it was happening. . . .

"The chief weakness of the play was in what should have been the most exciting scene, the rescue of the King. The fight sounded like a number of biscuit tins of various sizes and degrees of emptiness being thrown about accompanied by an odd noise like a sickle being sharpened. Throughout the play the noise effects were weak. The horses were good, but they might have been better; anyway theirs is an easy noise to achieve. . . . But if the effects were weak the management of the crowds was masterly . . . a triumph of Mr Peter Cresswell's imaginative skill. The music was on the whole well chosen, but there were moments when it undoubtedly did get in the way of the dialogue, either by being too loud or by not being absolutely appropriate to the moment. This, I may say, was a criticism that could equally have been made of the music to *Carnival*, where it was chosen for the sake of administering emotional punishment to the audience. . . . How much of the dialogue was Mr Holt Marvell's and how much Sir Anthony Hope's I do not know . . . but whether the younger writer or the older writer was responsible for the bigger half there was no sign of a schism; when one remembers what a master of dialogue Sir Anthony Hope was, this is to pay Mr Holt Marvell something of a compliment. Some of us may have forgotten that *The Dolly Dialogues* was the first book in which ordinary cultivated people were made to talk as they really did talk. . . . Was Mr Holt Marvell or Sir Anthony Hope responsible for the priests singing

Masses for the dead? I have yet to visit a church where a number of
sung requiems were being conducted simultaneously.

"And now after what I fear will read like a rather poky criticism
of small details we have to ask ourselves what further avenues of
exploration the broadcast of *The Prisoner of Zenda* has opened up to
would-be radio dramatists. The coronation scene may put into the
minds of some the fancy of using a background of crowds to contrive
for the imagination of the listener an appropriate emotional condition in which to follow the course of the action. . . . I have my
visions, or perhaps I should say my auditions of possible future
triumphs of sound. Stage crowds are always absurd, and I say that
with the knowledge of one who has himself driven through an angry
mob and been himself the prime object of their hostility. That
experience cured me of ever being deluded again by the noise of the
French Revolution off-stage. But I believe the effect of terror will be
possible over the microphone, and there are so many other emotions
that a crowd can evoke—elation, grief, anger, fear, lust, and the rest
of humanity's simple emotions; a crowd is never sophisticated.

"But that fight! We shall have to do better than that if we want to
stand up to the British Drama League. We must get rid once and for
all of the impression that our fights are being conducted in a biscuit
factory."

By June *Gallipoli Memories* was finished and Cassell's would be
able to bring the book out in the late autumn. I was to sell it outright
for £500.

I think it was about now that I wrote an article for the *Sunday
Pictorial*, advocating a small fixed sum for travelling by train far and
near like the old Twopenny Tube and the equalization of railway
freights on the model of the General Post Office. I must have been
fired to emulate the achievement of my kinsman Sir Rowland Hill
with the penny post. Letters of agreement and applause filled our
mail bag, and Macwhirter telegraphed I was to follow up my article
with another on the same subject.

The following day a telegram arrived cancelling this request. I
heard privately that the railways had protested and that Lord
Rothermere had forbidden any further mention of the subject.

Today I believe more firmly than ever that cheap travel and
equalized freight charges is the remedy for the present mess that has
been made of British Railways; now that they have been nationalized private interests are no longer affected.

The attempt to make the railways pay by raising fares, raising freight-charges and destroying numbers of lines would be funny if it were not such a serious menace to the nation's vitality by encouraging the festering concentration of urban life.

However, the damage already done to the English countryside, to Wales and to Scotland may already be irreparable and we must comfort ourselves with the reflection that presently business men will be able to get to Australia a few hours quicker than they can at present.

At the supersonic rate at which aeroplanes are moving some heroic lunatic will probably reach the moon before I finish *My Life and Times*. It is amusing to reflect that, when a couple of hundred years hence or even earlier the whole of Great Britain will be a suburb of London, the moon will be a suburb of the overcrowded earth.

At the beginning of June I went to Cambridge to take part in a debate at the Union. The retiring President, Mr H. M. Foot of St John's College, was to propose 'That Democracy is a Farce'. He would be opposed by Mr E. V. Knox of Corpus Christi College, Oxford. I was to speak third in support of the motion and Canon Raven, D.D., of Gonville and Caius College, would speak up for democracy fourth.

I extract from the almost illegible names on the menu of an excellent dinner before the Debate those of Geoffrey Crowther, Lionel Gamlin and Lord Pentland. The retiring President, Hugh Foot, is now Lord Caradon.

I do not recollect the course of the Debate, nor whether it was decided that democracy was a farce, but I seem to remember that Evoe of *Punch* was not bubbling over with the wit we had a right to expect from him. He and I were staying at the Blue Boar and I was surprised when we got back after the debate to hear him ordering two double whiskies for us. After another double he suddenly came to life and we sat up till half-past four in the morning in a conversation of which I recall not a word but which I know was one of the most stimulating marathons of talk I ever enjoyed. His brother Ronnie told me later that Evoe always required two double-whiskies before he could let himself go. In spite of that late night at the Blue Boar we were both at breakfast with the President at nine o'clock to the minute.

I think it was in this June that I met Gwilym Lloyd George,[1] who was interested in a scheme to imitate Luxemburg with a commercial broadcasting station by starting one in Guernsey. I rallied an

[1] Viscount Tenby.

influential group of Guernseymen to support it, but the G.P.O. managed to stop it; after the inroads Luxemburg was already making, the notion of another rival in Guernsey did not appeal to the Governors of the B.B.C.

I gave three or four broadcasts that July while I was in London for a week before going to Scotland. The one I remember most clearly is the unscripted debate which Lionel Fielden had devised for what was then a daring experiment. The subject was to be Town and Country. Beverley Nicholls was to be the advocate of life in town as a richer life than the country could give; I was to oppose him. The experiment of having a small audience in the studio was also made. I thought then that this was a mistake and I am surer than ever to-day that studio audiences are a mistake. The microphone is the only audience that should be allowed, and the only successful broadcaster is he who recognizes this.

Lloyd George never mastered the microphone; he would only allow his words to be broadcast when he was addressing an audience. On the other hand Stanley Baldwin used the microphone perfectly and I feel sure that Winston Churchill learned from Baldwin how to use the microphone as an audience in the palm of his hand. I recall from May of this year, listening to Baldwin's last words on the eve of the General Election:

"You trusted me once. Won't you trust me again?"

I can hear now that richly confidential Cambridge voice of the period and I could imagine the way it would appeal to elderly voters all over the country, who as they turned on their pillows that night would decide, whatever the weather might be to-morrow, to vote for the Conservatives.

The argument in favour of a studio audience is that the comic who gets a laugh from it is encouraged to feel he really is being funny and therefore becomes funnier and funnier. My reply to that would be that if a comic is not sure of a joke he would be wise to cut it out of his programme. Occasionally, of course, the laughter and applause does sound spontaneous because it *was* spontaneous; generally a studio audience sounds like what in effect it is—a claque.

Beverley Nicholls was nervous because he had written some juvenile silliness about me in his prematurely forced autobiography called *Twenty-Five*; he supposed that I should take the opportunity of scoring off him. He continually interrupted the argument by little asides to the audience which, being a studio audience, dutifully tittered. Then for no logical reason arising out of the argument he

suddenly launched forth in a denunciation of the horrors of war. I
tried to bring him back to the point, but he seemed on the verge of
tears as he told me and the studio audience what hell he had been
through when, just before the war ended, he had had to face the
Mess for the first time as the newest subaltern.

"And newly joined subalterns were known as warts," he exclaimed
in a passion of self-pity, the fashionable emotion of the moment for
young men on the lower slopes of Parnassus.

That first unscripted debate was a failure, but I console myself by
reflecting that whatever contribution I made to its failure was atoned
for by the possibility that it may have been the first step down the
garden path for Beverley Nicholls, to the delight of so many readers
who did not hear his advocacy of the town against the country.

I recall a cocktail party just before that debate given by Lionel
Fielden in Wilton Street at which I met for the first time Godfrey
Winn. He had seen the announcement of *Gallipoli Memories* and
was anxious to ask me about the effect of dysentery because he was
writing a novel in which his hero was struck down by dysentery.

"I'm asking Mr Mackenzie," he turned to explain to a young
woman who was standing next to us, "because he was at Gallipoli."

The young woman gaped.

"Oh, Gallipoli," she drawled. "Oh, then I suppose you hate the
Italians."

Godfrey Winn was on the verge of explaining to that young
woman what had happened at Gallipoli. Then he stopped abruptly.
I sensed that he felt himself defeated by such invincible ignorance.

Another job I did before I left for Scotland toward the end of that
July was to write an article for the *Radio Times* in answer to an
attack on broadcast drama by Gordon Craig which they were
printing. This is what I wrote:

"If Mr Gordon Craig will be consistent and admit that the
invention of printing was a major disaster for art, if he will accept
the proposition that every mechanical advance in the presentation
of drama has done its little bit to damage the externals of it, if
indeed he will accept my suggestion that the first and best drama was
played in the Garden of Eden and that every drama since has been
but a more or less superfluous variation of that original theme, I will
with pleasure join with him in what he calls his growling, though,
to be frank, that growling sounds to my ears more like the muttering
of a dear old lady in the chimney corner who cannot find her
spectacle case. I cordially associate myself with Mr Gordon Craig's

remarks about business men who run theatres, and if he wants to go on thumping a dead ass I am willing to stand by him and thump away at it too. At the same time I must remind him that, unless the drama were always liable to decay, it could never be blown by fly business men.

"To declare that drama is unaffected by whatever happens is to talk solemn nonsense; no expression of humanity was ever as much affected as drama by what happens. That is why in my opening sentence I have invited Mr Gordon Craig to accept that drama in the Garden of Eden as the first, the last, and the best. If he will do so, then I will nod a reverent assent to his solemn nonsense about the drama's not being affected by anything that happens. But will he agree to my proposition that his own method of dramatic presentation is entirely without influence? I doubt it. If he thinks it as unimportant as all that, why has he been making such a to-do about it for the last quarter of a century? I willingly admit that nearly all the plays written for a combination of voice and visible action will be affected unfavourably by broadcasting. Yet it would be rash to speculate prematurely upon what effect the restoration of the human voice to supremacy is likely to have upon the dramatic forms of the future.

"Mr Gordon Craig thinks that nobody is capable of speaking into a microphone without losing quality of expression. He tells us that in the year 1922 or 1923 he sat for many a day in a London hotel, listening to what was going on over the radio. Such an experience of listening-in sounds almost prehistoric to-day; it seems my fate to be invited to argue about broadcasting with people whose experience of broadcasting is too slight to count as experience. What would Mr Gordon Craig think if I were to condemn his method of dramatic presentation because fifteen years ago I had been in the habit of dropping in to the back of the pit every afternoon to turn a casual ear and eye upon one of his productions during a spare quarter of an hour when I was early for an appointment or for any other reason that induces one to sit still for a minute or two in London?

"There is probably little to choose between the amount of dramatic instinct inherited by Mr Gordon Craig and the amount inherited by myself, and I assure Mr Gordon Craig that his remarks about the failure of a speaker to give his best over the microphone are due to nothing but his own lack of practical experience. He has been so much preoccupied by the visual side of drama that his imagination has come to exaggerate its relative importance.

"Mr Gordon Craig waxes as merry as a school-master over the bad reading of an extract from Plato's *Phaedo*; it is an etiolated art which can find nothing more fresh at which to sneer than our old friend, the timid and underpaid curate. If Mr Gordon Craig himself had been as deeply affected by the *Phaedo* as he would have us believe, he should by now be above using such poor old 'property' similes. I gather Mr Craig wishes to maintain that the *Phaedo* would be better read by an actor on the stage of a theatre. I will wager that if Mr Craig can find an actor able to read Plato superlatively well and allows himself to be introduced to a good loud-speaker he will find that his actor, so far from losing through the medium of radio will have gained by being divorced from the tawdry associations of the modern theatre.

"There was a time when I regarded radio with aversion, fear, and contempt. Seven years ago when Mr Gordon Craig was toying with the earphones in that London hotel, I might have written in the same strain as his article of to-day, though I hope I should have avoided that dilapidated old sneer at curates. Gradually I have come to apprehend better and better the immeasurable power of this new medium of communication; I have realized that radio will give the artist the greatest opportunity he has had since the days of Homer to express himself without the mechanical barrier which the progress of inventiveness has raised higher and higher between the artist and his audience. Just when the cinema had dragged art down to the depths of debasement radio was born to restore the balance.

"For Mr Gordon Craig to write in one sentence 'the Radio, the Movie-Tones, the Cinema and all these things' argues such a confusion of mind, such a failure of imagination, and so much ill-informed prejudice as to make it seem hardly worth while for an intelligent man to argue with him. Nevertheless, if Mr Gordon Craig will give himself the trouble to listen intelligently to radio for a whole year, I will debate with him before the microphone at the end of that year, with one proviso, which is that there shall not sit between us and the real audience a small visible audience ready to titter at any jokes Mr Gordon Craig may make about curates and so render serious debating an impossibility."

From the point of view of the drama I regret television. I have listened to many plays broadcast and have seldom been disappointed. The Repertory Company built up by Val Gielgud rarely let me down. On the other hand, almost all the plays written specially for television have been to my taste pretentious failures, and with infrequent exceptions the television revivals of old plays have been feeble. One reason for this may be that the directors and producers had been corrupted in their youth by films. Sound broadcasting offered the challenge of a new medium; television seemed less a new medium than a way of bringing films to the fireside.

The live theatre was unquestionably devitalized by the ever grow-ing demand for visual appeal. The cinema was at last developing the art of producing visual appeal when the arrival of talkies barred further progress. When talkies arrived the directors should have insisted upon the camera's following the words; as it was they made the words follow the camera. And that is the threat to the future of television drama. It is much easier to give a good performance on television than on the stage, and if the directors of costume plays knew their job the actors would respond. But why should I be railing at the producers and directors of films and teledrama when the producers and directors of the live stage are making such a mess of Shakespeare, when charlatans of various nationalities are competing with one another to bring the world's greatest dramatist up to date? Does Shakespeare really need to be revivified with monkey glands? It is time to form a Society for the Prevention of Cruelty to Shake-speare. Even at Stratford these quacks of culture are allowed to dose their audiences with productions that make them feel how modern Shakespeare is after all, and how fashionably modern is their own pitiable ignorance of the past.

I read that at the Edinburgh Festival in 1965 the three witches in *Macbeth* were wearing bikinis. That must have made Banquo's words sound a little odd.

> *You should be women,*
> *And yet your beards forbid me to interpret*
> *That you are so.*

I read that after seeing a parody of *Much Ado About Nothing* some young jackass found a museum piece had been brought to life. I read of similar parodies of *Hamlet* and *Coriolanus* and I hear other young jackasses braying their delight. Presently we shall have King Lear playing golf to bring Shakespeare up to date and make him intelligible to contemporary taste.

But I have stepped out of 1929 into 1965 and must get back.

I was in Edinburgh by the last week in July and a little worried by what seemed to me the mistaken preoccupation of the National Party leaders with getting into Parliament. I was remembering what

Tim Healy had said to me in Dublin five years ago about the Irish Nationalists at Westminster being swept away in a night by the young men of Sinn Fein in 1918. I was irritated by the way members of the Council were going to such pains to disclaim any Popish or Irish influence on the policy of the National party. I began to suspect that some of these Council members were too much concerned with the temporary self-importance of being candidates for constituencies and that if any of them did succeed in getting into the Westminster Parliament they would be content with the same dilution of Home Rule as Northern Ireland. I did not want to see a glorified County Council in charge of Scotland's destiny. I felt that nothing less than the status of the Irish Free State was imaginable for Scotland's future. At the same time I was strongly against any idea of republicanism and felt that, although the Union of Parliaments was a disaster, the Union of Crowns should at all costs be maintained. Ruaridh Erskine of Marr and Christopher Grieve were both in sympathy with my fear of parochialism and we discussed the possibility of forming a society to be known as Clann Albain, the members of which would be pledged to do all they could to foster the Celtic Idea with a vision, on a far distant horizon at present, of rescuing the British Isles from being dominated by London. We were even prepared to regard as a Scotia irredenta the four northern counties of Northumberland, Durham, Cumberland and Westmorland. Grieve's particular quarrel with the Council now was its refusal to make Social Credit the main plank of its economic platform. He was also having a war on paper both with Lewis Spence and David Cleghorn Thomson of the B.B.C.

I must have had a soothing effect on David's ruffled feelings; at any rate he agreed to come with me to Barra, taking the road to the isles by Ballachulish where we were to pick up Father John Mac-Millan on our way to Oban.

We arrived at Oban on St James's eve and stayed at the St Columba hotel, the beginning of a long friendship with the Gillespies to whom it belonged. At this date the Roman Catholic cathedral in Oban was not yet ready for services, and we attended vespers in the little tin pro-cathedral. I recall Father John's moaning at the length of the solemn *Magnificat*.

"Oh dear, oh dear, wouldn't a simple little Benediction have been much better than all this to-do with the Magnificat?"

"It is a pro-cathedral, you know, and they must stick to the rules. Who was the good-looking youngish priest in the cope?"

"John MacQueen from Arisaig."

And that evening at Oban was the beginning of a close friendship which has lasted until to-day.

The boat for Castlebay left early next morning and I went up to David Cleghorn Thomson's room to make sure of his being up in time. He was still asleep, an anxious frown upon his forehead. No doubt he was wrestling with the problem of moving the Scottish headquarters of the B.B.C. from Blythswood Square, Glasgow, to Queen Street, Edinburgh, on which he was set and which he would achieve. They would return to Glasgow under the administration of his successor.

I think that crossing to Barra was made in the old *Cygnet*, which was as primitive a boat as any to which MacBraynes were still shamelessly clinging. Mercifully the Atlantic was in a friendly mood, although it began to rain heavily as we drew near to Castlebay. Father John was staying with his brother at Craigston; the hotel being full, David and I had to sleep in the tin annexe, where poor David was driven out of bed in the middle of the night by the rain dripping on to him through the tin roof.

Next morning the sun was shining again.

David was determined to catch a trout, which he managed to do; in trying to catch another he caught a telegraph pole instead. We were having tea with Father Macdonald at Northbay, the parish to which Father John MacMillan would be translated from Balla-chulish in September, to his unbounded joy. David begged to have his trout cooked for tea; I see that little fish on his plate now, about the size of a plump sardine. David did not remain in Barra but went on to Eigg where he had arranged to meet the Revd. Kenneth Macleod of Gigha, who was the guide for Mrs Kennedy Fraser and her songs of the Hebrides. I moved from the hotel to stay in Borve.

The great excitement for me was to see the coastguard-station on Ard Greine which on Armistice Day had been abandoned by the Navy to the Post Office and remained empty ever since. With the help of Father John I had bought it for £60 a few weeks before. On July 31st I was writing to Faith:

I am in a remote glen by the edge of the Atlantic staying with a dear old lady in a cottage. Calum MacSween is with me and in splendid form after a very sea-sick voyage from Tarbert. This is a delightful island. Even the dogs don't seem to fight.

The little house is wonderful. A supreme view. It's like a ship's cabin.
Even a mast for wireless. It cost £1,000 to build. Such seas and sands.

On August 3rd I was writing:

Father MacMillan has christened the house Faire na h'Abh, which means
the look out (faro) of the deep that lies beyond the ocean. It lies at the top of a
rolling grassy cliff covered with flowers. Primroses still in bloom. Gentians,
harebells, centaury, and many more. The walls are 2 ft 6 inches thick. Outside
shutters to all windows. Lined with pitch pine. Nothing to get except mattresses
and pillows for the 5 bunks and three wicker chairs. There are 5 wooden chairs
and lockers, toilet-flaps, tables, some pots and pans, some crockery, knives and
forks. There are telephone poles all the way, and only the line is needed to put
us on the 'phone again. The little middle room has one bunk and a desk. Even
the signal flags, flares, and some signal books are still there. The floor with the
best cork linoleum is damp because of course the linoleum should have been
taken up but there is no sign of damp anywhere else. The earth closet is
excellent with two pans, and even a cellar has some oddments of pails etc. Two
large freshwater tanks. Roof perfect. Every tile nailed with copper. Not a speck
on the ceiling. A range which has rusted a bit but only needs a few things. A
Tortoise stove in the 4-bunk bedroom. Lockers with brass chains and a pantry
with lamp-glasses and lamps still there, and even a spare wick!

Windows have a round hole for putting a telescope through in stormy
weather. It lies in the middle of the headland. Marvellous sands and dozens
of seals on the flat rocks. Inland a magnificent amphitheatre of hills. North-
ward the mountains of Uist across a blue sea. So I think I didn't spend my
£60 badly.

Calum MacSween has just opened a bottle of beer which has spurted all
over the old landlady.

An American lady arrived to stay in the Castlebay Hotel with an
outsize clarsach on which she twanged away at what she claimed
were the authentic accompaniments to the songs of Ossian, and
hearing that I was the Honorary President of the Glasgow University
Ossianic Society she twanged away for a whole evening, expecting
and being given my solemn attention.

"Man," said Calum MacSween to me on our way back to Borve,
"did you see the faces that strange woman was making with her
mouth when she was playing yon harp of hers?"

Apropos of the Ossianic Society, which was the oldest in the
University and only two years away from its centenary, I had presented them with a silver churchwarden pipe reputed to have

belonged to Dr Johnson. I was anxious to dispel the common belief that Dr Johnson had failed to appreciate the Highlands and Islands. In fact, as I pointed out, he could be called the first Englishman who had appreciated them, although his appreciation of Ossian was less marked.

From Barra I went on to Eriskay, for what I knew would be for me one of the great emotional experiences of my life. The evening before I left Borve I was taken to a small house under a roof that looked like the inside of an ebony boat, and here I heard a very old blind woman sing *The Silver Whistle*. "Sound the silver whistle," the song begins, "the son of my King has come to Alba." In that song the singer tells of all that a king's son shall have, how the sails of his ship shall be of golden web and the ropes of silk, and how the finest brandy kegs shall be broached for him and the plumpest bullock be killed for his banqueting. Verse after verse that old woman sang, each verse the expression of a people's joy, and when after she had sung for nearly a quarter of an hour I took her hand to thank her it seemed to me I was holding a piece of frail old ivory fashioned a thousand years ago.

The words of that song and the melody were preserved by Father John MacMillan, but those who hear it will not hear that rare old lady, nor see the ebony roof of her small house, nor hear the roar of the Atlantic upon the magical beaches of Barra when the music is stilled.

It was with the words of that song in my mind and the lilt of it in my ears that I went on to Eriskay. As we sailed to Loch Boisdale past the coast of the beloved island I had left I thought of the words of that old Barraman in the time of the great potato famine when more food was being offered to those who would abandon the Faith and turn Protestant.

"No, no," he said in refusal. "Almighty God has set a ring of gold round Barra and I would not be the one to break it."

How many people know that the Society for the Promotion of Christian Knowledge still draws £2,000 annually from the Royal bounty, given by George II to help their work of exterminating Gaelic and Latin in the West Highlands and Islands?

That brief sojourn on Eriskay is still as vivid as a waking dream of morn.

The parish priest was Father William Gillies, who had gone to the Scots College in Rome when he was only sixteen and who had a command of Italian dialects and Italian stories nobody else I have known came within leagues of approaching. To hear him giving an argument between an elderly priest from the Abruzzi and a conceited young priest from Florence was a masterpiece which even Peter Ustinov might have envied.

The Presbytery was a storm-swept granite house built by Father Allan McDonald, that figure revered by Gaelic scholars and still cherished in the memory of the people of Eriskay; the mere company of Father 'Willie' warmed it.

Alexander MacGill, my schoolmaster friend from Glasgow, had come to meet me with Margaret MacInnes, whose astonishing voice, the deepest contralto I ever heard, I had been successful in getting recorded. Here too was Mrs Macleod, a schoolmistress at blessed Morar who as a girl had sung for Mrs Kennedy Fraser the famous Eriskay love-lilt which would otherwise have been lost.

I could not have had a better companion for that emotional experience of mine than Alexander MacGill. As he reads that assertion I hope he will remember sitting in the Loch Boisdale Hotel with Father John MacMillan and when Father John went out of the room a small commercial traveller's coming up to us and asking if that portly priest with the resounding laugh was the Free Church Minister.

"Yes, yes," I quickly said, "that is the Free Church Minister."

And I still see the puzzled expression on the face of that little commercial traveller when Father John comes back and resumes his boisterous tales.

When I returned to London in the middle of August I gave a broadcast about Eriskay from which I quote:

"The island of Eriskay is not easily reached. So much by way of preface to what I can tell you about it. Hardly more than three miles long and not much more than a mile wide, it lies between the islands of South Uist and Barra in the southern half of the Outer Hebrides However, its accessibleness is of no importance to-night because I am not trying to lure visitors thither, and desire nothing more than to try to recapture for a few sympathetic listeners the landscape and the story of a dream. I shall probably not succeed. Dreams are incommunicable affairs.

"On that wet twenty-third of July in the year 1745 a French brig stood in from the East after eluding the English ships warned by Hanoverian spies of Prince Charles Edward's dash from France to win a crown for his father—*de jure* James the Eighth of Scotland and Third of England. Eriskay was chosen because from there it would

N

be easy to send word to Macdonald of Boisdale of the Prince's arrival
on this desperate quest. Boisdale's house was in South Uist just across
the Sound. The remains of the old walled garden are still visible.
The Clanranald Chieftains were Catholic; the Prince felt that if he
could count on the loyalty of any of his Scottish subjects he could
count on theirs.

"A fortnight later (but in years themselves one hundred and
eighty-four years later) I stood on the flowery knoll above that beach
of smooth white sand and saw in fancy the brig standing in once
more from the Minch, the south wind in her sails. It was not a grey
drizzling morning like that ill-fated twenty-third of July in 1745; it
was warm and radiant. The sea was calm, outspread in hues of vivid
green and blue and purple, of heliotrope and indigo and glittering
aquamarine. Full-breasted clouds of snowy cumulus idled across the
sky. It was June again up here, or so it seemed upon that knoll, so
sweet and sharp was the scent of the new-mown grass in the small
meadows among the braes sloping up from the sea. The bluebells
were out, the real bluebells, not the wild hyacinths called bluebells in
England, and up here a few primroses had lingered to greet them.
The crimson of the knapweed, the clouded yellow of lady's bedstraw
in profusion, corn-marigolds and clover, eyebright and ragged
robins, thyme and tansy and meadowsweet—oh, and far too many
other flowers to mention grew as thick as you may see them in the
picture of a child's fairy book. I have to search some time before I
found a flower of the famous convolvulus. I had been told it would
have bloomed away by now; but at last I found two blossoms. Legend
says that the Prince when he landed dropped the seeds of this convolvulus and that it has grown on this knoll and only on this knoll
ever since.

"I found later that this convolvulus grows on Belleisle where the
Prince waited wearily that summer for the promised brig and I have
no doubt that he idly picked some of the seed and put it in his pocket,
from which it fell when he stumbled ashore.

"That pink flower barred with white and shaped like an elfin
parachute is known as the Prince's Flower. It grows nowhere else
on any other island of the Hebrides. . . .

"I could believe in Eriskay many far less credible legends than that
of the Prince's convolvulus. I could believe that the rocks immediately
below the Prince's knoll did turn red on that fatal April morning
nine months later when the ungenerous Cumberland triumphed at
Culloden and turned himself into a butcher. Those red rocks strike

ominously upon the eye. Nowhere else are they to be seen on
Eriskay, which is indeed in the colour of its rocks of a grey that
might be called intense, such a positive, such a conspicuous greyness
is it. . . . Houses, rocks, sky, sea, and twilight all combine to produce
a grey which assails the senses with a more tremendous effect of
colour than the most lustrous scarlet could achieve. And in the grey
of twilight time stands motionless, nay rather it does not exist, so
that one walks along that narrow road, which seems to flow round
the island, more like a stream than a road, almost without being
aware of progress; and as from London I look back over last week I
seem to behold my wraith still walking in Eriskay, as when in childhood we fancied that one might enter the pattern of the curtains on
the wall-paper or the willow-pattern plate and live within it a quieter
and freer and yet always a more adventurous life. I did not find it
difficult to behold in those few red rocks among that immemorial
grey symbol of the blood that landing of the Prince was doomed to
shed."

Now as I record that first visit to Eriskay of nearly forty years ago
I play with the fancy that the *genius loci* approved of what I said that
night into the microphone and that it would reward me with the
inspiration to write *Whisky Galore* and so celebrate another landing
on Eriskay almost two centuries after the Prince's year. Once again
was heard *The Silver Whistle*, this time piped by a boatswain to
abandon ship and leave the cargo of the S.S. *Politician* to be enjoyed
by those who deserved to enjoy it. What is more, in memory of the
brig *Du Teillay* that brought the Prince to Eriskay, the *genius loci*
taught the French how to enjoy *Whisky à Gogo*. But the story of that
must wait until my eighth Octave.

I received a lot of kind letters after that broadcast, among them a
proposal of marriage which I discreetly destroyed. It came from a
young widow in the south of England who said she so much liked
the sound of my voice that she felt we should be well suited to one
another. I was not to suppose that she was a woman looking desperately for a husband. She had a beautiful house and an income of
£4,000. Could we not meet?

I wrote to thank her but had to tell her that there was an insuper-
able barrier to our marriage in that I was already married. So for
that charming young widow somewhere in the south of England I
remained *vox et praeterea nihil*.

And that brings me to the new paper. Five days after that broadcast a board meeting of the directors of *Vox* decided to offer me a

contract to contribute a weekly editorial at an annual salary of £2,000 as editor.

For some time Christopher Grieve had been feeling restless at Montrose, and I suggested that, if he was determined to move for a while to London, it would be a good idea for him to act as London editor of *Vox* in the same way as Christopher Stone was editor of *The Gramophone*. I felt that his salary as such should be my responsibility because apart from a weekly editorial, I was unable to devote myself entirely to *Vox* and carry on with my own work. Eric Maschwitz suggested that Philip Jordan should be taken on as sub-editor, in which position he did invaluable work.

As soon as *Gallipoli Memories* went off to Cassell's toward the end of June I started work on *Athenian Memories*, though with all my other interests work on it was much interrupted.

At the end of September I went up with Faith to the Mòd at Perth. I was naturally anxious to get her interested in Gaelic music and song and I was delighted when she and Lady Elspeth Campbell took to one another.

I was due to appear at Manchester in October at the Radio Exhibition that was being held there. We felt it was vital for me to do all I could to make the Radio manufacturers and dealers interested in *Vox*, the first number of which was due to appear at the beginning of November.

In answer to a request I sent the following message, which expresses perfectly my own feeling about what was still being regarded by the great majority as an amusing toy:

"Let us remember that the B.B.C. will celebrate only its seventh birthday next month. That means to say we are still many years away from being able to gauge its full social and cultural significance. It is because I feel with what is the missionary fervour of a convert that so much of the future of Art depends upon the way Radio is used that I am devoting myself to it. I believe profoundly that Radio (to which will undoubtedly be added Television) is going to revolutionize human thought and human action as completely as did the invention of printing.

"In the great future that lies before Radio the provincial centres will play a part of ever-increasing importance, and Manchester is to be wholeheartedly congratulated on realising this and initiating so splendid an exhibition."

I cannot remember exactly when it was, but I had been invited to see a demonstration of Baird's television. It was a queer experience sitting in the dark and watching ghostly figures with their bones showing wavering across the screen.

The day after I sent that message I attended the first lunch of the newly formed Wine and Food Society at the Connaught Rooms, at which, as I remember, Michael Sadleir was in the chair. I have regrettably lost the menu, but I recall a marvellous dish of quails with grapes all round them. I recall even more zestfully a Montrachet '22 the equal of which I have never drunk since. Now, 1922 was a poor year for all wines; why it should have produced that memorable white burgundy is a mystery. We wound up with two *marcs de Bourgogne* which I tasted for the first time; no wonder I left the menu behind me. The effect of those two *marcs* was that I swam out of the Connaught Rooms about two feet above the ground and continued to swim along Oxford Street until I swam through the iron gateway of Dryden Chambers and as with the wings of a dream reached our flat on the top floor. There Faith and Chrissie packed my suitcase; I swam down again into Oxford Street and alighted in a taxi which drove me to Euston. A porter took my suitcase and I swam along beside him to a first-class compartment, into which I swam through the opened door, to alight on a corner-seat where I fell instantly fast asleep, to wake up at Manchester as sober as the Lord Chancellor himself. That effect of wine was an unique experience and I have been sensible enough never to attempt to recapture it.

There was a jolly dinner at the Midland Hotel at which I met for the first time Edward Liveing who was head of the regional station of the B.B.C. at Manchester. 'Ted' Liveing was to remain a close friend of mine until his death. It may have been I who put him up for the Savile, of which he was a well-loved member. At this date B.B.C. regional stations always complained of too much interference from London, and next day, to Ted Liveing's gratification, I made a fiery speech, demanding more freedom for regional stations.

In November the first number of *Vox* appeared. The new weekly was given a friendly welcome by the Press but the failure of the radio manufacturers to support us as they should have done with advertisements made me ask myself whether I had been too soon with *Vox*. Were people yet ready to take Radio as seriously as they should take it? I had been so lucky in founding *The Gramophone* at exactly the right moment and the recording companies had had the foresight to recognize that it was the right moment by helping us with generous advertising. Had I mistimed the moment for *Vox*? The next few weeks would show. I was worried; I did not like the idea of people losing money through my optimism.

What seemed at first the breakdown of the whole economy of the United States on that disastrous October 23rd when the stock market crashed was having repercussions on this side of the Atlantic. I was disquieted to get a warning from the *Sunday Pictorial* that they might have to give up my weekly review of records unless they received better advertizing support. In the end I agreed to accept £750 a year for a shorter column in 1930, at the end of which time a decision would be made whether or not the feature should continue.

The publication of *Gallipoli Memories* took my mind away from worrying about *Vox*. It had been made the choice of the month by the newly formed Book Club, and I know it gave Hugh Walpole genuine pleasure to do this. The reviews were mostly favourable, but inevitably I had to be rebuked by a few for having apparently enjoyed so much of my experience. There were also the anti-Churchill lot; at this date he was not in favour, and when the 'National' Government was formed in 1931 he was left out of it. The *Civil and Military Gazette* of Lahore, Kipling's old paper, said "Mr Compton Mackenzie has some strange ideas of strategy, almost as strange as those of Mr Winston Churchill whom he seems to admire so much."

It was not until November 19th that Sir Ian Hamilton wrote:

After so many days it is pleasant to see you in your reach-me-down khaki and to tramp once more in your company the deck of the old Arcadian. So far I've only read about a quarter of the book but I feel moved to write you at once and let you know that if you can keep up to the end as you have begun, you will have beat yourself to blazes and put Achi Baba on to the top of Sinister Street.

My bones seem to tell me that by introducing Humour . . . you have produced nothing less than life. . . . Believe me, whatever the success or failure of your book may be at this moment, you have done a big thing which will live.

On November 22nd Sir Ian was writing in his own hand:

Still enjoying your book and feel I have so much to thank you for personally that I'd like to do it in person. My wife and I both hope you will be able to come and lunch with us on Wednesday next.

After that lunch Lady Hamilton told me that when my book arrived at 1 Hyde Park Gardens the General had left it unopened for over a fortnight. Then one night he had taken it up to his little bedroom, and when he came downstairs in the morning he was whistling.

"You don't know how happy you have made him."

There was a tear in my eye when I told that beautiful and great-hearted woman how fortunate I was to have been able to blot out that 'inkpot Iago', Ashmead Bartlett.

On December 12th Sir Ian wrote:

I only finished the book last night. My reason for taking so long over what I was tempted to devour at one sitting is, simply, that I began to get so many letters from people asking me this, that and the other that I found it a great help to be able to say to them truthfully that I had only read as far as the 70th page. . . .

As to the book itself, I can only say that it is inimitable. The world has been swamped with heavy, serious stuff and it is a relief to get away with you into the real life of the war-time which was half fun, half tragedy.

All through, I had it in my mind to try and make some suggestion as regards either the facts or the proportions you had mixed your bitters and your sweets but, really, I have nothing of that sort to say.

No one could put it better than yourself when you say if you had kept a proper diary you would have been tempted to overload the book. That's so perfectly right. . . .

You know how grateful I am to you for the way you have treated me. If ever it would interest you I could show you an extraordinarily veneomous leader written by Ashmead Bartlett in the American World *at the time my last despatch was published.*

I received a very large number of letters about *Gallipoli Memories*, and I indulge myself by printing two or three that gave me particular pleasure.

The late Lord Hankey wrote:

. . . Apart from meeting yourself and some other interesting people I look back to my visit with mixed feelings, which include bitter disappointment at the Suvla failure. It was a difficult mission which, though not unwelcome as bringing me into touch with realities, was unsought. In your kindly and friendly way you reveal the delicacy of my task. I think though that it did good, as, when I got home I had all sorts of things sent out—more small craft, a meteorologist, who forecast the right weather for the evacuation, and a lot of details.

It is interesting too to see oneself as others see one. I thought myself rather sprightly and almost debonair. Your picture is quite different! But I have no doubt it is the more correct one. Anyhow, it is very kindly, and I thank you for it. . . .

General Gouraud, the 'Lion of the Argonne', then Military
Governor of Paris, wrote from the Hôtel des Invalides:

Mon cher Camarade,

*Comme vous le pensez bien, tout ce qui se rapporte à l'Expedition de
Gallipoli m'interesse au plus haut point, puisque c'est là que j'ai connu de mes
yeux la bravoure britannique et l'accord parfait qui existait entre les hommes
aussi bien entre les États-Majors et les officiers. Cette amitié de guerre a tenu
jusqu'au bout et c'est ce qui nous a permis d'aller jusqu'à la victoire.*

*A mon avis, comme à celui de tous qui réfléchissent, elle est toujours aussi
nécessaire pour maintenir la Paix du monde.*

We had drifted apart from France during this decade. As I had
written bitterly, "The romantic liaison with France is over. England
wants to return to her loving wife, Germany. And now England is
hurt because a former mistress is asking for a financial settlement. It
is so unromantic. England will pay for this reconciliation as soon as
her dear wife feels secure enough to don the trousers again." Alas,
how right I was!

One of the most heart-warming letters I received came from
'Kiddy' Loring, now a Vice-Admiral retired. I included in Octave 5
some of what I wrote about my time with him in Tenedos when he
was temporarily Governor there after the loss of the battleship *Ocean*
in the March attempt to force the Dardanelles.

My dear old chap,

*How delightful of you and how like you to write such a charming epic of
our happy days together at Tenedos—to immortalize me as one of the central
figures in it. . . .*

*So you have not forgotten!! Nor indeed have I. And if it means anything
to you rest assured that you have held a very warm place in my affections, all
these years.*

*How often have I nearly written or taken some steps to get into touch with
you again! And if these impulses have remained unfulfilled I have in the meantime read with great pleasure all your published writings, and have recently
heard your voice here in this room telling about the charm of the Channel
Islands, the companionableness of Siamese cats, etc. . . . and the familiar
tones have reduced the last 14 years to as many days.*

*Your memory of detail . . . is marvellous. I thrilled to find even Tino
immortalized by name!* [Tino was a pony.] *And I have ridden (and raced!)
every mile of our adventures over again, and have laughed with you again as
we rode. . . . I have often wondered whether the book of those days would ever
be written. You sometimes talked of writing it after a lapse of years, but it*

might well have been crowded out by your many other post-war activities. Let us meet again. . . .

Yours ever

E. K. Loring

I was glad to get a letter from Sir Robert Graves[1] approving of the book. 'Bob' Graves, an uncle of the poet, had a mind of deadly accuracy and he would have jumped hard on any inaccuracy in my memory.

It is by far the best thing that has been written about the Dardanelles adventure and brings things back to me with amazing vividness. Also I am grateful to you for refraining from disquisitions on the morality or otherwise of War, and its reactions on those engaged in it, of which I think we have had too much of late. You tell a true story of things as you saw them and readers can draw their own conclusions.

Robert Graves, who was now over seventy, probably had a larger experience of the Levant than any man alive. Like myself, he was feeling contemptuous of those who following the fashion of the twittering 'twenties had dared to sneer at the 'romantic' young men who had died for their country. That attitude is recurrent in the sexy 'sixties when I am writing of my life and times.

It is a relief to quote a letter of 1960 from a former petty-officer of the Hood battalion of the Royal Naval Division:

You mentioned a few gentlemen (officers) which it was my great pleasure to be associated with as I knew them personally, being in contact with them each day, namely Arthur Asquith, F. S. Kelly, B. Freyberg, V.C., P. Shaw-Stewart, Charles Lister, Denis Brown, and many more. Well, you say that you would like to know what became of Hon. Charles Lister, well, he was killed in August or September 1915 in the trenches on the east side of Achi Baba. I was present when it happened in the afternoon. . . . Patrick-Shaw Stewart came from Gallipoli with us to France, and on December 17th, 1917, on Welsh Ridge he was killed in the morning about 5.30 a.m., he was at the time the commanding officer of the Hood Battalion and I write to say it was I who took the last order from him and that order was to contact Arthur Asquith to take charge, sorry to say Arthur Asquith took the report and we both went back to the line together, but young Asquith was wounded badly in the action started by the Germans, as they were dressed up in white smocks as you will see in grocery stores, and of course it was snowing at the time. Poor old Arthur Asquith, he was a good pal to me. . . . F. S. Kelly the pianist he was killed

[1] The late Sir Robert Graves, K.C.M.G.

at Beaucourt on November 13th, 1916. Poor old Kelly, he was always writing string music or something he told me, he was even writing it on the beach after we landed in Gallipoli. I remember them taking Rupert Brooke to the French Hospital Ship where he died in the afternoon April 23rd, 1915. I had one or two conversations with him as I was interested in poetry. Denis Brown the composer was killed on June 4th, 1915. I knew him well. Bernard Freyberg, V.C., the Hood boys worshipped him, always commanded respect, a real gentleman and first-class soldier. Hope I have enlightened you regarding Lister, Stewart, Kelly etc.

To me that letter is a fragment of the *Iliad*.

One more letter. This was from F. F. Urquhart, the much loved Sligger who had been my tutor when I was lucky enough to choose 919-1273 for my History School period. By that choice I was able to enjoy the essence of Balliol as well as that of Magdalen, my own college.

The Acland Nursing Home
Banbury Road
Oxford
27.12.29

Dear Monty,

   I read your book with intense interest and pleasure. It helped me through the first days here. I had to have an operation for rupture, which keeps me in bed for some time. The book reminded me of so many things I had been through twenty years ago for I was in Constantinople in 1909 and came back through the Dardanelles to Kavalla. I remember the Straits very well, but I was then more interested in the windy plains of Troy than in the hills of the Peninsula. I remember so well seeing Samothrace rising like a mountain in the middle of Imbros. We called at Dedesagatch and remained there till sunset. The western horizon had been clouded, but as the sun set the clouds thinned and the sunset was a golden crimson one. Just after the sun had gone down, I suddenly noticed a darker crimson cone in the middle of the sunset, becoming more and more clear as the sun sank lower. I think I guessed almost at once what it was, Athos, an experience very much parallel to yours in your last chapter. But of course the book interested me for more serious things than that. So full of people one knew, and also of people whom you make one know, and suggesting so many problems about the War and our conduct of it as a nation and as individuals, which I should like very much to discuss with you some day, though I shall probably never get the chance. Finally, let me say, as being a temporary invalid, that I was amazed at your power of overcoming the

*weakness and the despondency which your very bad health must have made at
times almost overpowering.*

Goodbye for the present,

Yours ever

F. F. U.

*This is the first real letter I have ever tried to dictate (Business letters are not
real letters). I should love to go on writing about your book.*

By chance a copy of the letter I dictated from Jethou on January
1st, 1930, has survived:

My dear Sligger,

*I shall have to dictate a letter to you because I am in bed myself at the
moment with one of those wretched goes of sciatica. I am very glad you
enjoyed* Gallipoli Memories, *but very sorry to hear you are in the Acland.
I can't somehow imagine your being ill, but I hope it is not going to last long.*

*I had a letter from the Master of Univ. the other day, asking me to present
a MS. to the Bodleian, and I have presented the second part of* Sinister
Street, *which I was writing when we had that walk I mentioned in* Gallipoli
Memories.

*One gets used to being ill and it becomes more or less easy to live outside
illness and pain. I am setting out on the task of writing* Athenian Memories,
*which I must confess for the moment almost dismays me with the difficulty of
their convincing presentation.*

Get well soon and enjoy a Happy New Year

Yours ever

Monty

On that same 1st January Sir Michael Sadler wrote from The
Master's Lodgings, University College, Oxford:

*May I say that I never got a letter which delighted me more than yours. . . .
We shall treasure your precious manuscript and will give it the best binding
we can devise. Please accept our grateful thanks on behalf of Bodley and the
future.*

On January 13th the Master wrote:

*The glorious gift for Bodley has come and I write again to say what a
privilege it is to hand over the precious document to the Librarian of the
Bodleian.*

November and December had been strenuous months. I did
several broadcasts. I was in Scotland for a fortnight where, apart
from political speeches in various town, I was the guest of various

associations with an after-dinner speech at each. I spoke in Glasgow at the dinner of the Caledonian Catholic Association to celebrate the centenary of Catholic Emancipation.

When the future of *Vox* became more clouded I made an effort to convince the Radio trade that *Vox* was a venture worthy of their support. Unfortunately the Radio trade was still under the delusion that only a few eccentrics wanted Radio to provide listeners with anything but light music and comic turns. Unfortunately, too, some of the high-ups at Savoy Hill resented some of the criticism in *Vox*. The result was that Eric Maschwitz was not allowed to give us the support of the *Radio Times* on which I had counted when I planned to start our weekly.

I nearly missed getting to Jethou for Christmas; so fierce was the weather I had to hire a stouter craft than the *Melusine* and somehow in the heaviest sea in which I had ever crossed from Guernsey, I managed to land on Jethou, feeling like a melting pillar of salt.

Then came the news that Christopher Grieve had fallen either in getting on or off a motor-bus and was suffering from concussion. However, he was back again in Soho Square within ten days, working as hard as ever with *Vox*.

I on the other hand was in bed and between bad goes of pain trying to get on with *Athenian Memories*.

Newman Flower wrote to say that, although *Gallipoli Memories* had been a success, he thought it would be wise to publish a novel in between my war memories. I was upset at first but on reflection I realized that Flower was right. I felt I could not count on *Vox's* lasting nor on the *Sunday Pictorial*, and the £500 apiece I should get for my books of war memories would need the financial buttress of a novel. Which novel should I write next? I was in such infernal pain on the edge of my forty-seventh birthday that I knew it would have to be a comic novel. For some odd reason the fight against pain always rallies beloved Thalia to my support. Even if I cannot laugh easily myself I can usually make other people laugh when I am in pain.

Apparently I did not waste any time in making up my mind which novel I should write next. In *More Than I Should* Faith wrote:

"For about ten minutes he was in a sort of despair but with his usual resilience decided that after all it was a good idea, dismissed *Athenian Memories* from his mind and began *April Fools*."

I am coming to the last year of my sixth Octave. When I started it I had intended to carry right on with my seventh. Now I realize that I am weary for the moment of reality and that I must retire into that comic world of my own from a sojourn in which I always emerge refreshed. I have been rebuked by one or two serious critics for failing to reveal my inner life in this long autobiography, but I cannot believe that pages of introversion, however subtly expressed, would be of the slightest interest even to myself. I have my own comic world which I enjoy so much that I want other people to enjoy it. So now in the mood that enabled me to put aside *Athenian Memories* and play with children in *April Fools* I am thinking of laying aside *My Life and Times* in order to take up the story of *The Red Tapeworm* and tell in *Paper Lives* how Sir Oliver Huffam, K.C.B., fared as Permanent Under-Secretary of the Ministry of Sanitation.

SOMEHOW I managed to get to London at the end of the month for a couple of nights and make one last desperate effort to persuade the Radio manufacturers to support *Vox*. It was no use. The directors had proposed to turn the paper into a monthly, but I felt sure that such a step would merely postpone the day of reckoning and that it would be wiser to surrender and allow the paper to die. The depression in the United States was having its effect on the gramophone trade and I knew that it might be all we could do presently to keep *The Gramophone* going. Indeed, I doubt if we should have managed to do so without the prudent skill of Cecil Pollard.

The people I was most sorry for were Togo Maclaurin and Jack Barrow, whose enthusiasm had ended in failure, not in any way from their own fault. Christopher Grieve was philosophic and having found a temporary job in Liverpool, wrote hopefully of other jobs in view.

"I am very grateful for the promise 'to see me through' if I fail to get placed. You have worries and difficulties enough without my adding to them."

Philip Jordan was soon at work again.

At the beginning of January I had cancelled all speaking engagements for the next four months, and among those I had to cancel was a series of gardening talks for the B.B.C. It was as well I took a gloomy prospect about my health. I was in bed from February 8th until March 24th, but I was able to send *April Fools* to Newman Flower on March 21st. It is as depressing to write about being ill as to be ill. I turn with relief to a letter from Sir Herbert Samuel in that January:

Here are three more examples of the misuse of literally I have come across recently;

1. 'He is literally here, there and everywhere.' (Paragraph in the News about myself, Feb. 1929.)

2. 'To this day I see his face exactly as I saw it then—stricken and defiant, blazing with an anger that seemed literally volcanic.' (J. A. Spender of Parnell in 1890. Life, Journalism and Politics, Vol. 1, p. 44.)

3. 'In this case, the wish was literally father to the thought.' (Oxford Undergraduate's Essay.)

In February he sent me a literally from the *Manchester Guardian* from the notice of a play called *Frankenstein*.

> *'The Monster, made in the laboratory, slowly coming to life makes a perfect scene of Grand Guignol, and his death in an avalanche on the Jura Mountains is noisy enough literally to bring down the house.'*

I particularly enjoyed this example because it was so typical of a *Manchester Guardian* writer to avoid a split infinitive with his 'literally'.

I replied with a 'swarm' of literallys.

> *Somebody who had involved himself in political trouble in Rumania was said to have reached the frontier and found he had literally driven into a hornets' nest. Last Sunday in the* Sunday Pictorial *the forwards of some team literally swarmed round the goal, and in another Sunday paper readers were told that Savoy Hill was literally a hive.*

On April 3 Charles Morgan wrote from the Garrick:

> *I'm going to Athens for* The Times, *leaving England on April 22. I'm taking my wife with me, and, when my job is done, about May 8 or 9, we contemplate a holiday in that part of the world. We must be in England again by June 17 so we cannot go far afield, and should be eternally grateful if you would suggest a good place where we can be lazy and swim and not be pestered by tourists. We thought of Rhodes, but are in fear lest it be too hot . . . moreover, the Italians may have converted it into a Lido.*

I have a copy of the letter I wrote:

> *Rhodes is enchanting, completely enchanting. The Italians have, I believe, put up a big hotel there which is, I am told, very comfortable. The climate is perfection. Rhodes is like Oxford with olives instead of elms and palms instead of planes. Of course, I was only there during the war when there was no big hotel.*
>
> *Another excellent place is the Island of Poros (not Paros) which is quite close to the mainland of Greece and, as no doubt you will remember, is where Hippolytus was trying to do a Kaye Don trick along the beach, and was laid out by Aphrodite. There are orange groves at one point almost down to the water's edge. I don't know if your wife is a good sailor (you of course must be) but if she is it seems a pity you shouldn't get round to several of the islands, in which case Syra is the best centre, though it can be as hot as hell in June. Don't forget that the Aegean is rough four days out of a week in the summer; it is only always calm for about a fortnight in April and in October. Should*

you visit any islands do not miss Delos which is an amazing experience and is most easily reached from Syra via Mykonos.

When you start one off talking about Greece, I want to tell you to see so much that I had better shut up. Let me beg you not to drink any wine except retsinato, however unpleasant you find it at first, and eat plenty of garlic if you can. Be sure to take a mosquito net and get a lightly-smoked pair of glasses. Forgive me if I am sending golden apples to the Hesperides with this advice; when I came back from Greece the south of Italy seemed almost misty compared with that brilliant air, and smoked glasses at mid-day are necessary. Rhodes has a softer climate; if you go there be sure not to miss Cos, but Calymnos is hardly worth getting off the boat for nowadays. And you must *see Patmos.*

Charles Morgan wrote back from 6 More's Garden, Cheyne Walk:

It was good of you to trouble to tell me so much—and to tell it in a way that makes the travellers eager for their journey. Rhodes it shall be . . . Oxford with olives and palms is irresistible.

Whether I can face retsinato I doubt. I tried once in Corfu. It is worse than OZO (which I can't spell or drink). Why do the Greeks drink such filthy drinks? I will struggle with garlic and certainly shall bless you whenever I look out of smoked glasses or crawl inside a mosquito net. Your letter shall go with us and be our bible.

I have taken an opportunity to print that letter of mine because I get a good many letters from people asking my advice about a holiday in Greece, and now I can refer them to this page.

I gave myself the pleasure of dedicating *April Fools* to P. G. Wodehouse. He wrote on March 27th from the Beefsteak Club:

Dear Monty,

How awfully nice of you. I can't think of anything I should appreciate more. A sequel to Poor Relations *is almost too good to be true, even without its being dedicated to me. Golly, how I shall devour it. . . . You can't realize how bucked I am about that dedication.*

Yours ever

Plum

On August 21st I was writing to Wodehouse:

My dear Plummy:

I have just seen a copy of the American edition of April Fools *in which Dorans have made an April Fool of me and you by printing at the head of it 'Dedicated with affection and gratitude to Raymond Savage'. I don't know who Raymond Savage is, and I now wonder which of Doran's authors has his*

book dedicated to you. It is almost a theme for one of your short stories. Your
English copy of April Fools *is waiting until you come back from Hollywood.*

But Wodehouse did not come as soon as I hoped and I sent the
English edition to 724 Linden Drive, Beverley Hills, California.

On October 25, 1930 he wrote:

Dear Monty,

*The book has just arrived and I am most awfully bucked by the dedication.
I read it in the American edition directly it came out and howled with laughter
over it. It is every bit as good as Poor Relations and what a treat it is to meet
my favourite characters again.*

How curious that was about the dedication in the American edition. . . .

*Why don't you come out here and look the place over? I rather shrank from
coming here, but I have enjoyed my first six months very much and am starting
another six next week.*

*Till you get used to it, you have a forlorn feeling of being landed in some
outlying colony, like Hongkong, but one soon settles down. We have a nice
house with a small garden, which contains a big swimming-pool, and that
makes all the difference. I swim four times a day, and as far as I can make out,
shall be able to all through the winter.*

*I don't have to go to the studio unless I want to, and what work they have
given me so far has been very easy.*

*I see absolutely nothing of Hollywood life. I am about as secluded as you
are at Jethou. The only drawback is that the place is exactly like a London
suburb, long rows of houses each with a small garden. I do long sometimes for
a bit of open country. . . .*

Yours ever

Plum

The proofs of *April Fools* were corrected by April 20th and I was
able to brag that in spite of bronchitis, a vile eczema and the usual
attacks of sciatica, I had written a novel of 120,000 words and seen
it through to press in three months. Newman Flower's encouragement and financial help through that difficult time had been priceless and I am glad to remember that a year later I was able to give
that tormented manuscript as a wedding present to young Desmond
Flower whose own beautiful handwriting was such a contrast to
mine. I look back too with gratitude to the laughter of Chrissie and
Nellie when I read it to them chapter by chapter: I was in such
damnable discomfort myself that I could hardly believe I was
managing to be funny.

o

While I was writing, besides the continuous accompaniment of music from the gramophone, I was able with a portable wireless to listen to opera in Rome, Milan, Prague and elsewhere.

Faith was at Dryden Chambers for most of the spring, working hard at her life of Christina of Sweden. I was glad when she was able to go to Capri at Easter with John and Christine Mavrogordato and their two boys.

Earlier this year the Adjutant of the 1st Bn. The Sikh Regiment (King George's Own) had written to Cassell's to ask for an autographed copy of *Gallipoli Memories* for the mess, and I was lucky enough to find among my papers the original despatch I had written after the battle of the Fourth of June, which was printed in the *Westminster Gazette*. This I sent to the regiment.

From Colonel Heath I received the following:

> Nowshera
> N.W. Frontier
> India
> 23 March 1930

Dear Mr Compton Mackenzie,

It is difficult to express, adequately, how deeply we appreciate the valuable gift you have made to the officers of the Battalion which it is now my privilege to command, a privilege I might add which would never have fallen to my lot had it not been for that very action of the 4th June 1915 described so vividly by you in Gallipoli Memories. There is but one British Officer, Capt. R. A. Savory,[1] surviving to-day and he, yet, too junior to be considered for command.

Your inspiring account of the part played by the 14th Sikhs will, I know, have results infinitely more far reaching than you could have foreseen when the events of that day were recorded by you.

In the words of our Infantry Training Manual, 'Battle is above everything else a struggle for morale'.

To cultivate morale is, thus, our foremost duty and one which we endeavour to accomplish by inculcating discipline and that mainly through the medium of drill and such comparatively dull devices.

There is, however, a further, a more penetrating and durable method and that is by recounting the past deeds of the Regiment, a means which, unfortunately, is generally beyond the scope of the average officer whose imagination needs to be stimulated to enable him to make the desired impression upon his audience.

It is the good fortune of but few Regiments to have in their possession an

---

[1] Lt.-Gen. Sir Reginald Savory, K.C.I.E., C.B., D.S.O., M.C.

account of any one of its Actions described by a master hand with just that vision and touch which stirs the imagination and gives the requisite stimulus to enable one object to be achieved.

We are now, through your hand, the proud possessors of just such an account, and, when in the future we are confronted by the acid test of battle, we shall have the certain knowledge that a fixed determination to maintain the tradition of the regiment, whatever the cost, will have been so instilled through the medium of your writing, that there can be no question as to what the result will be.

I am, Sir,
Very gratefully yours

L. M. Heath[1]

I should not meet 'Piggy' Heath until 1948 in Kenya. He had commanded the 3rd India Corps in Malaya and endured imprisonment by the Japanese. What a pleasure it was to tell him how much my own morale had been stimulated by receiving that letter of his eighteen years earlier. What paladins they were, those officers of the old Indian Army! That letter I have quoted makes me feel very humble.

At the end of April I went north where after speechifying in three or four places I was due in Inverness to open the Northern Counties Musical Festival at the beginning of May. Sir Richard Terry was the adjudicator and we were both staying in the Station Hotel.

One morning at breakfast he said to me,

"What a relief it is to talk to a dyed in the wool Catholic. I get very tired of converts."

"Yes," I agreed. "I must confess I do sometimes find converts a bit too earnest. Yes, it's been great fun talking to you."

"But I *am* a convert," Terry said.

"So am I," I told him.

We had a good laugh.

"I've just had news of another convert this morning—Ronnie Knox has written to Lady Lovat," said Terry. "She is coming to Inverness for the festival and I'm to lunch with her here."

That lunch at the Station Hotel was to be a landmark in my life.

With their mother were Magdalen,[2] Hugh[3] and Veronica,[4] and I felt immediately as if I had known them all my life.

[1] The late Lt.-Gen. Sir Lewis Heath, K.B.E., C.B., C.I.E., D.S.O., M.C.
[2] Countess of Eldon.
[3] Rt. Hon. Hugh Fraser, M.P.
[4] Hon. Lady Maclean.

Magdalen was now not far from seventeen and already as tall as Mary, Queen of Scots; Hugh was at Ampleforth Junior School. It had been decided it was time he went to a prep. school after he and Veronica had gone up to the top of the tower at Beaufort Castle with the intention of parachuting from it under a couple of umbrellas. They were stopped just as they were stepping off.

"Isn't Hugh lucky?" Veronica exclaimed that May day.

I asked her what particular stroke of luck he had enjoyed.

"He was born before the war was over—nearly a year before it was over," she added with a sigh.

"When were you born?"

"Not for more than two years after the Armistice. But I'll be ten in December."

I have written of my fortunate friendships with little girls. With this confidence of a little girl's regret began another.

I was fascinated by the atmosphere of Beaufort Castle. Laura Lovat was about ten years younger than myself but her taste coincided exactly with mine; the Medici prints of great pre-Raphaelite painters; the Morris wall-papers; the love of flowers: the world of what seemed already once upon a time. We talked of that Oxford just before the war, of her brother Charles Lister, of Patrick Shaw Stewart and how many others. When she heard that I was bent on finding a house in the North she said what a pity it was that Eilean Aigas was let, although there was a chance that the present tenants might be giving it up in the autumn. This was the house built on an island of the Beauly river by a previous Lord Lovat for that fantastic pair of dreamers, the Sobieski Stuarts. We went to look at Eilean Aigas, and I made up my mind that if by chance it should be given up I would become the tenant of it. I shall not describe Eilean Aigas in this Octave; it must wait until Octave 7, which will be dedicated to Frasers and Maxwells galore.

One day we drove up Glen Strathfarrar, now almost desolate for all its fourteen miles. Two hundred men from Strathfarrar had fought at Waterloo, fifty had fought in the Crimea; there had been only two to fight in the Great War. Half way up the Glen was an empty shepherd's cottage. I asked if I might have it as a retreat. Veronica thought this was a capital notion and immediately announced she would come and live there with me.

That time in May was all too brief. By the eighth of the month I was bound for Glasgow, where I was due to meet Faith and Chrissie for a visit to Iona.

I had my first letter from Veronica:

Keir House
Sunday May 11
1930

Dear Mr Comp. etc.

I have arrived here safely, and I hope you have.

It is not a very nice country and too flat for my liking, I don't feel as free and wild as at Beaufort, but still we have great fun as there are lots of nice trees to climb and ponies to ride so we have great fun. There are such lots of glass and china and other valuable things in the house, that I am sure to breack fifty before I go away and come to Kile to catch the boat.

Do hurry up and send me the parcel with a long, long, letter.

I cannot send you the list of the house-hold things as I have to catch the post.

Lots of love

From

Veronica

She was staying with her aunt, Mrs Stirling of Keir; the Irene in her next letter is her cousin. She too would be a delight to me when we went to Eilean Aigas. The allusion to 'Barrar' in the next letter and to 'Kile' was a possibility of coming with Faith, Chrissie and me to Barra; but that was not to be for another two or three years.

Keir
Dunblane
Scotland
May 18th 1930

Dear Mr Comp. etc.

Thank you very very *much for the lovely book. I am longing to be at Barrar especially when I am at lessons. I wish I was doing Galic instead of beastly fractions and decimals and french verbs. Uch!*

I am having great fun when it is not lesson time, yesterday we went to a cinema and had a nice time there. Besides, I had someone to quarrel which is very nice, and although Irene wrestles pretty well she cannot get me on the ground very often. The worst of it is that I can't get her down as she is a good stone heavier and a bit broader.

Thanks awfully for book and postcard

Your loving

Veronica

By the time this letter reached me Faith, Chrissie and I were in Barra, staying with Father John MacMillan at the Presbytery in

Northbay. Faith and Chrissie had met me in Glasgow, whence we had gone by way of Oban to Iona. I had commissioned Mr A. Ritchie to design and make a silver challenge shield to be won at the Mòd by the school that gave the best performance of action songs. Mr Ritchie promised that this beautiful example of his art should be ready in time for this year's Mòd at the end of September in Dunoon. Father John provided the Gaelic inscription.

> *Thig Gaol is Ceol a Iar*
> *Gu latha na Seachd Sian*
> *Sgiath Chompton MhicCoinnich*
> *As na Eileanan Sianta*

> Love and music shall come from the West
> Until the day of the Seven Whirlwinds
> The shield of Compton Mackenzie
> Of the Shiant Islands

I reflect with gratitude that as I record the design of that shield it will be competed for at the Mòd in Larg in this year 1965.

From Iona we drove across Mull to Tobermory and boarded the *Dunara Castle* for Barra. I shall say no more about that beloved island in this Octave because there will be so much about it in the next two Octaves.

Chrissie won Father John's heart by being able to aspirate 'l', the ability to do which was apparently by now confined to the people of Scarp.

I see her now on a June day demonstrating at Father John's instigation the aspirated 'l' to D. J. Macleod, the Chief Inspector of Schools for Inverness-shire, of whose visits to Kingussie Academy she had been in such awe not so long ago.

> Keir
> Dunblane
> Scotland
> *Sun. 8 June*
> *1930*

Dear Mr Comp. etc.

Thank you very *much for your* lovely *letter. Please don't explore the bay till I come.*

I am reading all your lovely stories in the Joy Street books. I like the Blanket Land and Candlelight Cottage best and I love all the others.

Do come soon to Keir it will be fun.

Don't come at half past 9, because I have my music lesson then and I like that but come at half past ten because I am doing beastly fractions then and I hate them.

Here is a list of the things we shall need for Tigh na da. [Tigh nan damh, House of the Stags, equally suitable for Mackenzies or Frasers.]

    The Kitchen

Tiles red and white a sheep-skin heart-rug.

Two cosy chairs and three wood ones, a round table, a dresser and Chinese curtains the same stuff as the arm-chairs.

    Your study oposite the kitchen.

    Also the library. On one side books.

    In the middle your desk, at the side a table for my sewing.

    Two other cosy chairs on each side of the fire.

    Your Bedroom

    A nice soft bed with an eiderdown and wash-stand.

    A sofa at the bottom of your bed Chince. A dressing-table and two chairs a window-box, Chinse curtains.

    My Bedroom

Nice soft bed. My own eider a sofa at the bottom of the bed washstand dressing-table.

    A cosy chair.

      The shed beside scullery.

                Your

                loving

                Veronica

P.S. Can you read it?

From Barra we went to Loch Boisdale where Christopher arrived in the *Dunara Castle*. On board was Wilson Ramsay, the member for the Western Isles, who was on his way to St Kilda to enquire into the contemplated evacuation of the island. Christopher and I decided to make the voyage to St Kilda, leaving Faith and Chrissie to go on to Tarbert where the *Dunara Castle* would be calling on her way back.

Wilson Ramsay, Christopher and I made our way slowly up the great amphitheatre of cultivated land surrounded by sheer cliffs about a thousand feet high by the edge of which at the summit we sat down, exhausted.

"You'd find a climb like this easier, Ramsay," I observed, "if you sported a kilt."

The Liberal member for the Western Isles was wearing the black coat and waistcoat and pin-striped trousers which a member of parliament felt was the correct attire in which to visit his constituency if he wanted his constituents to believe he really was an M.P.

"Oh, I do wear the kilt," he assured me as he mopped the sweat on his forehead. "Yes, indeed, Ramsay MacDonald congratulated me only the other day when I wore my kilt at a League of Nations banquet in Geneva. But in my constituency, well, you know, my dear fellow, how critical they are up here. They might suspect me of playing the laird if I wore the kilt."

As we walked down toward the straggling little street of this isolated community we saw the fishing-cruiser *Minna* dropping anchor, and presently a prostrate figure being carried ashore.

"Good heavens, do you see who that is?" Wilson Ramsay exclaimed. "It's Tom Johnston. I do hope there hasn't been an accident.

The Under-Secretary of State for Scotland had not been injured. He had merely been prostrated by sea-sickness during the voyage from the mainland. Soon he recovered sufficiently to confer with the islanders about their evacuation, to which they were strongly opposed.

By the shore was a gun emplacement in which was a virgin 9-inch gun. I was amused to hear that it had been landed and established to defend the island against German submarines on the day the Armistice was signed. I suppose that virgin gun is still there.

We had glorious weather when we got back to Tarbert next day, so glorious that we were able to go to the Shiants and spend two nights on the islands. Then Faith and Christopher went back south, crossing the Minch from Stornoway, and I settled down to work at *Athenian Memories*, answer innumerable letters, write articles and keep going my weekly review of gramophone records in the *Sunday Pictorial*. Nellie, who had been staying with friends in Aberdeenshire, joined Chrissie and me.

We left Tarbert at the end of July to go back to Jethou and stayed for a day or two at the Station Hotel in Mallaig, presided over by Monsieur Dauthieu and his two daughters, Marie and Rose. Here we enjoyed the best table in all Scotland. Ah, those *rillettes de Tours*, ah, those galantines! And with the wonderful food wonderful wines. Yet the miserable tourists were utterly unappreciative.

"Yes, it seems fairly good, but I wish they had some decent tinned tongue. I like a plate of tinned tongue or a ham that isn't too fat, better than this Frenchified food."

Just after that maddening remark I read Tom Johnston's speech

in the House of Commons explaining the reasons for the proposed
evacuation of St Kilda; I sent a letter to the *Oban Times*:

"Mr Tom Johnston landed on St Kilda with a mind obscured by
sea-sickness and he was in no condition to appreciate the real state
of affairs on the island; a more pusillanimous admission by the
member of any Government that his Party was incompetent to deal
with the problems of modern Scotland than Mr Johnston's statement
in the House of Commons on the subject of St Kilda I never read.
. . . Sentimental eloquence over nurses cannot disguise the feeble
handling of the St Kilda business, which is a clear sign that the town-
obsessed Labour Party intends to shirk all land problems. However,
my criticism of the Labour Government is not inspired by the least
respect or belief in either of its two rivals."

I must add as a postscript to that letter that ten years later I
should recognize Tom Johnston as the finest Secretary of State Scotland had ever had, and that he was right to evacuate the people of
St Kilda.

Most of them were settled in Morvern and stories abounded of
the way they were puzzled by 'civilization'. My favourites were of
one of the older women who after being initiated in the mysteries of
the water-closet decided what a time-saving device it offered for
washing up her crockery. And then there was the aged St Kildan
who, having been told how to use the water-closet on a train, pulled
the communication cord instead of the plug.

After one of my broadcasts that summer, I received a letter which
filled me with humble gratitude for an opportunity to give somebody
a happy month. She wrote from Deptford:

*A friend allowed me to listen over the wireless to you and it has come into
my mind somehow that being so much a lover of the country as yourself my
appeal would be perhaps kindly listened to and so I try.*

*It is 17 years since I had even a day in the country. I am so poor all alone
and next Wed. I shall be 67 years and oh if I could only give you a slight idea
of the longing I have just once more to have a short stay in the country but
unless someone will help I can never do so. Things are never likely to mend
for me now. All thro' the war hard for us and when that was over my husband
was struck with paralisis and for 4 years he lay helpless and when he was gone
I was a complete wreck of nerves. . . . He was very many years older than I
and the war and his illness took our little savings and bit by bit our little
home . . . thank God he never realized how things were but things have been
very hard for me since and now I feel if I could have just a change from this*

*one back room I could be braced up to face the winter. I suffer from bronchitis
so very badly. . . . You have so much to be thankful for. Will you spare me a
little bit of your Thank-offering?*

*My husband worked hard all his life from 13 and he was stricken down
at 77-8 months died at 82 and yet he had so little. Life is so hard. . . .*

*On the 21st of August my landlady and family are going away for their
holidays and I shall be left here alone and instead I should so like to go to
some quiet place for a time. I know some people who might take me cheaply.
Now you have got back to your lovely surroundings will you take pity on poor
old me and give me a week or two I should be so grateful.*

*I have got a small Crystal set but I could not afford the licence and so it
has got a bit out of order lying by or else I loved it so and time seemed much
happier. You when you are surrounded with all your beauties of possession
try to imagine what it is to be old, ailing, poor so poor and oh so lonely. Pray
forgive me for the liberty I am taking*
                    and believe me yours respectfully
                                                          M— W—

Alas, in spite of much that has been done there are still too many
poor and too many lonely old people.

Back in Jethou poor Faith had some anxious moments when I
received from the London firm of house agents details about the
forthcoming sale of the Calf of Man.

"The area of the island is approximately 616 acres and is about
5 miles in circumference. There are 89 acres of well-fenced land, of
which 51 acres are pasture and about 27 arable land. The remainder
of the Island, apart from the buildings, consists of rough heathy
pastures.

"The buildings in the Island comprise a residential house, a farm
house and farm buildings and a little cottage.

"The Island contains a newly constructed wharf which can be
approached at high or low tide, and a road runs straight across the
Island connecting the buildings and the harbour.

"The price that will be accepted is £6,500."

It did seem a tremendous bargain, and after all Manx was Gaelic.
Moreover, the Isle of Man had an almost independent status. My
mind went back to boyhood's days in Douglas, and to Twinkle, my
dearly loved Manx cat at Burford.

Two days later on August 20th came a telegram from Laura Lovat
to say that Eilean Aigas would be free in October. I wrote at once
to that firm of house agents to thank them for their information
but to add that I had enough islands for the present.

Only a week before this I had had a long wrestle with the Assistant General Manager of the Westminster Bank in Lombard Street, and I find the rough copy of a letter to Ralph Pinker:

I have had a terrible time with my bank. Finally I have managed to get my payments reduced from two thousand a year to one thousand a year, so that by next June my overdraft must be reduced to seven thousand. Meanwhile, I have pledged myself not to go above eight thousand, and at the present moment I am £7,800 overdrawn and it is vital for me to get the money in from America at the earliest possible moment. It is well overdue now. I had a talk with Newman Flower who is pleased with the way April Fools *has gone and as always was anxious to help. There is no chance of finishing* Athenian Memories *in time for publication before next year, but I have told Flower I will do my utmost to let him have a couple of novels for next year as well as* Athenian Memories.

My decision to give up Jethou gave me reason to suppose that I would soon receive a large enough sum for the lease to reduce my overdraft. So I was not greatly worried by my financial position. Moreover, I knew that if the worst came to the worst I could raise a good sum from the insurance people by surrendering my life and endowment policy.

That September Blackwell's published under the dull title *Told* a collection of my children's stories, mostly written for the annual *Joy Street*. I sent a copy for Veronica Fraser and at the beginning of September received a letter from Beaufort:

Dear Comp etc
Thank you terribly for 'Told'. I do like it very much indeed.
The term begins at the end of this month so you must come for the day as soon as you can. I suppose you have heard about poor Mummie. She was walking in the courtyard on the flags when Baba ran up to her and Mum lifted her up. It was then that Mummie's foot caught in a stone and down she came right on her side. And that's how she broke her leg.
I have not thought of a book except suppose Puck has written his life and it would be great fun if a kind witch or you perhaps might interpretate or whatever its called for me to write down.
I hope you will think this a good idea

Lots of love
Veronica

I was at Beaufort before term began and spent a couple of nights there. Simon Lovat was away, but Ronnie Knox was with them, doing crossword puzzles faster than I ever knew anyone do them. He was writing one of his 'whodunits', a sinless enough occupation for what leisure a priest could enjoy but frowned upon in upper ecclesiastical circles; not long after this he would in deference to their feelings abstain from writing any more.

Poor Laura Lovat was lying in a sort of hammock. I recall from that September of long ago Magdalen's saying that Jane Austen's novels bored her.

"At your age, Magdalen, I was bored by *Emma*, but even then I did enjoy *Pride and Prejudice*."

Laura Lovat suggested my reading some of *Pride and Prejudice* aloud.

I cannot remember what bits of *Pride and Prejudice* I read on that sunny September afternoon, but I still see the expressions on the faces of Magdalen and Veronica, and Laura Lovat lying in that kind of hammock, and the Medici print of Botticelli's Primavera on the wall.

I went over Eilean Aigas with Major Dewar, the factor of the Lovat properties, and it was arranged I should rent it from November.

I was enchanted by Eilean Aigas and Faith wrote in *More Than I Should*:

"The picture he gave me of it was so fantastic that I could only suppose his imagination was rioting, as it was wont to do when a new scene captured it. It was an island covered with magnificent trees, firs, larches, spruce and silver birches, surrounded by foaming rapids up which salmon leapt in great abundance."

At the beginning of October I heard from Neil Shaw, the Secretary of An Comunn Gaidhealach that the Shiant Shield had been won at the Mòd in Dunoon by the Luing junior choir with a 'wonderful characterization of Mrs Kennedy Fraser's version of "An Fideag Airgiod" '. The headmaster of the Luing school wrote:

I am the conductor of the children's choir which won the silver targe presented by you for the action-song competition.

I cannot forbear writing to you to express my admiration of this exquisitely beautiful trophy and the delight I have in knowing that I am to possess it for a year.

I wrote to tell the headmaster what a pleasure it was that the Shield should have been won by an island school and what an added pleasure it was that the song chosen should have been *The Silver Whistle*, one of my favourites for music, words and sentiment.

That first week in October was darkened by the loss of the airship

R 101 on an experimental flight to India when Lord Thomson, the
Air Minister, and Sir Sefton Brancker, the Director of Civil Aviation,
were both killed. Although the loss of life was nothing comparable,
the loss of the R 101 cast such a shadow over the country as the loss
of the *Titanic*.

There was a turgid retrospect of literature in the *Annual Register*
of 1930 which tried to suggest that novelists who were merely
observers were inferior to the wonderful new mood of 'dissent, un-
rest, protest, harshness and bitterness', and that the observers were
'disinclined to analyse and probe below the surface, a movement so
marked as already to have the name of "The abdication of
Intelligence" '.

I had not read this nonsense when a woman journalist came to
interview me in Jethou but I find a note from her of various things
I had said, asking me to cut anything I did not want put into print.

One sentence seems an apposite comment on that *Annual Register*
retrospect. I was talking of the younger generation of novelists.

"They are so curious and so knowing about the human works that
most of their novels are really studies for novels. They lift the bonnets
of their motor-cars so easily that they are apt to think the bonnet of
life is just as easy to lift. Precocity is for them the mother of invention
—and Freud the father."

While I was at Beaufort in September Veronica had expressed to
me her intention of never getting married.

"That's rather a rash resolve," I observed.

"Well, the only person I'd like to marry is Hugh. And apparently
I can't marry Hugh."

If that remark had been made to D. H. Lawrence he would
immediately have discerned in it some dark fantasy of the uncon-
scious. To enjoy the innocence of an enchanting little girl would
have seemed to that ass in the *Annual Register* an 'Abdication of the
Intelligence'. Incidentally, books by J. B. Priestley and A. P. Herbert
were cited by that critic of the *Annual Register* as examples of novels
published in 1930 by observers who had abdicated from intelligence.

I turn with relief from that braying of thirty-five years ago to one
more letter from Veronica:

> *2 Nov. 1930   Beaufort   Sunday*
> *Dear Monty*
>   *Thank you very much for your rude letter. Luckily I could not read it well
> enough to observe the many unpolite remarks. This is somewhat eloquent
> language but I hope you will comprehend it.*

I began you a letter the other day but it got lost.

We have just got home from (At least we had got home but now it is 5 o'clock) Beauly Church. Irene grumbled at going out for it was raining so Zelle (Mademoiselle) said she could stay in. Poor Irene was rather stuck here and we all teased her about it.

Mummy got up for lunch with us to-day for the first time and we all (Father Geddes[1] also) gave a thanks giving to the Sacred Heart in the Chapel. I am going to Keir on Tuesday and wont' be back till Dec. 10 or thereabouts and I shall be ten when you come.

Lots of love

Veronica

Fraser

I was again in Scotland in October and November, speaking at one dinner after another and at various Nationalist meetings. I feel guilty in not paying adequate tribute to so many people in Edinburgh whose hospitality was continuous. I recall those Sunday lunches with Andre Raffalovich in Whitehouse Terrace after Mass at St Peter's that beautiful church of which Canon Gray was the incumbent. Canon Gray had been a young poet of the 'nineties who had become a priest and between him and Raffalovich there had been a lifetime's friendship. 'Raffie' had published his first volume of poems in the 'eighties. I recall great evenings with W. G. Burn-Murdoch, the artist whose recreations in *Who's Who* were 'whaling, fencing and piping' and who had written a book about polar bear hunting. I recall a visit to Miss Craigie-Halkett at Cramond House in a large park surrounded by new little houses. When one rang the ancient bell and the door was opened, about three dozen Pekinese terriers rushed out to greet the visitor with friendly snuffles. Years later I would commemorate that Pekery in my novels about the Highlands. I recall evenings in York Place with David Cleghorn Thomson, but I am reproached by some reviewers for introducing too many people into *My Life and Times*; in the words of Sir Thomas Malory it is time to say 'Ho!'

Faith, who had at last taken to gardening with enthusiasm, was rather depressed at having to forsake the little garden she had made on Jethou, but when Newman Flower accepted *The Sybil of the North* for publication next spring she was cheered. On top of that a volume of her short stories called *Mandolinata* was to be published by Cope and Fenwick, where Colin Summerford was trying to make Sandys Wason's acquisition of a mummified firm a practical business.

[1] The late Canon Aeneas Geddes.

Faith had the additional diversion in London of learning to drive a motor-car; on the recommendation of Nicolas Mavrogordato, now a fifteen-year-old Etonian, she urged me to acquire a Hornet Sports car as the best value for money on the market. Most people who do not learn to drive a car until they are over fifty remain cautious drivers. Faith drove a car as well as she used to drive a horse, but seldom at less than fifty miles an hour. I decided against the Hornet for the moment and bought a second-hand Austin in Inverness which should be chauffeur-driven, for I was still quite unjustifiably nervous of Faith's prowess at the wheel.

Somehow or other I managed to finish *Athenian Memories* and start *Buttercups and Daisies* before I left Jethou in the middle of December.

The departure from Jethou was in the nature of a migration. Only Macdonald and his wife were left; they were to come north as soon as Jethou was sold.

Faith wrote in *As Much as I Dare*:

"On a sunny morning in December Chrissie MacSween and I, the vanguard, were driven the sixteen miles from Inverness in a huge Daimler with a prodigious load of luggage. Down a stony drive to a white bridge, with the rapids roaring beneath it. Then a steep drive curved upwards in a semicircle to the house. . . .

"The island was incredibly, wildly romantic. On the north side rugged purple and grey cliffs flanked the narrow turbulent river, small pines hung at all angles over the water from rock crevices. Walking against the stream up on the grassy path of the cliff, you went suddenly downhill, and came upon the same river, tranquil as a pool, on fine days reflecting the trees above it as though in a looking-glass. Now you were on a level with it, and a broad track shaded by oaks and larches went parallel with the tranquil stream until the round of the island had been completed; the river went mad again and rushed under the white bridge, and you would return through dense rhododendron walks up to the house."

The next party to leave for the North was Nellie Boyte, Honor, Keegan and his wife, with six cats. Mr and Mrs Boyte went at the same time to London, where they were going to live with their son.

The day on which I myself left Jethou was blue and breathless. We had been having savage weather all through November until the beginning of December but this was indeed the December halcyon. I told in Octave Four of seeing two kingfishers fly out to sea from Capri as on halcyon days the ancient Greeks had seen them fly, so they supposed, to nest on the outspread blue Aegean. Incidentally, in a moment of incomprehensible aberration, I wrote swallows for kingfishers which was noticed only by one reviewer, evidently as much surprised by that aberration as I was myself. I told in Octave Five of seeing two kingfishers fly out to sea from Herm in the direction of Jethou on another halcyon day. To my amazement, as I was being rowed out to the *Melusine* on this December morning, I saw two kingfishers fly across the Percée between Jethou and Herm.

'Winged with blue fire the urgent halcyon flies,' I wrote long ago in an early poem. There was no tradition that such a sight was a favourable omen, but I who have indulged myself in omens all my life decided, perhaps to reassure myself, that I was doing the right thing by forsaking that much loved little island, that the sight of those kingfishers was indeed of good omen.

Nevertheless, I felt a deserter.

Seven and a half years earlier I had left Herm with the responsibility, apart from my own debts, of trying to avert the bankruptcy of my mother, who had started her Nottingham repertory theatre with as much optimism as I had acquired the lease of Herm. In those seven and a half years I had written fourteen books and innumerable articles for the Press. Here I had seen *The Gramophone* thrive. Here I had been captivated by the future of radio. Here I had been granted the fulfilment of a dream when I was able to buy the Shiant Islands. To be sure, I had had plenty of illness and pain, but no more on Jethou than I had had for the last twenty years, and always deeply conscious of and deeply grateful for my own good fortune I offered illness and pain to placate the jealousy of the gods.

And now I reflect that if I had remained on Jethou I should have been carted off it ten years later to be interned in Naziland.

I have never landed on Jethou since I left it on that halcyon December morning thirty-five years ago, but its trees and its flowers, its birds and its butterflies still leaf and bloom and sing and flutter in my heart.

I shall not end on this elegiac note. Let Faith write of the New Year:

"The first event of any importance at Eilean Aigas was a children's party on New Year's Day 1931. It was the noisiest and most high-spirited party imaginable, and consisted entirely of the Fraser family, three sets of cousins, of ages varying from eighteen to four. Lady Lovat came with her children, Shimi (now Lord Lovat),

Magdalen, Hugh and Veronica. They brought Maurice Baring, Father Ronald Knox and Lord Eldon, who in 1934 would marry his beautiful cousin Magdalen. I forget how many of their cousins, the Constable Maxwells, were there. I think about half a dozen. The youngest child present was Rory Fraser, aged four, whose mother Lady Sybil Fraser brought five children. Rory screamed throughout the afternoon, for pure joy and high spirits, wearing a dress Fraser kilt, the tiniest ever seen. His sister Fanny, also wearing the kilt, danced solo reels. Monty did conjuring tricks which didn't come off. Bombs full of presents were flung into the midst of the uproar with deafening reports, bagpipes shrieked, fireworks banged, the gramophone grumbled, and the evening ended with a game of Hunt the Slipper. Rory fell blissfully asleep almost before he was packed into the car with his brothers and sisters, and an equally delicious exhaustion sent everyone in Eilean Aigas early to bed that night."

I recall saying to Michael Maxwell, a fourteen-year-old schoolboy at Ampleforth, who had made some remark about school terms seeming so long, that he would find time went by faster and faster the older he got.

"I believe it doesn't go quite so fast when you're ninety," he said, being even then as he still is to-day always anxious to help.

I hope dear Michael Maxwell is right. My eighties are galloping along terribly fast.

P

APPENDIX A

THE RECTORIAL CONTEST
By Bernard Shaw

From *The Student Leader* No. 2, October, 1925

Rectorial contests are not very accountable things. I am occasionally asked to present myself as a candidate; but the well known vehemence of my conviction that what is called university education is destructive to all but the strongest minds, and seriously injurious even to them (unless they protect themselves by a resolute neglect of their studies and an implacable scepticism as to university doctrine on every subject) would put me in a false position if by any extraordinary mischance I were elected; so I have always refused the opening. The arguments advanced to overcome my reluctance are always that the Rector is not really a Rector; that he has nothing whatever to do with or at the University; that he need never have heard of it before nor need ever hear of it again; and that his Rectorial Address may, if he pleases, be of a nature to cause the university authorities to expire in convulsions, and to make Karl Marx protest from his grave on behalf of Law and Order.

As far as I can make out, the real use of the Rectorial election is to enable the University to make a periodical gesture of insult to academic education. A representative of party politics pure and simple is put up in the person of a parliamentary figurehead who is, as far as the public knows, totally ignorant of and indifferent to everything else. Against him is put up a distinguished representative of liberal education, an eminent classical scholar and poet like Professor Gilbert Murray, a foremost man of letters with a philosophy of history like Mr Chesterton or Mr Wells, a sociologist of European authority like Mr Sidney Webb: in short, anybody who opposes to the mere party parliamentarian the culture of which the university professes to be the temple. And with a rush and a roar of derision the academic electorate boots the representative of enlightenment downstairs and into the gutter, and carries the politician shoulder high to the rectorial chair with shouts of triumph. The Rector thus becomes an Abbot of Misrule. If his constituents could not thus for once in a way let loose their intense hatred for the sham learning of the schools they would go mad, or burst.

This time, however, the situation is complicated by the appearance in the field of three candidates. The parliamentary one, Mr

Austen Chamberlain, is ideal for the purpose, and is certain to win hands down unless he unexpectedly betrays cultural interests and knowledge of other things than the Party Game before polling day. I call for three cheers for Mr Austen Chamberlain.

In wildest contrast to him stands Mr Chesterton, who by sheer literary force has taken the position in London created in the eighteenth century by Dr Johnson, and left vacant at his death until the accession of G. K. Chesterton's experience of what is technically called public life is, as far as I know, limited to a single appearance as a juryman; but in the true and general sense he, by a prodigious sort of journalism which is his bow of Ulysses, is perhaps the greatest publicist we possess. He began with a generous Liberalism, and was presently confronted with Socialism. But Socialism was neither magnanimous nor romantic enough for him. He repudiated it as an elephant might repudiate a set of toy chains, and reinvented it for himself as the Distributive State, a more accurate and less pedantic term than the Collectivist State, as the Socialists of his youthful day called it. Every man shall sit down under his own vine and figtree; and none shall make him afraid, saith the Word; and Chesterton saw that the Word is good, and left details to take care of themselves.

Finally he made the startling gesture of joining the Church of Rome!

Whenever I have been asked why, being so inveterately Catholic, I do not join the Church, I reply that the experiment of having two Popes was exhaustively tried in the fourteenth century, and was, in spite of the vaunted advantages of competition, on the whole a ghastly failure, like Capitalism. Chesterton took that risk without hesitation; perhaps because he was too modest to be conscious of his own inveterate pontificality. And through G. K. C.'s Weekly he hurls fifty-two encyclicals a year from his Avignon in Buckinghamshire. To make him Rector of Glasgow University would at lowest be a magnificent lark. One foresees the headlines: GLASGOW COMES TO CANOSSA, etc., etc., etc.

Sidney Webb, the *tertium quid*, is more unlike Chesterton than seems possible. Chesterton, by nature, a modest, friendly, affable, unassuming soul, is by sheer weight and stature and energy and gaiety enormously pretentious, colossally self-assertive, all style (and such a whacking style!) and all art. To Webb a man with a style, like Oscar Wilde (also all style, though a different style from Chesterton's because he was so different a person) is simply a man making a fool of himself. His motto might be "Madam: I will use no art". Go to Chesterton for instruction, and he will most courteously impress you, persuade you, dazzle you, and delight you until you are incapable of noticing that he has totally changed the subject. Go to Webb, and he will hardly conceal his impatience with the importunities of an imbecile asking for explanations of what must be obvious to any moderately intelligent person; but he will tell you exactly what you want to know and what you ought to do, and how to do it, and tell you so disinterestedly that you will be disgusted with him for not taking more interest in you personally. If Webb, being in Glasgow, has business in Kelvingrove, he will walk thither prosaically or take a tram; and nobody will stare after him, or be moved, as the spectators used to be moved when Count D'Orsay passed, to stop him and say "I beg your pardon, sir; but are you anybody in particular?" What is more, he will arrive there. Chesterton, on the like errand, would have an ecstatic crowd following him in two minutes, and would eventually reach Dalmarnock Bridge and forget all about Kelvingrove. Anyhow, he would not notice the difference. Chesterton would address two corner boys, a woman and a baby, as if they were a grand demonstration in the St Andrew's Hall: Webb would address the biggest demonstration as if he were telling the boots what to do with the luggage. People adore Chesterton's irrelevancies: Webb's efficiencies infuriate them. They invent affectionate stories of Chesterton's extravagances: they revile Webb as a soulless instrument of precision. Chesterton's weaknesses encourage: Webb's powers humiliate, all the more unbearably because he cannot see why everyone should not be as clever as himself, and persists in behaving like an ordinary person. He has the maddening effect of a Napoleon who will not cock his hat, a Newton who will not wrinkle his brows, a rescuer of drowning heroines who walks away without giving his name to the reporters. He might as well be a nobody, for all the fun there is in it for himself or the spectators. One feels that no man of such complex ability should have such an extraordinarily simple character, and that no man with such a simple character should have any ability at all. He violates all the decencies of congruity. He entraps experienced politicians into underrating him almost as if he were doing it on purpose. When they find him out they feel that if they are to confess his superiority and accept his leadership, he must really behave like it or they will look like fools. And they end by doing that anyhow.

Webb, like Chesterton, began as a Liberal. Confronted presently

with Marxist Socialism, he tackled the monster, and in an apparently
effortless manner changed it into a constitutional movement and
codified it for parliamentary use. German Revisionism, European
parliamentary Socialism, colonial Labour government, British
Fabianism and the Labour Party, are all forms of the order brought
into the Socialist chaos by Sidney Webb. Public life is mere porridge-
for-breakfast to him. He and Lord Olivier were the ablest civil
servants in the Colonial Office before they came to grips with Socialism. When Webb left the civil service he manipulated the new
Technical Education Committee of the London County Council for
years with undisputed mastery as its chairman. Out of a few thousand
pounds bequeathed to him by an ex-town clerk (who was a good
judge of men) to do some good with, he built up the London School
of Economics and added it to the University of London: the greatest
one-man achievement of the kind since the Middle Ages. He married
the right woman, and with her help produced a monumental series
of standard treatises on political science, industrial history, and the
evolution of British local government. He established an unpre-
cedented and invincible electoral majority in a huge mining constituency, virtually a non-party Sidney Webb majority, and paid the
penalty by having to waste his valuable time for a year as a cabinet
minister at the head of the Board of Trade.

Throughout all this staggering public activity his fertility in finding working solutions for political and industrial problems and keeping the solutions in line with their historic evolution could have been
possible only to an omnivorous high speed reader with a prodigious
memory. I doubt whether such a portentous man should be allowed
to contest elections. It is not fair: he should be declared *hors concours*,
and placed *ex officio* on every governing body in the country or out
of it. He is the only man I ever met qualified to be a Universal
Alderman. Neither Chamberlain nor Chesterton would have a
dog's chance if the Glasgow academic electorate were capable of
taking in Webb's career, or if Webb could be induced to advertize
effectively.

As it is, one can only look on somewhat cynically, and wonder
what will happen. For no election in our time has produced three
candidates so piquantly contrasted as these three. And this, at least,
I hope the University will appreciate however foolishly—that is to
say, academically—it may give effect to its appreciation.

      SCOURIE,   G. B. S.
SUTHERLAND, *4th August, 1925.*

   P*

APPENDIX B

In Octave Four I wrote about the children of a Sunday School I started in Cornwall in 1908. Mr F. J. L. Timmins, the husband of Beatrice Bolitho, wrote to say he was going to give the book to his wife on her 70th birthday and asked me to autograph it. I was naturally moved by that letter, and in replying to it I asked Mr Timmins for news of the rest of the Bolitho children. From 'Drop Anchor', 7 Dracaena Avenue, Falmouth, he kindly wrote me a long letter from which I quote:

I will start with *Ernest* the eldest now 72 years old and very fit and well; he is a great worker and local preacher for the Full Gospel Church along this road, a very good living man, non-smoker and strictly teetotal. When he left school he entered your service as page boy and after leaving Phillack went out to Butte City, Montana, U.S.A., to an uncle, and he worked on top at the copper mines. He was a G.I. in the first world war and became an American citizen; he came back to England and married a girl from Helston called Gluyas, returned to the States, and had 2 sons. He lost all his savings in the slump about 1930, came back home and became a British subject and worked at the local ship repairing yard, as a rigger and boatman until he retired 7 years ago. His sons have made the grade very well, one is working as an engineer in the Harwell Atomic Station. He served his apprenticeship as a Marine engineer, went to sea, and College, obtained his chief ticket, and worked on Atomic Boilers, nice steady, Christian fellow, married with one son, this son of Ernie's is called Dennis. The other son Robert, served his apprenticeship with a smaller marine engineering firm, and went through the whole of the business, welding, drawing, tuning and fitting and is present working at Wimbledon as an engineer designer, goes abroad and places, representing his firm, he married a Wimbledon lass and have 3 children 2 boys and 1 girl. He also is a good Christian lad and a joy and credit to his Dad and Mum.

Percy. After leaving school he worked for some years at the Mullion Golf Links and then he went to the States, to Akron, Ohio. He was head Green Keeper at the Firestone Golf Links, married an American girl, descendant from a Scottish family called Livingstone. They had 3 sons, one John is still at Akron an Elec. Engineer, and his wife has a floral shop, have one daughter. The other son George is a carpenter, has twin daughters, lives at Penryn, the 3rd boy David,

married, a painter, has 2 daughters, lives at Redruth. Percy and
family also returned to England after losing all his savings during
the slump of 1930. All are fit and well. He worked at the Falmouth
Golf Course. He is 71 years old.

Beatrice, 70 years old. When she left school she went to live with
the Rev. Paine, curate of St Mary Church Penzance, then went to
live at the Vicarage, Lanteglos, Fowey, when he was appointed
vicar. My sister worked at the vicarage as his cook, that is how I met
my wife Beatrice. We were married at Gunwallow Church April
22nd 1922 by the Rev. Wagner. We have one big regret, we have no
children and we love them so much, as much as you and your wife
Faith used to love and do so much. The Mission Hall is still in good
order, but is not used, at least to my knowledge. Beat is a very clever
woman, needlework, knitting and especially cooking; her pasties are
excellent and have been enjoyed by many people such as Sir Hartley
and Lady Shawcross. I was chauffeur to the Silley family and office
of the docks for 42 years, have driven such V.I.P.s as the late Duke
of Kent, Lord and Lady Inchcape, and many, many others. I
retired 3 years ago and we have bought a plot of land opposite
The Bowling Club designed our own Bungalow had it built and
have lived in it for about 2 years, very nice, small, and pleasant,
just lovely for Bowling. Beat and myself are very keen bowlers, and
I am proud to say she has this year received her County Badge.
She plays a very good consistant game as lead.

Bessie, aged 68 or 69. She is fit and well but lost her husband some
4 years ago, silocosis, he was a granite stone mason, worked on
memorials, was a very clever man expecially on raised letters,
anchor and chains, etc. When she left school she went to work as a
nursemaid for the son of the Rev. Vawdrewy, Vicar of Budock, was
married at Malie and has 2 children 1 son 1 daughter, her son has
a business as haulage contractor, married, with 1 boy and 1 girl.
Her daughter is married to a monumental Quarry Owner, they
have 1 daughter. Bessie lives alone at Malie and is fit and well.

Alec aged 67 a Bachelor. When he left school, he too went to
America, to Butte City, and worked in the Gas Works as engineer.
Lost his savings in the slump, returned home and worked in the
local ship yard as Pivot man, that's mooring up ships etc. He served
in the First World War in the Duke of Cornwall's Light Infantry,
was O.K. Percy also served in the 1st War in the Royal Field
Artillery was O.K. I myself served in the 1st World War in the
K.R.R.C. served in Italy and France was taken prisoner at Bapaume

in March 1918. Alec is a great worker for the local British Legion.
He organises all the football competitions and Dart matches, has
done very well, won lots of cups.

Lily, aged 65, a Spinster. She stayed at home, had Infantile
Paralysis and was crippled in her left leg, also had rheumatic fever.
She struggles along and keep remarkably well, nursed her Mum and
Dad until they passed on. Father was 75, and Mother 88 when she
passed away about 3 years ago. My, Lily is a worker, she lives for
her broom and bucket of water, washes clothes twice a week, and
cooks every day, you see she has 3 bachelor brothers to look after
and, believe me, no wonder they never get married, they are a happy
well cared for family. She has just this minute arrived to spend the
afternoon with us. All the Bolitho's are a united family, visit one
another every week, Bessie comes in and spends the weekend every
week, with Lily and the boys. I never saw such a glutton for work as
our maid Lily, sewing, mending, washing, ironing and cooking all
the time.

Leonard, aged 63 a Bachelor. He too went to America, and worked
in the Firestone Tyre Factory, lost his savings in the slump and
returned home with the others. He works at the local shipyard as a
tinkerman and Sawyer, a steady comfortable home bird, has a craze
for boats and fishing, makes his own crab pots and nets, works like a
horse and is as strong as a bull, he owns a large store on the water
front at Falmouth, has a 30 ft long fishing boat with 1 diesel engine
and one petrol engine, spends all his spare time especially during the
winter painting and improving his boats (4 in all).

George, aged 55 or 56 a Bachelor. The baby of the family, when he
left school he worked at the Falmouth Docks as a locomotive boy,
greasing etc, then he worked in the Water Dept supplying fresh
water, fine hoses, etc, now he is Foreman, and also Model maker. He
is very very clever at model making, has made models of deep sea
tugs (they have been to Plymouth and London on Exhibition) made
models of the fuel oil installation at Falmouth Docks, one is in the
London Office of R. & H. Green Silley Weir London, a model of
the whole of the Falmouth Docks, with the ships of different lines
in the docks and alongside wharves (tankers, cargo, and passenger
liners) every one to scale, and he makes everything from the winches,
to anchor and chain (or cable) loco's, cranes, and breakwaters, and
men, is now engaged on making a model of Mr Silley's schooner
yacht, he has made models of a housing estate for the firm "Civil
Engineering Co" and, believe me, it is beautiful, I wish you could

see the finish on the yachts, the high polish on the hulls and the putty made waves, painted blue with white crested tops, it is a wonderful gift and he does it so easily. He is a very good golfer and snooker player and has won several trophies.

They are a grand bunch and no wonder they stick together. Now enough of this, so a bit about the excitement of reading your book, Ernie called in yesterday to see if it had arrived. Of course the wife now knows all about it, and opens the front porch door every morning, so that the post man can ring the front door bell. These past few days have been all memories, about the Christmas stockings, the Christmas tree in the mission hall, the Christmas Pudding with brandy set alight, the dogs, and pony, the swimming lessons on the beach, and oh so many delightful things. Of course, Sir Compton, in those days children had to make their own fun and games, and the thought of having some one in their midst to play with them, and invent games for them as you did, must not and cannot be forgotten.

That those beloved children of long ago should have grown up to set a Christian example to every family in the country makes me feel humbly grateful. When in a letter to my wife Mr Timmins wrote that Beatrice remembered the sound of my voice reading *Alice in Wonderland* to them I regret that so few children today read *Alice in Wonderland*.

INDEX

OCTAVES FIVE AND SIX